DAVE GORMAN is an award-winning comedian, storyteller and writer. He has numerous TV writing credits and was part of the double BAFTA-winning team behind *The Mrs Merton Show*. His live shows have won many awards and he is the only performer to twice win the Jury Prize for Best One Person Show at America's prestigious HBO US Comedy Arts Festival. He was the host of *Genius* for five series – three on Radio 4 and two on BBC2. He has made numerous other appearances on TV and radio including *Absolutely Fabulous*, *The Frank Skinner Show*, *The Late Show with David Letterman*, *The Tonight Show with Jay Leno*, and *The Daily Show with Jon Stewart* where he has appeared both as a guest and as the show's 'resident statistician'. His documentary film, *America Unchained*, won the Audience Award for Best Documentary Feature at the Austin Film Festival. He hosts a Sunday morning show on Absolute Radio. He enjoys cycling, darts, poker, photography and cryptic crosswords. His ambition is to one day become a team captain on *Call My Bluff*.

www.davegorman.com

Also by Dave Gorman:

Are You Dave Gorman?
Dave Gorman's Googlewhack Adventure
America Unchained

DAVE GORMAN

VS. THE REST OF THE WORLD

EBURY
PRESS

3 5 7 9 10 8 6 4 2

This edition published 2012
First published in 2011 by Ebury Press, an imprint of Ebury Publishing
A Random House Group company

The Random House Group Limited Reg. No. 954009

Addresses for companies within the Random House Group can be found at
www.randomhouse.co.uk

A CIP catalogue record for this book is available from the British Library

The Random House Group Limited supports The Forest Stewardship
Council (FSC®), the leading international forest certification organisation.
Our books carrying the FSC label are printed on FSC® certified paper.
FSC is the only forest certification scheme endorsed by the leading
environmental organisations, including Greenpeace.
Our paper procurement policy can be found at
www.randomhouse.co.uk/environment

Printed and bound by CPI Group (UK) Ltd, Croydon, CR0 4YY

ISBN 9780091928483

To buy books by your favourite authors and register for offers visit
www.randomhouse.co.uk

To Beth

acknowledgements

I'd like to thank Jake Lingwood, Charlie Brown, Ali Nightingale, Ed Griffiths and everyone at Ebury, especially the ladies and gents of Mondeoland. Rob Aslett, Cath Gagon, Dan Lloyd and all at Avalon, too: I'll be more likely to pick up the phone or answer your emails now.

Thanks to Matt Welton for his advice, guidance, encouragement and constancy and for reminding me that while it's all just words it's never *just* words. Both my Mum and David Smiedt read an early draft and offered useful insights for which I am hugely grateful. My wife, Beth, did likewise but also had to put up with my nocturnal writing habits. Thanks Beth: YLTMYYA.

But my biggest thanks must go to the many, many games players who made me so very welcome. There isn't space in this book to describe every game I played. But I'm very grateful to all my hosts and opponents. Thank you.

I've changed the names – and some small, inconsequential details – of three people. Twice this was done at their request. Once it was done as a courtesy.

"Life is the name of the game,
And I wanna play the game with you.
Life can be terribly tame,
If you don't play the game with two.

Yeah, life is a go-as-you-please
And I need some place to go with you.
Life can be oh, such a tease,
If you don't play the game with two."

Bruce Forsyth

'Okay, children, just stand back and let these people through.'

The female voice wasn't raised but the clipped tones, honed no doubt by a few years in the classroom, easily cut through the thrum of commuters and the squeaking, grunting tube train doors.

Her charges: a crocodile of tiny, hand-holding infants – boys and girls in matching bright blue sweatshirts – obediently scrunched up to the wall as the tidal wave of suits, briefcases and backpacks surged past them.

'Remember, these people are on their way to work,' she continued, 'so they might be a *bit* grumpy.'

It might have been a harsh lesson in reality for ones so young but the bald honesty of the statement brought a chuckle to my lips as I passed by. So I guess at least one of the crowd didn't look grumpy.

But then, this member of the crowd wasn't on his way to work. I was on my way to play a game. I was on my way to play … 'Egyptian Laser Chess'.

Having never played it before I didn't know what to expect from a game of Egyptian Laser Chess although for the record, I dislike chess, like lasers and am entirely neutral when it comes to Egyptians. I'd never met my prospective opponent before either. In fact, I really wasn't sure what I was doing. Or why I was doing it. But I can tell you that – like so many things in this modern world – it had started with a tweet.

CHAPTER 1

Does anyone play any games?
Real life, not computer games.
Would you like a game?

That was the text of a tweet I'd posted on the social networking website, Twitter. For those of you unfamiliar with Twitter in particular, or social networking sites in general (or the online world in even generaller), you don't need to get bogged down in any details as to what that actually means; just think of sending a tweet as the online equivalent of pinning a message on a notice board outside the village hall. You know every villager won't see it – it's not like putting a postcard through everyone's letterbox – but those who choose to wander by and look *will* see it and that's what really counts.

At the time I had just shy of 76,000 people 'following' me on Twitter. How many of them saw the tweet is unknowable – it depends on how many of them were online at that particular moment and how many of *them* were likely to be paying me any heed – but even so, the sudden barrage of replies was overwhelming.

The thing is, I like games. Physical and mental. I like to compete. I like the way they engage the brain. I like the fact that while I'm playing a game I'm not thinking of other things and yet I *am* thinking. I don't like it when my brain is at rest. Doesn't it *have* to be thinking of something? If I'm alone I like a cryptic crossword and if I'm in company I like a game.

It's probably worth pointing out that I'm a pretty competitive sort. I beat children. Only at games, you understand. I'll cheerfully beat my nephew at draughts because I think it means more to him when he then beats me at Mario Kart on the Nintendo Wii. Which he does. Regularly.

But, as competitive as I am, I'm also a very good loser. I've had to be. I spent my childhood as the permanent underdog, the runt of the litter. I was always going to be slower and weaker than my two older brothers, Jon and Rich, but I was also slower and weaker than my twin, Nick. We're not identical. He's always been a more physical specimen. If you could see the series of scratchy pencil marks our parents had made on the kitchen wall to mark our growth over the years, you'd see that wherever there was a line marked with a 'D' for David, there was always another line an inch or two above it marked 'N' for Nicholas. Sometimes I'd stand on my tiptoes to try and nudge my Mum's pencil a little higher; I'd concentrate on my back, hoping to think my spine a little longer. But I never caught up with him. Older brothers might occasionally feel protective of their younger siblings. Twins don't. Why would they? They compete. They exercise every advantage they have. In physical games my twin won out. And on the rare occasions I somehow lucked out and came out on top, he'd punch me for daring to challenge the natural order of things. It's okay. We're friends now.

You'd think this would have put me off games for life. It didn't. But while I liked them, I didn't seem to know many people who agreed with me. My wife Beth and I play games. Card games mostly. Our first date – a Saturday morning stroll around an East London market – became a Saturday afternoon game of Rummy and a bottle of red in a small café bar nearby, and that in turn turned into a Saturday evening game of Rummy and another bottle of red at mine. She won. Although so did I. Obviously.

We played Rummy the day we got engaged, too. We were at Dunnet Head, the northernmost point of the British mainland: a windswept, rainswept, desolate place with nothing much to do but plenty of sea to stare at.

There is romance in desolation, but I wouldn't have chosen to take Beth to the ends of the earth – or the ends of the British earth at least – for that reason. Dunnet Head was the finishing line of my midlife-crisis bike ride. A lot of men don the lycra and have one as they approach forty, and I was no different. And while Lands End to John O'Groats is the most popular route on these shores, once I discovered that they weren't actually the southernmost and northernmost points of Britain I decided I'd do it 'properly'. So I cycled from Lizard Point to Dunnet Head instead and to really tick the boxes I took in the easternmost and westernmost points, too: Lowestoft Ness and Ardnamurchan respectively.

I did the 1,600 miles in thirty-three days and if you think that's a bit slow, my excuse is that I'd been persuaded to do a two-hour stage show every night at theatres along the way, too.

For the first thirty-two days I'd enlisted the help of various strangers: local cyclists who volunteered to show me the way. But, knowing I'd feel a bit emotional, on the final day I'd eschewed that idea. Instead I'd been joined by the one person I *was* willing to share that exhilaration with: Beth. I already knew she was the one – and the fact that she wanted to travel all that way to be there at the end of my journey only helped to cement my feelings.

With the help of a friend I had a bottle of champagne, a bowl of strawberries and a bicycle bell hidden in the shadows of the Dunnet Head lighthouse. The champagne and strawberries were to be consumed, while the bicycle bell was the only thing I could find to act as a makeshift engagement ring.

As I led Beth towards the hidden stash, the whole ride transformed itself into a Greek myth: a trial by which a man had proven his physical worth in order to win the hand of the one he loves.

I was physically drained but mentally strong. I went down on bended knee … unsure that I'd be able to get up again.

That night we stayed in what I think is the only hotel in the town, a creaky old place that seemed more surprised to see us than anything. We tried going for a walk on the beach but the wind, uninterrupted since Iceland, was whipping the salty sea water into our eyes and we soon retreated to the hotel where a log fire, hot chocolate, the occasional rum and lots more Rummy was the order of the day. I won. Although so did she. Obviously.

As I've got older, the game-playing connections in my social network seem to have diminished. When you're a kid you're allowed to knock on a friend's front door and ask, 'Is Timmy playing?' but as an adult, wanting to *play* seems almost frowned upon. You can arrange to meet for food any time. You can meet for a pint of an evening or a coffee of an afternoon. There are certain friends I can go to the theatre or a gallery with and there are others where a gig is deemed more acceptable fare. But that's kind of the point. The connections with my friends have become more fixed. The common ground is known. And I was finding that when I asked a non-game-playing friend if they wanted to play a game, they seemed to view me with suspicion. A *but-I'm-the-friend-you-go-for-a-drink-with-so-why-do-we-need-to-change-anything?* kind of suspicion.

I used to have a regular Tuesday night game of football, but what had once been seven-a-side soon fell away to five-, four- and then three-a-side and then to utter pointlessness. I play at a friend's poker night when I can, which amounts to maybe six times a year if I'm lucky. Not that I'm often lucky. Then there's a friend I used to play Scrabble with but he no longer lives in London. I used to play Scrabble with my mum and stepdad, too, but in recent years they've introduced their own innovative house rules – they use a small, handheld electronic word-finding device and a dictionary to work out what word they should play on *every single go* – which has turned it into a letter-lottery and removed any sense of actual game-play from it. If you ever meet them, do tell them how ridiculous their system is.

My latest love affair with a game had been with darts. I've always enjoyed it on the TV but hadn't really played as an adult. I was watching the World Championships on TV one year, when it suddenly struck me as faintly ridiculous that I didn't play a game so cheap and accessible. I bought a set of darts the next day and skipped over to the Kings Arms, one of the few pubs near my Bethnal Green home that has a board.

It was an afternoon and the only other customers in that day were three old boys, in their sixties or seventies, each of them nursing a pint of bitter and a betting slip. They were glued to the horse racing on the TV screen that hung from the ceiling in the far corner, and from what I could gather the nags hadn't given any of them much cause to celebrate. Not today. Not for a long time.

While the three of them were able to discuss the horse racing in low mumbles and grunts, as I started to throw my first darts in twenty years they suddenly turned up the volume.

I don't think they did it on purpose but I might be wrong ...

'Do you play darts, Bill?'

'Have done.'

'Y'any good?'

'I'm better than that twat.'

The next day, I bought a dartboard to go with my darts and took my game into the spare room, away from prying eyes. I asked around amongst friends to see if anyone fancied a game but takers were thin on the ground. Few amongst them could muster anything more than an ironic appreciation for the game. Darts, it seemed, was deemed naff. But then I used Twitter to help me.

When my day job as a stand-up comic took me on a two-month tour of the UK, I took my darts with me. Touring is a largely enjoyable endeavour but, like any job, it involves moments of *ennui*. You get odd lumps of time off in towns and cities where you're a stranger. It's never long enough to see the sights but it's always too long to be spent in a grotty dressing room. So, you've travelled from Aberdeen to Glasgow, say. You've checked into your hotel, been to the theatre and dealt with the technical side of things. You've done an interview with a local radio station and had a bite to eat and then you find there's a ninety-minute gap before you need to be backstage getting ready. It doesn't sound like much, but when this sort of day is stacked up one after another, day after day, these moments become quite isolating, not to mention tedious.

On several occasions, I used that time by putting a message out on Twitter asking if anyone could tell me if they knew of a nearby pub with a dartboard. (I used to think that every pub had a dartboard; it was only when I started playing that I discovered how false that impression was.) Sometimes I found one and played alone for a while but most of the time I found someone who wanted a game, too. They were generally lovely encounters that helped to keep the *ennui* at bay.

Of course, there's a risk involved with meeting strangers and there was one oaf in York who rather took the shine off things for a while ... but in hindsight, even he just served to make the day a little more colourful. Much more often than not it was a good way of making a tour a little less lonely.

I had a small window of time off. I'd been working seven days a week for three or four months, only to suddenly stumble into a two-day week. I presented a radio show on Sunday mornings that also required a midweek meeting and … um … that was it! The sudden rush of free time was unsettling. Like a pit pony seeing daylight for the first time, I didn't particularly know what to do with myself.

Oh. I did have a wedding to help plan. Beth and I were not yet man and wife. But we could only really do that when we were both around, and Beth had just accepted a job that was taking her away from home a fair bit. I was spending my days rattling around the place, twiddling my thumbs, awaiting her return. So I decided to knock on a door and ask if anyone was playing. The door I chose was the internet: the world's door.

It's not a huge leap from a tweet saying: 'In Glasgow. Anyone know a pub near the Pavilion with a dartboard?' to: 'Does anyone play any games? Real life, not computer games. Would you like a game?'

I know one is quite specific and the other more open-ended but … well … it was the same *sort* of thing, wasn't it? Wasn't it?

No. Not really. I knew full well what I was doing. I was bored. I wanted to *do* something, to *go* somewhere … but I didn't know what or where. This was a way of letting others decide for me. I knew that if I hit 'Send' I would be opening a portal. I knew there would be quite a lot of replies. I knew there was every chance there would be more than I could read. But it didn't matter. I only needed to follow up one or two. It was my own little random-day-out generator.

Many of the responses were frustratingly devoid of specifics. I found myself looking at pages and pages of, 'What have you got in mind?', 'When you say "game" what exactly do you mean?' and 'I like some games but not others – is that useful?' All reasonable reactions to my question, I suppose, and yet all exactly what I wasn't looking for. I didn't *know* what I had in mind. I didn't know exactly what I meant. And I wasn't conducting a survey.

But not all the replies were as vague as the question. Dotted in amongst them were messages from people with real offers of real games they wanted to play in the real world.

The first one I saw that I could actually act on came from a man called Rhys. He lived only ninety minutes away by train, was free the next day, and wondered if I wanted to try Khet.

'What's Khet?' I'd tweeted back cautiously. I didn't know for sure that Rhys's message was about a game and I didn't want to find myself inadvertently accepting an invitation to attend an illicit ketamine party. Not again.

'It's a board game,' came the reassuring reply. 'It's kind of like chess. Only with an Egyptian theme. And it involves lasers.'

Well, if you put it like that …!

Khet? Meh … Egyptian Laser Chess? Sold.

CHAPTER 2

'Are you sure about this?' Beth asked.

'Of course,' I said. 'What harm can it do?'

'What do you mean, "What harm can it do?"' she sighed. 'You're meeting a stranger. That you met on the internet! You know, that thing everyone tells people not to do. "*What harm can it do?*" Are you serious?'

'Oh, I don't worry about things like that,' I said, brushing her concerns aside. 'I'm thirty-nine! I've taken bigger risks than this in my life. I've been to plenty of strangers' houses before. Most people are pretty nice.'

'What about the few people who aren't nice?'

'He wants to play a game,' I said. 'Only nice people want to play games.'

'News flash: not-nice people don't always tell the truth.'

'Well, he *seems* nice,' I said. 'Y'know … in his tweets and stuff.'

'Well, that's all right then,' came the sarcastic reply. Beth paused. 'Look, if I told you I was going to meet a stranger I'd met on the internet, what would you say?'

Hmm. She had a point.

'You've got a point,' I said. 'But I promise you it's safe. I've done this sort of thing before. It's always been safe. I'm a good judge of character. Please don't worry.'

I was worried. Worried that I had the wrong address. There was no sign that the front garden had been tended, there were no curtains or blinds and through the undressed windows I could see only a sparse collection of furniture: a bare table and mismatched chairs. There were no nick-nacks, no personal objects, no signs of life. The place looked to be unoccupied.

What if it was? What if Rhys didn't live here? What if he'd just sent me on a wild goose chase to an empty house as some kind of prank – a reverse engineered knock and run? There was only one way to find out.

I rang the bell. I waited. I waited. And was relieved to find the door being flung open by an imposing figure of a man with a warm handshake and a grin to match.

Rhys turned out to be one half of a magical double act. Or, as he describes himself online, 'Half of "Morgan & West" if done by people. Two-thirds if done by body mass.' In fairness, that says as much about the slight frame of his partner in illusion as it does about his own sizeable girth.

Morgan & West – or Rhys and Rob – describe themselves as 'Victorian magicians', which I think means they do their stuff while wearing waistcoats, frock coats and extravagant facial hair. Not that they were wearing such things when I met them. Apart from the facial hair. Rhys had an impressive set of mutton chops that had met in the middle to discuss a long-term future as a moustache, while Rob had a spiky cavalier's beard and a waxable, eminently twiddleable moustache: a wiry, spry combo to match his wiry, spry physique.

Looking round the house, I could see they'd only just moved in. In the back room the cardboard boxes were stacked up and odd props, hats and domestic paraphernalia spilled out.

'We're renting this place because it's cheaper than Oxford,' Rhys explained.

'We've just qualified as teachers,' Rob continued, 'so we're going to do some work and save some money – ideally, enough to allow us to take ten months off.'

'Then we'll really go for it with the magic.'

A third, female, voice came from behind me, 'Do you want a drink or anything?'

I turned to find a short girl with light brown hair pulled back from her face by a pair of glasses, offering me a handshake. 'I'm Amy.'

I smiled and shook the proffered hand. 'I'd love a cuppa,' I said gratefully. 'Milk and none.'

'Biscuit?'

I paused ever so slightly. Ridiculously, I was weighing up whether or not it was polite to accept biscuits on a first visit to a stranger's house. They'd been very freely offered but somehow I think the sparseness of the furniture had created an illusion of austerity.

'We've always got a lot of biscuits,' said Rhys, as if sensing my quandary. Either that or he just wanted to avoid being the only one chomping biscuits.

'We do a biscuit trick,' explained Rob, making the situation clearer and yet somehow less clear at the same time. 'We produce a member of the audience's favourite biscuit.'

Light dawned. 'Then, yes,' I chuckled, 'I'll have a biscuit.'

We briefly discussed the difficulties of biscuit-predictions. Apparently, you have to be careful which member of the audience you choose. Children are best avoided. You can't produce someone's favourite biscuit out of thin air without secretly having several different biscuits hidden away, ready to appear. While adults can be counted on to name one of the classics – y'know: a digestive, HobNob, ginger, bourbon or maybe a Jammy Dodger – kids are significantly less predictable. Kids have no sense of biscuit history. Kids know obscure, new biscuits. They know the odd brand names that have only been on supermarket shelves for two weeks and will be discontinued in another two weeks' time. Pick a child as your volunteer and you're more than likely heading for biscuit-trick disaster. I'm pretty sure the same is true with animals.

By the time our discussion of trick logistics was done, the tea and biscuits had arrived and I'd been introduced to

Rebecca, the final piece in the housemate jigsaw. Rob then placed a game board on top of the table.

'This,' he said with a flourish (I imagine magicians do a lot of things with a flourish), 'is Khet.'

'Okay.' I rubbed my palms together in anticipation. 'Bring it on.'

Between them, Rob and Rhys explained the rules but, as with almost every game, it only served to make it sound more complicated than it really was.

Learning the rules to a game without seeing them put into practice is like being taught a language without ever having a go at speaking it. There's no point someone trying to teach you how to conjugate French verbs if you haven't yet got a simple, *'Bonjour, je m'appelle David,'* down pat.

That being the case, I suspect there's little point in me trying to explain the rules to you, either. Instead, allow me to direct interested parties towards this brief overview:

Khet

An abstract strategy board game for two players.

The board is 10 x 8 squares in size.

You each have a laser – an **actual** laser! – built into the board. Your laser – your **actual** laser! – always fires in the same direction.

You each have 14 pieces.

These pieces might have Egyptian names but you can ignore that – the important thing isn't what they're called but how many mirrors they have.

Djed: Two sides, both mirrored

Pyramid: Four sides, one mirrored

Obelisk: No mirrors

Pharaoh: No mirrors

On your turn you can do one of the following:
a) Move a piece one square in any direction
b) Rotate a piece through 90°
c) Have a Djed swap places with any adjacent Obelisk or Pyramid.

At the end of your turn you must fire your laser.

The laser bounces off mirrors but if it hits a solid surface that piece is lost.

If your Pharaoh is lost, the game is lost.

Duration: 10–30mins.

The rules had sounded confusing but as I watched Rob and Rhys play an example game, my bam was rapidly unboozled. Ten minutes later, with Rob the victor, they were replacing the pieces in the starting position and it was my turn to play.

I looked down at the board and tried to work out what my first move should be. The raised outer edge of the board was decorated with various hieroglyphs – an ankh, a hawk, a bird with a boy's head, an ibis – that kind of thing, but there was another that seemed, well, a little phallic. (If it's an authentic hieroglyph it proves that childish graffiti artists have been scrawling the classic cock-and-balls pictogram on walls for many years. If it's not, it proves that somewhere in the Khet design team there beats a mischievous heart.) Ack. So easily distracted. I looked down at the board again. This time I ignored the decoration. This time I tried to work out what my first move should be. I moved a Pyramid. I was playing Khet.

In total, I played three games. My first was against Rob. I thought I was doing okay to begin with. I quickly gained a numerical advantage, eliminating three or four of his pieces before he managed to remove one of mine. But he wasn't perturbed. He was quietly structuring his own defence while allowing me to tie myself up in knots. It was like watching a seven-foot-tall giant holding off a four-foot assailant by the head as their arms flail around wildly, unable to connect, until they exhaust themselves and can be swatted away with one tiny flick of the wrist.

In the end I lost the game by an act of suicide. Or was it regicide? Or deicide? It depends on your point of view and how immersive you want the Egyptian theme to be. Reluctantly, I'd moved a Pyramid into the path of Rob's laser, prepared to sacrifice it in order to protect my Pharaoh, only to discover that when I fired my laser, it hit the same Pyramid from the other side, hitting the mirror and being deflected towards the very Pharaoh I was trying to protect. It was a useful lesson. I'd only really thought about defending myself from my opponent's laser and I'd only really thought about attacking with my own. They were both weapons. They both needed to be defended. They could both be used to attack.

In my next game I played Amy. This time the momentum swung to and fro: it was a nip-and-tuck, tit-for-tat game that could have gone either way – but went mine. And then finally I played Rhys in another tight, nail-biting game.

During the first two games the conversation had been flowing and I'd learned a lot about my hosts but during this third game the flow became a trickle. I had learned that the four of them had met at university. They had explained that their fondness for board games in general – and Khet in particular – was probably to do with the fact that they were all science geeks … and then they had lightly teased Amy for not being a science geek at all. It turned out she'd studied the only thing 'squarer' than science: theology. Amy accepted the teasing the same way she accepted Rob's inability to notice that she'd had her hair done: with a wry, affectionate smile. I learned about the schools they were working at, the month-long run they were about to embark on at the Edinburgh Fringe Festival, and about the show they were doing that night. I had also drunk two cups of tea and eaten an inordinate number of biscuits.

But now the conversation began to dry up. Not because there was nothing left to say but because Rhys and I were both concentrating hard. This was the main fight on the bill. Rhys vs Dave. Morgan vs Gorman. Mutton chops vs beard.

I was enjoying the game. With each turn played, the puzzle I was solving altered subtly. It was absorbing. And I really wanted to win. I was sure I was losing. Especially when my Pharaoh went on the run: it was the first time anyone had actually moved their Pharaoh. Sending him out into open space seemed like a desperate move but I couldn't see any other way of defending him.

And then something happened. The atmosphere changed. I looked around at the faces of my new friends and saw that they were all thinking the same thing. I just didn't know what that thing was. Amy, Rebecca and Rob were hiding smiles behind their eyes while Rhys's look of calm was so studied it had to be the look of a man who was *trying* to look calm.

I stared at the board some more, desperately trying to see what they could see, but no matter how hard I stared it was impossible to see anything other than my own Pharaoh in peril. I had no choice but to defend him: should I move him again, sending him out into a wider expanse of uncluttered space or should I block the path? I decided to block the path. I picked up a Pyramid and moved it one square to the left, not letting go, just resting my index finger in contact with its apex, unprepared to commit to the move until I'd considered all the implications.

I lifted my finger. I lost contact with the Pyramid. Had I done all that I could? Too late now. If Rhys was about to destroy me with his next move then so be it. *Que sera, sera.* I pressed the button. I fired my laser. It bounced once, twice, thrice and then four times ... and hit Rhys's Pharaoh.

'Agh,' said Rhys, through gritted teeth, 'I didn't think you were going to spot that. Well played.'

Should I admit to him that I *hadn't* actually seen it, that my move had been intended only as a means of defence? Of course not. I took the congratulations. I pretended I was better than I was.

'Thanks. I *nearly* didn't see it,' I said, shaking the hand he'd offered. 'I was a bit distracted by the cock-and-balls hieroglyph for a moment.' I gulped down the rest of my tea. 'I don't know what I was thinking.'

Rhys and Rob had to prepare for a show and I had to return to London, so with our afternoon's play over we decided to call it a day.

'I'm really glad I did this,' I said.

'I think we are, too,' said Rhys. 'It's a weird thing to do ... but ... but ... but ... well, there's no reason why it should be, is there?'

'No reason at all.'

With the sun shining and four red kites putting on an imperious aeronautical display in the clear blue sky above, I let my sense of direction guide me back to the train station. Didcot Parkway.

I found myself muttering the words aloud as I wandered. 'Didcot Parkway. Didcot Parkway. Didcot Parkway, Didcot Parkway, Didcot Parkway, Didcot Parkway ...'

If you say them quickly enough you start to sound like an old-fashioned steam train building up to a sprint. Is there a more onomatopoeic train station in the land? I very much doubt it.[1]

'Didcot Parkway, Didcot Parkway, Didcot Parkway,' I continued as I passed rows of pretty 1930s semis with stained-glass sunrises sitting atop neatly painted front doors and bay windows overlooking dainty front lawns. I was in a good mood. I had a spring in my step. I felt like I was walking away from a great first date. The kind of date that you just know will lead to other things.

I contemplated what a thoroughly fantastic couple of hours it had been. Far better than anything I would have done if I'd stayed at home in London. Mentally, I ticked off the positives. It had been a cheap day out. Tick. I'd played a very enjoyable game. Tick. It had been a great excuse to meet some really lovely people. Tick. I couldn't think of a negative. This had been a good day. Excellent!

And of course I was a winner. Lost one, won two. Not that I was keeping score. Competitive I may be, but I'm not a child.

---

1. Incidentally, 'Parkway' has always struck me as a particularly ugly and pointlessly modern term. It's a compound word and yet, unusually, it contrives to mean less than the sum of its parts. It feels hollow, as if a focus group has been given the task of inventing a word that means nothing but *sounds* full of meaning so as to not arouse suspicion (I imagine the rejected candidates were things like 'lakegarden', 'fieldscape' and 'dalewinton').

Given its vagueness, it's perhaps unsurprising that the word is used in different parts of the world to mean entirely different, and sometimes contradictory, things. In some places, a parkway is a rural road and in others it's a motorway. And in Britain, 'parkway' is used to describe a particular type of train station. Bristol Parkway was the first of them but these days there are nearly twenty park-and-ride stations that carry the suffix, ranging from Aylesbury Vale Parkway to Whittlesford Parkway.

In essence I've always understood it to mean train-station-that-isn't-actually-in-the-town-just-mentioned-but-does-have-a-big-car-park. Which makes Luton Airport Parkway my favourite of the bunch. It seems fitting that an enterprise that brazenly brands itself *London* Luton Airport despite lying thirty miles north of the capital should be served by a train station that's also not quite on target.

Okay. I *was* keeping score.

Rest of the World: **1**

Me: **2**

CHAPTER 3

Buoyed by the relaxed, easy, loveliness of my Didcot excursion I returned home and went straight to my computer. It was time to fire up the Random Day Out Generator. AKA Twitter.

In no time at all, I'd set up three play-dates for the next two days. I didn't do much picking and choosing; I just selected things based on their convenience.

As it happened, however, there was not one board game amongst them. In fact, things were taking a distinctly sporty turn. Well, sort of. If you consider table tennis, pool and territorial skittles to be sporty. (They are all things you can do in long trousers, after all.)

The first game was with a man called Clive. Clive had tweeted to tell me about an initiative called 'Ping London'. The aim of Ping London was to get people playing table tennis. To that end, they'd placed 100 hardy, weatherproof ping-pong tables in various public spaces around the capital. They could be found in parks, train stations, pubs and plazas and one of them had been placed directly outside the building where Clive worked.

I wonder how they arrived at the name, 'Ping London'. I assume it was a process of elimination. They probably thought 'Table Tennis London' sounded a bit too formal and 'Ping Pong London' a bit of a mouthful. They obviously couldn't go with 'Pong London' because that just sounds like an aftershave for people who want to smell of London[2] ... which left only one option. So Ping London it was.

---

2. As I write, there's an easterly wind, and London has the distinct whiff of fast food and diesel fumes, with a pigeon shit top-note.

I had two meetings to attend that day – I know! Two whole meetings! Poor me! – one in the centre of town, and the other just five minutes from the west London office where Clive worked, in White City. I had a ninety-minute gap between my two meetings, a window of opportunity that coincided perfectly with the time Clive said he could be free. It couldn't have been more convenient. It was clearly meant to be.

You don't have to have visited this particular office block to know what it looked like. Buildings just like it have been sprouting up all over Britain these last few years; it's not just an office block, it's a 'modern village'. It's the kind of place that looks so suspiciously like the architect's drawing that you suspect they've got someone on the payroll who pops along after dark to paint the leaves on the trees that particular shade of green. To keep the incoming traffic at a sedate pace there are bollards, but you're not entirely sure they really are bollards because they might just be particularly innocuous pieces of formless modern art. The ground-floor units have been given over to a collection of shops and there must be a local by-law stating that every catering outlet has to feature avocado and salmon, if not on the menu, then as a colour scheme. There's a wine bar decorated to make itself feel older than it is but it doesn't fool anyone because nineteenth-century taverns are rarely found inside twenty-first-century buildings. And it's all situated around an open, paved boulevard and a patch of grass. It is essentially a motorway service station with offices on top. And no motorway.

When I arrived I found small clusters of people gathered in the cool breeze: early-lunchers, late-arrivers and the occasional clutch of let's-take-this-meeting-outsiders, too. They were a peculiar mixture of smart and edgy. The people wearing suits all had some aesthetic quirk – spectacular frames to their spectacles, bright yellow trainers on their feet, an asymmetric haircut – to show they were creative, while the people in jeans all carried laptops and had smart phones pressed to their ears to show they meant business.

Clive didn't look like one of them. Clive wore raggedy jeans, a long-sleeved, loose-fitting, plain red shirt and had a huge mop of rock-God hair that billowed in the breeze.

Our game had to wait five minutes as I struggled to get my new table-tennis bat out of its wrapping. After my first meeting of the day, I'd nipped into a high street sports shop and picked up a decent bat for just three quid. It was a bargain for sure, but as Clive stood there, patiently bouncing a ball first on his bat, then the table, then his bat – *kadinkidonk*, *kadinkidonk*, *kadinkidonk* – I'd have gladly paid someone three times that price to open up the heat-sealed, clear plastic shell that encased it. Eventually a combination attack of teeth and keys did the job. We began to play.

Even before a ball had been struck I realised I was almost certainly going to lose. Clive stood ready to return my serve: one arm raised, the other held in front of his body as a counter-balance, looking more like a freeze-frame from the World Air Guitar Championships than anything else. But it wasn't his stance that gave him away as a player. It was his grip.

He held the bat in the oriental style. I hold a table-tennis bat like I'm shaking hands with it. He was holding his as if it was a pen. A big pen. With a nib the size of a table-tennis bat. That's not the grip of a casual, occasional player. That's the grip of someone with form.

He might not have looked very businesslike but he meant business.

'You've played before, I see.'

'What, this?' Clive adopted a look of wide-eyed innocence. 'This is how I was taught.'

I recognised his tone of voice. I might have been approaching forty but I could still remember the pre-exam conversations from my schooldays: '*Me? I* haven't done any revision!'

'Do you play?' Clive asked.

'Not really,' I said, serving the ball his way. *Kadonk.* 'The last time I played was about eight years ago.' *Kadink.* 'I played a nine-year-old boy in Boston.' *Kadonk.*

'Really?'

Kadink.

'It's a long story.' *Kadonk.* 'What about you?'

We were just patting soft shots across the net, battling the wind more than each other as we just tried to establish a rally.

'I used to work for a company that had a table.' *Kadink.* 'The boss ...' *Kadonk.* ' ... was really into it.' *Kadink.* 'He was Swedish.'

I furrowed my brow, confused at the idea that being Swedish was somehow sufficient explanation for someone's passion for ping pong. Saunas? Yes. Meatballs? Uh huh. Designer furniture? Okay. Table tennis? News to me. The ball seemed to be equally confused. So much so that it suddenly forgot the laws of physics and stopped in mid flight, hovering briefly before jerking backwards and then spiralling down-wards as if riding an invisible helter-skelter. Okay, maybe it wasn't confused; maybe it had just been caught in a peculiar current of wind. Either way, it pinged off the edge of a paving stone and into a low bush behind me.

'He used to organise tournaments at work,' Clive continued, as I scrabbled around trying to retrieve the ball. 'I was the doubles champion for a while.'

'Oh, aye!'

'That was more to do with my partner than me, though.'

'Really?' I stood up, ball in hand. 'Who was that then?'

'The boss,' said Clive. He gestured for me to start a new rally. I did. *Kadonk.* 'He used to play for the Swedish Olympic team, I think.' *Kadink.*

'Really?' *Kadonk.*

'Something like that.'

The ball sat up obediently at Clive's shoulder. It was too tempting for him to continue our polite tippety-tap rally-building so he unleashed a smash, the whole of his body rolling over and through the ball in an instant. *Thwack! Donk!*

I turned, approached the ball-swallowing bush and dropped to my haunches once more.

With the ball back in hand we checked that we both understood the rules the same way – first to 21 with serve alternating every five points – and then we started the game proper.

Clive served first.

Less than a minute later and he was 4–1 up. I'd only made contact with the ball a handful of times and I hadn't hit a winner. My one point had been secured not by any brilliance on my part, but by Clive uncharacteristically misfiring a serve into the base of the net.

With my five serves I got myself back into the game, even playing an audacious drop shot to win one of the points that left me just 6–4 down. The wind decided to help me out in the next two service cinques and, remarkably, at the halfway stage I found myself level. 10–10.

It surely couldn't last. But it did. I took the next three points against the serve before dollying up two sitters that Clive dispatched with clinical, flashing, top-spin smashes. *Thwack! Thwack!* I was in the lead but only just. 13–12 and serving.

Serving into the net. Twice. Agh. I got the next three serves in, but in making sure that I at least put the ball in play, they had little or no bite and I'd effectively surrendered control, gifting him another three points. I was 17–13 down.

17–14, good. 17–15, nice, then, with a shot that landed so perfectly on the edge of the table that it just zinged horizontally into Clive's crotch, 17–16. That seemed to prompt Clive to push the ball further towards the edges, too, and he immediately returned the favour with his next shot doing the exact same thing at my end of the table before, *thwack,* another smash and he was 19–16 up.

My life was on the line. I had five serves. Or at least I would have five serves if I won enough of them. I could just as easily lose the game in two.

Kadonkidink. 20–16. Arse.

Kadonkidink kadonkidink kadonk. 20–17.

Kadonkidink kadonkidink kadonkidink ka-swish donk – the ball landed and, with a surprisingly vicious backhand slice, it deceived Clive's eye, jumping sharply to the left and under his bat. 20–18. I was still in the game. I wanted to win.

I served into the corner – *kadonk* – Clive, returned it with interest – *kadink* – I took the pace off the ball – *kadonk* – and then a small breeze got up, slowing the ball further, foreshortening its path. Clive adjusted quickly, lunging forwards, his weight on the balls of his feet as he batted the ball back my way – *kadiiiiink.* It was my turn to go for the smash – the ball was hanging in the air begging to be hit – I jumped, rolling my shoulder as I did so – *thwack* – the ball accelerated away from me and then spun on and on and on, missing the edge of the table not by a hair's width, not by an inch but by a yard or more. It was a frankly awful shot.

Defeat. 21–18.

Rest of the World:	2
Me:	2

As competitive as I am – and I *bet* I'm more competitive than you – I couldn't walk away from the game feeling unhappy. It had, after all, been a quite marvellous distraction. I don't know what you do for a living but whatever it is, if your working day serves up a one-off ninety-minute interval I doubt you can think of many ways to use that time that would pip a game of ping pong. Besides, if you're going to play strangers at games of their choosing, it stands to reason that you're going to lose more often than not.

If the only point of playing games is to win then there'd have been no point at all in me boarding a train that evening and heading to Twickenham to meet Rob. This wasn't the Rob I'd met in Didcot. This was a different Rob. This Rob had invited me to play pool.

I am categorically awful at pool. I had to assume Rob wasn't awful. It would have been peculiarly masochistic of him to suggest it if he was. I have never been good at any cue sport. It has not been for want of trying.

Like most people in Britain, I was carried away with the snooker boom of the 1980s. The sport regularly secured huge ratings on TV, most famously with the 1985 World Championships. The final was contested by Steve Davis and Dennis Taylor, two players who were portrayed in simple terms: Davis was the man with loads of ability but – at that time – no discernible personality, while Taylor ... well, let's just say he had bags of personality.

Davis stormed into an 8–0 lead and everyone thought the game was going to end earlier than normal. But, amazingly, Taylor clawed his way back into it. The match went the distance. It couldn't have been any closer: it didn't just go down to the final, 35th, frame ... it went down to the final ball. One ball. Whoever pots it, wins. Whoever pots it is crowned champion of the world.

The official figures say that 18.5 million people were watching when, long after midnight, Dennis Taylor finally sank that ball. He raised his cue aloft, gripping it with both hands, his knuckles white, half punching the air like a man who'd seen other people celebrate and was now trying to remember how it was done.

Nobody really knows how many people were watching. There's no accurate way of knowing how many TVs were turned on, let alone what channel they were tuned to. And even if 'they' had known that our TV was on BBC2, how could they possibly know how many people were in the living room watching it?

We were *all* watching it. Nick and I were fourteen. Do fourteen year olds have bedtime any more? We certainly did back then. At the time, I was convinced that Mum was so engrossed in the game she'd forgotten we were there, but with hindsight it seems more likely that she was just making an exception. Most parents did. The next day at school even the kids with no interest in snooker had seen it. Not because they wanted to but because their parents had *made* them stay up. It was an event. It had to be witnessed. It was our moon landing.

It was around that time that Nick and I were given a snooker table. A joint present in every way: his and mine, Christmas *and* birthday. It obviously wasn't a proper snooker table. It was only four feet long and with a chipboard base that warped in no time at all. It was rubbish. But we were rubbisher and we loved it. We saved up our pocket money and bought our own cues from Argos. Mine was made of ash and 'signed' by Alex Higgins. I convinced myself that it made me a better player. It didn't. It really didn't.

Occasionally we'd take a trip into town and play on a proper table at the local snooker club. It was on the far side of town somewhere near to Stafford Prison and, to my innocent eyes, most of the clientele looked like that was where they belonged. I think they liked to give that impression and I don't think they liked us being there. We ruined the carefully crafted atmosphere just by existing in it. Sitting in the triangular shadows, their low voices hanging in the air with the same lack of distinction enjoyed by the thick fug of cigarette smoke that drifted lazily around the green canopied lights, they were extras in a gangster movie. But the illusion was shattered by the arrival of two smartly turned-out, middle-class boys with unbroken voices. Snooker only had itself to blame. It had gone mainstream.

Snooker might have a gentleman's dress code but at heart it belongs to the rogues. If it's for children at all, it's for the wild ones who bunk off school and play old men for beer. The wildest thing about me was the Alex Higgins 'signature' on my catalogue-shop cue.

But they let us in. They took our money. And they didn't let us on the good tables. (And if I was in their shoes today I'd do the same thing.)

If you've never played on a full-size snooker table before, I recommend you try it at least once. Especially if you think you're a half-decent pool player. You'll be astounded by your own lack of ability. On TV, the table just doesn't look as vast as it truly is. That shot you think of as a tricky long pot on your pub pool table is the same length as a shot across the width of a proper snooker table – the type of shots you think are sitters when you're in your armchair. It's four times bigger. And consequently so are all your inaccuracies.

In all our visits to the snooker club, I don't think either of us had a break involving more than four consecutive balls. At the end of a frame the scores would be embarrassingly low, 37–26, say, and half of those points would have been the result of 4-point penalties for foul shots. We were so bad it's hard to fathom why we went back for more. I really can't see that we ever played competently enough to make it satisfying.

These were the memories that flooded through me as I descended the stairs towards the Twickenham basement where I was meeting Rob that evening. I was expecting to open the door at the foot of the stairs and enter the same, smoky, dingy, wannabe-gangster atmosphere I'd been cowed by as a child. But of course it wasn't smoky. Public buildings in Britain aren't any more. Not unless they're on fire, and I make a point of not walking downstairs towards basements that are on fire. It's one of the things you should know about me.

It was huge, occupying the same footprint as several of the shop units above ground combined. It was bright. Brightly lit and with bright red walls; most of them decorated with brightly coloured posters advertising brightly coloured drinks. There must have been ten, twelve, maybe fifteen pool tables evenly spread throughout the room and, on the far wall, a solitary dartboard. And this was just the frivolous end of things. The *snooker* tables didn't breathe the same alcopop-tinged air as the pool tables, no: they were lined up, like a bunch of high-end sports cars in a special air-controlled garage, on the other side of a darkened glass wall.

It wasn't smoky. It wasn't dark or dingy. And there were no wannabe gangsters to be seen. In fact, it was almost empty. There were just three people in the whole place: one member of staff, one man playing pool by himself and one man, presumably Rob, propping up the bar.

Rob looked to be in his late thirties, with sandy hair, a stubbly beard and broad shoulders. Our eyebrows did the 'I'm-meeting-someone-are-you-meeting-someone-because-if-you-are-it's-probably-me-that-you're-meeting' manoeuvre and then, having swapped hellos, we shook hands with shy smiles, our shoulders doing the 'I'm-sorry-about-that-thing-I-just-did-with-my-eyebrows' shrug.

Rob had a soft Yorkshire accent: years of living in London meant his flat vowels were now wrapped up in consonants with smooth edges. He was a graphic designer but he'd made the move down south not for work but for a girl.

I'd moved to London from Manchester when I was 28, so we had plenty in common.

London doesn't have *one* identity. London is many places and has many tribes. When you don't really know the place but have to choose which part of it to move to, it's an almost entirely random choice. Rob and I had made our moves down south at a similar time. He'd ended up in the south-western suburbs and I'd ended up in the East End. It seemed to me we had more in common with each other than with our respective choices, and yet we were both amusingly adamant that we'd found the best part of London for us.

Twickenham doesn't feel like London at all to me: it's not connected to the tube for a start. I can't quite accept the idea of taking an overground train – not a tube, not a bus, not a tram but a train – and using it to travel to another part of the *same* city. Twickenham, along with Kingston, Richmond and Hampton Wick, is really Surrey in disguise. It's the stock-broker belt. In these parts, the Thames is a wide playground for rich people's leisure boats; not the industrial-looking river you find slicing through the city from Battersea to Greenwich docks. In Twickenham, the postcode begins with TW. That's not a London postcode! *Real* London postcodes – N2, NW3, EC4 – tell you where they are relative to the rest of London: N (north), NW (north west), W (west), SE (south east), SW (south west), WC (west central), EC (east central) or, the finest of the lot, E (east). Twickenham is where I expect to meet posh yobs: public schoolboys with a sense of entitlement and their collars turned up almost as much as their noses.

Rob, of course, was nothing of the sort. I don't think I appear to be a part of the Bethnal Green tribe either. I'm not a trust-fund artist/poet/dj/nightclub-promoter. I don't wear skin-tight jeans or vintage clothes. I don't have an ironic 80s haircut or any primary-coloured plastic jewellery.

If you had been in the snooker club that night you'd have seen two men wearing interchangeable outfits: blue jeans, trainers, the kind of loose-fitting shirt that hides a recently developed paunch – both approaching forty, both with grey flecks in their reddish beards, both having moved to London from different parts of the North and both passionately convinced that they'd chosen the right part of London to live in. And, I suspect, both knowing that deep down it didn't really matter.

You would also have been witness to a near whitewash: we played ten frames of pool. I won one of them.

As every pub pool player knows, there's a point in the night when your level of alcohol consumption is just right and you are suddenly transformed into a cue-wielding, computer-programmed robot. All at once, the pockets are huge and welcoming, your cue arm is fluid, and the balls simply do your bidding. And then, just half a drink later, your form disappears and you are human once more. For me, the right amount appears to be exactly two-and-a-quarter rum and cokes. The window closed by the time that third drink was done. For that brief time I was good. For that brief time, I was better than Rob.

He probably had a similar moment during the evening when things went especially well for him. I didn't notice, though, because when we were both human, he was still, clearly, much, much better than me. In fact he was sort of good.

Rest of the World:	**11**
Me:	**3**

Ouch.

CHAPTER 4

The next day I completed my mildly sporting, long-trousered triathlon by playing the game I referred to earlier as territorial skittles. The game in question is actually called 'Kubb'. It's Swedish. (So I imagine it loves table tennis.)

To play Kubb you will need:

RULES

- An opponent. Obviously.

- A patch of grass about eight metres x five metres in size. (If you want to visualise it, that's about two-thirds the size of a badminton court.)

- Ten kubbs: square-ended wooden skittles about fifteen centimetres tall.

- 1 king: a thicker, larger skittle about thirty centimetres tall.

- Six wooden rods, about fifteen centimetres long and similar in diameter to the baton you might use in a relay race.

- Six life-size concrete cows.

Okay ... I lied about the concrete cows. You don't actually *need* them. But we had them and I think they added a certain *something* to the experience. Seeing as there's only one set of famous concrete cows that I know of, you might have sensibly deduced that my game of Kubb was played in Milton Keynes. You'd be right.

I like Milton Keynes.

There, I've said it.

It's not a fashionable opinion I know and, given some of my comments about Didcot, you might even detect the whiff of hypocrisy about it, but it's true all the same.

It wasn't ever thus. Some of my father's family were based in Milton Keynes, and when the Gormans went to visit I'd look out of the car at the ordered houses and think it a soulless place. Or did I? Did I *really* think that for myself or was I just buying into the Milton Keynes mythology? After all, that's what we're supposed to think, isn't it?

To many people, Milton Keynes will always be more a punch-line than it is a place. It is to British urban centres what the marque 'Skoda' is to cars. But just as these days Skodas tend to be perfectly acceptable motorcars, so it's true that Milton Keynes is a perfectly acceptable town. In fact, these days, I think it's a place with real confidence and swagger.

Of course, as I was a child when I first visited the place, it's possible that it just looked different through grown-up eyes. More likely, I suspect, it's Milton Keynes itself that's grown up. The Milton Keynes we know today is only in its early forties. Only now is there a generation of adults who feel they *belong* to Milton Keynes. That makes a difference. Milton Keynes is no longer embarrassed by its newness.

Other towns – with their ring roads and spider's-web maps – can sneer all they like because Milton Keynesians know their road system does that most un-British of things: it works. And if that makes it sound like a non-stop urban-tartan of tarmac and concrete, well, I don't find that popular myth to be true either. There's surely more greenery there than in most towns of equivalent size, with cycle paths stretching their way through lush parkland that has emerged from its awkward teenage years looking mature and assured.

Its most famous residents, those famous concrete cows, are situated in some of that parkland. Or at least the main set are. (I believe there are a few different sets round and about; some in a local shopping centre, some in a hotel lobby and so on. Maybe it's like when Field Marshal Montgomery employed a lookalike during the war: it helps to keep people guessing.)

I was playing against Andy, who had found the game through his work. He's a youth worker and had deliberately sought out games that would be good for children of different ages. Kubb did the job because, unlike a lot of games of its ilk, it doesn't necessarily favour the biggest, strongest player. There's guile involved, too. And some luck.

With the gentle trickle of water in the nearby brook acting as our soundtrack and with that herd of concrete cows and the occasional dog walker as our spectators, my game of Kubb began.

Unlike skittles, where both players throw at the same target, in Kubb you face one another, playing from opposite ends of the improvised court. You start with five kubbs lined up on each baseline and the king standing halfway between the two of you, right on the notional centre spot. The winner is the first person to knock over all of their opponent's kubbs and *then* the king. But the king is like the black ball in a game of pool: you can't take it out until you've downed all the others. If you do, you lose the game. Of course, in pool, when you pot a ball it's no longer a part of the game. The equivalent isn't true of toppled kubbs. At the end of a round they're thrown back into the opposing court and then, wherever they land, they're stood up again to become targets for the round that follows.

There are intricacies to this stage of the game that mean delicate tactical decisions have to be made. It really is about far more than just throwing bits of wood at other bits of wood (indeed, its Swedish origins and tactical nature have earned the game the nickname 'Viking chess'). Which part of the court do you throw the kubbs to? Do you try to group them? Leave them near the halfway line? Or throw towards the back of the court? If one bounces out of bounds you get to try again. But if it's out of bounds a second time, your opponent gets to place the kubb wherever *he* likes. (So long as it's in his half of the court, obviously. He can't take it home and put it in the fridge. That'd be silly.)

If, during your round, you fail to knock over one of the kubbs you've thrown into court, then when it comes to your opponent's turn he no longer has to throw from the baseline. He can advance to a line level with the furthest standing pin, making his throws shorter and therefore considerably easier.

The end result of all this is that control of the game tends to ebb and flow. Just as you think you've seized a numerical advantage, just as victory seems to be in your sights, your opponent invariably comes back strongly and it's you who's fighting to stay alive.

In our first game there were four occasions when Andy was left with just one kubb standing – while I was just two throws from triumph – but on all four occasions he was able to rally. And he definitely *wanted* to rally.

Andy was a competitive soul. He left me in no doubt of that when he suddenly employed the most dastardly of tactics. The ground was relatively hard under foot and things were bouncing erratically, scooting off at odd, unpredictable angles. I had twice failed to lob a kubb safely back into Andy's half – both times it had landed somewhere in the middle of the court, only to kick, spin, thud and bundle its way out of bounds. So I knew I was in trouble when Andy picked up the disobedient piece of wood and a mischievous Jack-Nicholson-'Here's-Johnny!'-style grin spread across his face.

'Now,' he said, 'I get to place this one *anywhere* I like ...'
'Yeah.'
'So ... I'm going to put it, mmmmm ... *here*.'
He placed the kubb directly behind the king.
'Ah, come on!' I squealed. 'You can't do that!'

'Yeah, of course I can.'

'I can't even see it! If I go for it and knock the king over I lose the game ...'

'Yup.'

' ... and if I don't knock it over you'll be able to throw from the halfway line ...'

'Yup.'

'Bloody hell!'

'Well ...' Andy chuckled. 'I wouldn't do this if I was playing a ten year old – I go easy then. But you're not ten. And you've got to learn.'

'Fair enough,' I said. Because it was.

It was the Kubb equivalent of being snookered. If I didn't knock the kubb over the game was as good as lost.

I went for death or glory.

I moved as far to the right as I could to give myself the best angle and lined up my arm with care. With a short backstroke, I lofted the baton towards the target and – to my amazement – it managed to pass within an inch of the king, clipping the kubb on the top edge and knocking it safely away.

The rush of adrenaline was real. I actually did a small fist pump as a growled, 'Yessss!' fell from my lips.

Andy rubbed his hands together. Game on. Suddenly this game of Kubb was serious.

This game of Kubb was seriously fun.

I liked Andy. It was easy to like him because he seemed to like life.

People who really like their jobs tend to have an enviable sense of ease with the world. It makes them ... well, easy to be around. I don't think Andy liked his work. I think he loved it. Perhaps it was because he hadn't simply glided into it. People who've travelled a harder road are often more excited about the destination when they get there: ex-smokers are always more passionately anti-tobacco than those of us who've never had the habit.

'I failed all my A-levels and didn't really know what I wanted to do when I left school,' he told me as the kubbs bounced around our ankles. 'I got a job at the Royal Mail. It was good money. Especially as I was still living at home. I liked the people and all that, but all I did was spend five days in a sorting office looking forward to the weekend … when I'd spend the money getting drunk. I wasn't going anywhere.'

'And now you're a youth worker … So what happened?'

'I was in the pub one night, in a hell of a state, when someone came in …' Andy's voice trailed off. I couldn't tell if it was because he was weighing up what to do with his next throw or because he was caught in a moment of embarrassed reflection on that drunken night of the past.

'Go on,' I said, nudging the chat gently on. 'Who was it?'

'Paul.' Andy's smile was rueful. 'He used to be *my* youth worker. He reminded me that I'd said I wanted to work with young people and …'

Another pause. Another embarrassed smile.

'And,' I guessed, 'you were good at it?'

'Yeah,' said Andy quietly. Shyly. And then, with a bit more confidence, he said it again. 'Yeah!'

'Wanting to do it and actually doing it are different things.' I picked up a kubb and tossed it back into Andy's half of the court. 'How do you go from being a postman with no A-levels to being a youth worker?'

'It's hard work. Paul sent me some details of a course that could be a springboard to university. It was two years and I was still doing forty hours a week at the Royal Mail, but I knew it was what I wanted. It was a steep learning curve. Learning about myself, too. *Really* hard work. But with lots of volunteering and practical experience … it was fantastic to actually be *doing* something.'

Andy's two-year course had been followed by a three-year vocational degree at a university in Leicester. His first job was in Leicester, too, but it hadn't been long before the gravitational pull of his home town had eventually drawn him back to Milton Keynes.

As our game continued Andy told me about the day-to-day nature of his job. Occasionally he'd slip into jargon but then he'd catch himself doing it and, with an apologetic grin, quickly rephrase it using more everyday language. He didn't put it as plainly as *this* but my understanding is that the job really calls for two qualities. One: being there for people, and two: not being a dick.

Everyone needs some advice and guidance as they negotiate the tricky path from childhood into adulthood. The lucky ones get all they need in this area from their parents, extended families, teachers and so on, but there are always going to be some who either reject these role models or for whom they're simply absent in the first place. Having an adult like Andy around for *those* kids to talk to – someone who isn't an authority figure and who isn't a dungaree-wearing, happy-clappy, children's entertainer, either – can only be a good thing.

It's got to be the kind of job that you get more effective at the longer you do it, too. It makes sense to me that young lads might look on you with suspicion if you're the-man-who's-come-to-talk-to-them-now-that-they're-fifteen-and-getting-into-a-spot-of-bother – but if you've been in their orbit for five years already, then there's an existing connection and they're more likely to meet your eye.

Andy was clearly passionate about his job and the positive effects it could have, but his self-deprecating nature meant he was never in danger of getting carried away with himself. There are people in the world – the high-on-life evangelists – who exhibit such superhuman levels of happiness and self-confidence that it's actually more off-putting than anything else. Andy wasn't one of them. Instead, he exuded a quiet confidence, warmth and a sense of contentment.

Little wonder, really. He's an ordinary bloke whose job is to be an ordinary bloke. I think that's got to be the best way of helping young people to be the best blokes – and blokesses – they can be. Which is pretty extraordinary when you think about it.

I seem to have stopped telling you about the game. Except I haven't, really. Because with some games the fun is in the stuff that goes on *while* you're playing them. It's about the interaction and the conversation. It's about the sharing of time and space. And Andy's time and space were worth sharing. I certainly couldn't be unhappy about the fact that he'd beaten me in a game of Kubb.

Especially as I won the one after that.

I wished we'd had time for a third, but Andy had to race off as he was heading to a music festival later that day. We'd had an hour of play. Honours were even. We left it at that.

Rest of the World:	12
Me:	4

CHAPTER 5

At the age of twenty I existed in a state of permanent awkwardness. I hadn't yet settled in my own skin. I wasn't remotely confident of my ability to negotiate the adult world but, because my teens were behind me, I no longer felt I was entitled to ask. I felt like an impostor, bluffing my way from day to day, always just moments away from being exposed. I felt like a gatecrasher at a party even when I was sitting alone in my own room.

I'd started performing stand-up comedy at the age of nineteen. I had nothing to talk about. I hadn't been anywhere. I hadn't *done* anything. I hadn't worked out who I was. So instead of writing about *stuff*, I wrote about *words*. It was smart-alec stuff that I delivered with an emotional detachment; I hid my lack of confidence behind a deadpan mask. It was a defence mechanism: if I looked like I didn't care then the audience couldn't hurt me … If they didn't like it – I didn't care. Or so I told myself. Of course I cared. But I was young. And caring made me look vulnerable. I didn't dare to look vulnerable.

Most of the time it worked. Most of the time I got away with it. But sometimes the deadpan mask got in the way. Sometimes an audience looked at me and seemed to think, 'Well, if you don't care, why should we?' And they were right.

It wasn't until I was in my late twenties that I found the confidence to be myself on stage. I showed that I cared. I let the audience see that I was vulnerable. It wasn't a sign of weakness after all. It was a sign of strength. It wasn't until I was in my late twenties that I grew up.

*

Elliott must have been about twenty. But he was fresh-faced enough to have passed for fifteen. He wore a red, white and blue cotton sweatband on his right wrist, while his left was decorated with a rag-tag collection of plaited string bangles. A small chain hung round his neck and with the top two or three buttons undone on his baggy grey shirt, I could see the plectrum-shaped pendant that hung from it. If I tried to get away with that kind of laid-back, gap-year chic I'd look like a midlife-crisis beach-bum, but on Elliott it was cool. (Or whatever word the youngsters use to mean 'cool' these days.) It was the look of a troubadour: a singer–songwriter with conviction in his soul and hope in his smouldering eyes. Which was a good look for Elliott, because that was exactly what he was.

The day after we met I searched for him online and found some of his music.[3] His guitar playing is intricate and skilful and his voice is strong and honest – something it needs to be for his heartfelt style of folky pop. If I hadn't liked him I'd have hated him for making me feel so old. He's not just good at what he does; he's good at being who he is. How dare he!

We met in an east London pub that sits in the shadow of Liverpool Street station. A real ale pub. A proper boozer. It had an almost exclusively male clientele: men of different ages but all of a certain type … a type who probably wouldn't use the word *clientele*.

While I'd been waiting for Elliott to show up I'd bought myself a coffee and been faintly amused by the number of disapproving glances my teetotal choice had garnered. But when Elliott asked for a pint of Owd Wobberley Jowls (or whatever peculiar concoction it was) I was glad. No more coffee for me, either. I, too, was ready to imbibe. It wasn't peer pressure *per se* – it was more a simple counter-balance to what was about to happen.

---

3. http://www.myspace.com/elliottmorris

This was a venue for inconspicuous adults to be doing inconspicuous, keep-yourself-to-yourself things. But Elliott's game of choice was ... 'Guess Who?' I was about to play a children's game – a brightly coloured, hard to miss, children's game – with someone close to being half my age. So any stamp of adulthood – any sign that we were aware of our own surroundings – was more than welcome.

Once upon a time, many years ago, I spent a couple of hours sitting in a photographer's studio pretending to play the children's game, Guess Who? I sat there with wide eyes and a rictus grin, feigning high excitement while the scene was captured on film from every conceivable angle. The resulting photos were used as part of a book cover which parodied the game's own packaging. (It must have been a little too accurate a parody because a few years after the book was published, lawyers representing the game's manufacturer, MB Games, got in touch. I believe our cheeky choice of cover ended up getting my publisher into a spot of bother. Oops.)

Despite all that pretending, I'd never actually played the game. A classic it might be, but not one my brothers or I had ever owned. Of course, I had a rough idea as to how it worked. I knew there was a cast of fictional characters and that you had to identify one of them by a process of elimination and guesswork, but I didn't know any more than that.

It turns out there is nothing more than that to actually know.

I'd always assumed there was some extra dimension to it, that it involved some level of skill and tactics, *something* that meant it wasn't *just* about luck and guesswork. I couldn't really understand how it had become quite such a popular game if it didn't have any of those qualities: qualities that, to me, *define* a game.

There is nothing I can write that will inject even a hint of drama into proceedings. There were no nail-biting moments.

There were no *moments* of any kind. Three games passed by in fifteen minutes or so but it was just a tit-for-tat, bit-for-bat, exchange of questions: 'Does he have black hair?', 'Is she wearing a hat?', 'Does he have a big nose?' Neither of us employed tactics – there are none – and neither of us could say we played well. Or badly. You can't. You can only play.

Game one. I lost and yet didn't feel defeated. Game two. I lost again and simply didn't care.

'Am I missing something here?' I took a sip of rum. 'I mean … we are just both *guessing*, aren't we?'

'Yeah. Basically.'

'So what made you suggest Guess Who?' I asked. The game seemed genuinely at odds with the confident young man sitting in front of me.

'I thought it might be a bit different,' he shrugged. 'I didn't think anybody else was likely to come up with it …'

I smiled. I'd been bombarded with a few hundred tweets in such a short space of time that I had no idea what I had and hadn't been invited to play. I hadn't analysed them. I hadn't quantified, filtered or filed them. I'd just taken a lucky dip, seen whatever was convenient and gone with it. I was about to explain as much but I figured it might sound a bit brusque, a tad ungrateful.

'Well, I think you're right there,' I said.

Elliott gulped at his ale. 'Do you want another game?'

'Um … yeah, okay!' I don't know where *that* came from. I definitely didn't want another game. But I didn't not-want one, either.

We shuffled the cards. I picked first. Bill. Stupid Bill. With his egg-shaped face, rosy cheeks, bald head and ginger beard. Elliott picked a card. Elliot guessed first.

'Does your character have red hair?'

'Yes.'

My turn to guess.

'Is your character male?'

'Yes.'

Whoop. De. Do.

Hmm, I realise I could be starting to look a bit mardy here: I appear to be painting a picture of myself as something of a bad loser. Please believe me when I say that in all honesty, winning or losing didn't really come into it. I wish I had won a game, not because I think there'd be any pleasure in that victory but because it would allow me to demonstrate how unmoved I was by *that* as well. Because being unmoved by the game was really the dominant sensation. I wasn't enjoying Guess Who? ... but neither was I actively *not*-enjoying it. I was simply nonplussed by it all.

The conversation was sort of flowing but then it had to, because the game wasn't. All performers, be they musicians, comics, actors or anything else, have a store of self-flagellating tales to trade with one another. These stories of backstage disaster, of early performances to near-empty rooms and of dodgy fly-by-night promoters who don't pay on the day and then disappear without trace, are usually enjoyable to share. It's just that whilst doing so we were also having to play ... no, no, *play* isn't the right word, um, *participate in* ... nope, that's not right either, um ... I know ... *say the words required by* – yep, that's it – *say-the-words-required-by* ... the so-called-game Guess Who? If asking 'Is he bald?' is playing a game, well, then you might as well say that when my mum's cat, Banjax, scurries around the living-room floor chasing a ball of wool he's actually knitting.

After three 'games' and three 'defeats', I was trying to work out whether or not it would be rude to leave already. It was all right for me; I was only a twenty-minute walk from home. But Elliott had travelled 130-odd miles from Lincoln. He hadn't made that journey just to play me at Guess Who? you understand; he was in London to play a couple of gigs but, even so, it would have been rude to cut and run too soon. Luckily I didn't have to.

'I guess that's that for Guess Who?' he said, picking up the pieces and packing them carefully away in his satchel.

Ah, I was off the hook. He was clearly about to steer the conversation towards the goodbyes himself.

Or was he?

'I did bring another game with me … if you're interested …?'

I was.

'You might not have heard of it,' he continued. 'My dad had it. I've played it a couple of times. It's called "Kensington".'

I shrugged. The name meant nothing to me, but then, as I saw the game being drawn out of his canvas bag, I almost yelped with delight as a fully formed memory rushed excitedly to the front of my brain.

I'd played this game before. I remembered playing my middle brother, Rich, at this; the two of us hunching over the board as it rested precariously on top of his crumpled bed – the only semi-flat surface available in his ludicrously tiny box room.

There's something oddly energising about sparking a memory from nowhere like that. I don't think it's the memory itself that does it. I think it's the excitement at discovering your brain is so much bigger than you realised. The game Kensington had been locked away in a darkened corner of unused memory space. Seeing it for real had turned a light on, instantly illuminating not just the game but whichever other long-lost fragments of my past were occupying the same dusty brainhole. Suddenly I could recall the bedspread with the diamond pattern of little cotton loops and the bald patches on it where one of us kids had idly plucked the loops away. The glass panel above the door that my mum had painted black with thick, unfussy brush strokes, the smell of the house, the sound of the phone, the tartan slippers with the rubber soles that we didn't really wear except when Gran was coming to stay when we'd have to pretend we always wore them ... all these and more came flooding back to me: a mini tsunami of fond reminiscence. All things that had been long forgotten. All things I'd forgotten I'd forgotten. All things I didn't know I'd ever known. If one object can trigger all that, then how many other darkened recesses are there lurking in my brain? How many other memories lie there dormant just waiting for a stranger to strike a match? Is everything I've ever seen, heard, touched, smelled and felt available to me, given the right stimulus?

'Wow!' I said (because that sums up everything I've just shared with you). 'We *did* have this. My brother had this game! Wow!'

Elliott grinned.

'My brother got this for Christmas one year,' I continued, still bubbling with what must have seemed to be inexplicable levels of excitement. 'He was *really* disappointed!'

Elliott's eyes narrowed and his jaw dropped, momentarily perplexed by my upbeat tone and downbeat words. I *was* excited by the game. And my brother *had* been disappointed by it. But that's not because the game itself is disappointing; it's because the game's packaging flatters to deceive.

It was in the same dimensions as an LP. It weighed about the same as an LP. And its packaging – a cardboard, gatefold sleeve contained within a clear plastic wallet – was identical to the packaging you'd find on an LP.

To the game's manufacturers this must have seemed like a masterstroke of cost-effective design. Surely it would have saved them a fortune. The LP was the definitive music format of the day. Machines could print, cut and fold cardboard sleeves in huge numbers at low cost. Why pay to have something bespoke made for you when the infrastructure required to produce cheap packaging that could be made to work was already available?

The problem was that back then, an LP was a highly treasured item. In this age of disposable, dirt-cheap downloads and free online file-sharing, it's hard to remember quite how much we used to lust after those unwieldy vinyl discs. They were gold dust. Gold dust that in late-70s, early-80s Stafford, we could only really get from three shops: WHSmith, Woolworths or, more oddly, Boots the chemist.

A single was almost impossibly exciting but an album, well, that was out of this world. An album involved a real commitment. It took two or three weeks' pocket money to buy an album so you'd think every duff track would be bitterly resented. But it was worse than that. Every duff track was *denied*. The emotional and financial commitment involved in buying an LP was so great you would convince yourself you loved every single second of it *no matter what*. Admitting to my parents that I'd found the two or three inevitable filler tracks a bit dull would have been like telling them I'd stood in the street and set fire to my pocket money. The very thought was too much to bear so instead I would pretend – to myself as well as to them – that the jazz experiments and introspective noodly nonsense were exactly what I was after. I had to. Because it was *an album*.

Giving a child a gift-wrapped version of Kensington for Christmas in 1982 was, effectively, an unwitting practical joke that verged on the cruel. I remember seeing Rich as he held the present aloft. His eyes were wide, awestruck. He was almost salivating, his imagination doing back-flips as he contemplated what vinyl glory was about to be unleashed. Rich was a rocker, the only one in the house, but that just meant his tastes were easily defined. It was probably the latest Iron Maiden album. They were his big thing. Or maybe Motorhead? AC/DC? But most likely Maiden.

His sweaty fingers tore at the paper, his face a vision of premature glee, but all that was revealed was ... a board game. A board game that boasted it could be played by people of all ages '... from 7 to 107'. On the back cover of this board game – where the track listing clearly should have been – was a photograph that could have been calculated to make young boys yawn. It was a picture of two boring old men sitting by the boring old Albert Memorial: a monument *so* boring and old it's actually a tribute to an old, boring man: a man who was so boring he married the most famously unamused woman the world has ever known and so old he was actually bloody dead. I mean ... *pfft*!

How could it ever have been anything but a disappointment? It didn't matter how good the game was, once a young boy had been led to believe he was getting an album, the fact that it was a game – any game – could only be a let-down.

Kensington

Kensington's board is made up of interlocking squares and triangles that combine to form seven larger hexagons. The three central hexagons are white in colour while the two on either side are either red or blue. Each player has fifteen small discs. Not the exciting discs you'd hoped would be inside the sleeve, but small counters about the size of your fingernail. One of you plays with the red counters, the other with the blue. The idea is to slide these discs around the board so that you occupy all three points of a triangle, all four points of a square or all six points of a hexagon. If you take control of a triangle you get to move one of your opponent's pieces. If you complete a square you get to move two of them, and if you complete a hexagon you win the game – so long as the hexagon is one of your own colour, or one of the three neutral whites.

It's abstract. And it's tactical. And because every piece moves in the same way it's also exceedingly simple to grasp. Which makes it the kind of game

I have a bit of a soft spot for. It requires a lot of concentration: you have to work just as hard to frustrate your opponent's moves as you do on building your own, and it's very easy to become so focused on blocking a square that you forget two of its nodes are also corners of the neighbouring triangle. Or vice versa. I suppose it's a bit like Khet. A bit. A tiny bit. Only with much smaller, fiddlier pieces. And no lasers.

As Elliott and I set up and began to play our first game, I started to enjoy the distracted, abstract feeling that comes as your brain properly engages in an activity. Now *this* was a sensible thing for two men to meet in a pub for. Mind you, it wasn't necessarily the most sensible thing for two *strangers* to meet in a pub for. It's not the kind of game that incubates a getting-to-know-you conversation. It requires too much focus for that. I like it. But it's probably best played with someone you know really well. Or someone you don't really like.

I doubt you've heard of Kensington. I don't think it made much of an impact on the public's consciousness. It certainly doesn't seem to have endured. I can't say I'm surprised. I genuinely enjoyed playing it – both as a kid and in the pub with Elliott that day – but looking at the packaging it does seem to have been doomed to failure. Of course, it's easy to say that now I have the benefit of hindsight, but really, there's not a lot right about the way they sold it to the world. Some of it is down to simple misfortune. For a start they launched their product, gimmickily packaged to resemble an LP, just before the dawn of compact discs came along to make it look old-fashioned and cumbersome. But there are other mistakes, too.

I've scoured the front and back cover looking for a description of the game and come up with nothing. You can see some hexagons on the front and there's a rosette of some description telling you that somebody, somewhere, has deemed it Game of the Year, but there's really nothing telling you what the game actually involves.

On the back cover, over the Albert Memorial photo, there's a long small-print essay – it must be 800 words at least – titled 'Kensington AND ITS INVENTORS'. Their use of capital letters tells you quite a lot there. Because the vast majority of those words are indeed about the two men: Brian Taylor, a 'short, thick-set Welshman', and Peter Forbes, a 'lanky young half-Scandinavian',[4] rather than the game they created. They sound like nice guys. Charming. Eccentric. But unless they're offering to come round to your house and play it with you, all that is surely irrelevant. It reads more like a pitch for a cheesy *Odd Couple*-style sitcom than anything else. I can hear the theme music and jaunty voice-over explaining the 'sit' already: '*Meet Peter. He's an academic. You think he's straight-laced but you're wrong ... he once tried to persuade his university to buy a racehorse! And this is Brian. He's a bit of a scruff. But don't be fooled, he lives in a fifteen-room mansion in Wales. Oh,* and *a council house on the South Coast! He's definitely not your average guy. He once took a transatlantic flight wearing a bathrobe and slippers! But together, these pals are dynamite ... because together they're inventing a brand new game!*' I've added some exclamation marks and a tone of voice but I haven't invented any of the self-consciously quirky facts ... that's just how it reads to me.

I suppose the blurb *does* tell you a bit about the game. It tells you that they based the board design on some ancient Islamic patterns they'd found in a book on Portobello Road Market (and isn't that another detail just bound to excite the pre-teen kids of Stafford?), and also that they were 'satisfied

---

4. I wonder if he likes table tennis?

at last that they had invented the greatest board game in a thousand years ...' But nope, no details on how you actually play the bloody thing!

Inside the gatefold sleeve it gets better still. One side is given over to a photograph designed, presumably, to demonstrate the game's broad appeal. The photo is taken looking upwards, as if it was shot from beneath a transparent version of the game. Six people – six almost comically diverse people – loom over the board, all eager spectators or players of the game. There's a man in a business suit next to a cute seven-year-old girl with pigtails. There's a hip young woman wearing a hat at a jaunty angle and a grey-haired old duffer with a pipe clamped tight between his smiling lips. But the *pièce de résistance* has to be the Eric Idle-esque vicar and the Rastafarian standing next to him, beaming broadly, his dreadlocks bundled inside a big woollen hat with red, gold and green trim ... because at the end of the 70s that was the epitome of black British culture. It really is a picture of rare beauty and charm. It says everything they wanted it to say – 'Look, this game is for everyone!' – but it does so with such heavy-handed deliberateness that it now looks like a parody.

The other half of the inside cover is given over to the rules. Here you can't fault them for ambition because they're listed in six or seven languages, with French, Spanish and Arabic amongst them.

But surely calling the game Kensington doesn't quite display the same multilingual outlook? Global businesses employ brand analysts who work hard at naming new products, always striving to find – or create – words that transcend international and cultural barriers. It's not really my field but something in my gut tells me the word Kensington – with its clumsy junction of hard consonants – must sound peculiarly British. I can't imagine that Fiat Kensingtons will be rolling out across Europe any time soon.

But my favourite detail on the sleeve is the manufacturer's address and phone number. 'Whale Games' lists its address without a postcode, while their phone number is given simply as 'Cambridge-355-****'. The postcode scheme was only finalised on a national scale as late as 1974 so I guess people weren't yet using them habitually, but there's something quite mind-bogglingly quaint and stoically British about listing a phone number whilst not giving people *all* the digits actually needed. Were we still calling the operator and asking to be put through to 'Whitehall five-oh five-oh' at the end of the 70s? I don't remember that. It feels more like a relic from the 1930s to me.

Bless Messrs Taylor and Forbes – Kensington was a perfectly fine game, but everything about the way it was presented seems now to have been on the cusp of extinction.

It took Elliott and me thirty minutes to play a game out. We started chattily but by the time the endgame was upon us, we were both silently scanning the board with intense *Robocop* eyes, massaging our temples, our brains now fully occupied. I'd managed to build up a two-pronged attack and was slowly bullying my way into a position of strength. Elliott's pieces had been spread too far apart from each other, scattered around the board's winding perimeter – a thin, useless, blue-disc diaspora that couldn't get a foothold. So long as I didn't make a mistake, I was going to be okay.

I didn't. I was okay. Eventually, cautiously, I was able to seize the central white hexagon with relative ease.

'Well played,' said Elliott, his features relaxing from the tense, focused stare of moments ago. 'That was ... kind of *exhausting*, wasn't it?'

He was right. As puzzling as it seemed, it was.

'Totally,' I agreed. 'I feel drained by that. I can see why we didn't play it all that much as kids. It takes over your head, it's just ... so ...'

'Exhausting?'

'Yeah. Exhausting. Draining.'

'Yeah. Draining.'

We sounded like two Speak and Spell machines running low on batteries. The vacuous nothingness of Guess Who? had been redeemed by the full-on intensity of Kensington. It felt like a proper session of gaming had been achieved after all, but now we were winding down.

For the second time I sensed that our goodbyes were imminent, but for the second time I was wrong.

'I enjoyed it, though.' Elliott ran his left index finger under the sweatband on his right wrist like an old man trying to stretch the waistband of his too-tight trousers after a particularly filling Christmas feast.

'Me, too.'

'Do you ... do you ... want to play again?'

I think we were both surprised that he'd asked.

'Yeah ... go on,' I said, and again I think we were both surprised. 'I reckon I can go one more. Do you want another drink?'

'It's my round.'

'You brought the games,' I said. 'I just walked here. Let me.'

'Okay. Thanks. I'll have the same again then.'

Our drinks were the same. And so was the game's outcome. I couldn't get a look in with Guess Who? but I was the undefeated king of Kensington ... the greatest board game in a thousand years.

Rest of the World: **15**
Me: **6**

CHAPTER 6

The studios of Absolute Radio – my Sunday morning employers – are in Golden Square. Given its Soho location, it's a surprisingly quiet little enclave. It lies just south of the authentic-New-London-cool-meets-ersatz-swinging-60s-grooviness of Carnaby Street, and just north of Piccadilly Circus, which is so busy it's like bloody Piccadilly Circus round there. And yet, while both those spots continue to hustle and bustle at all hours of the day, seven days a week, when I look out of the studio window on a Sunday it is rare to spot a soul.

Although the buildings there have changed their shape and purpose many times over the years – it was once a square full of grand Georgian townhouses and is now dominated by offices in more recently built shells – the open space at its centre means Golden Square still retains a certain gentrified aura.

After our show, the team (my two co-presenters, Martin and Danielle, our producer, Chris, and assistant, Rich) and I often go for a bite to eat together, but not this day. Beth had a rare weekend off. The two of us were going to have Sunday lunch together. At home. Like a proper couple.

I stepped into the bright, still, sunlit square alone. I paused for a moment to breathe in the fresh air and enjoy the unlikely silence. Or near silence. A light, gentle breeze whispered in my ears and somewhere there was the unlikely chirrup of a couple of songbirds. And – and there was something else ...

Kadink ... idonk. Kadiiiink ... idonk.

Surely not.

Kadiiiink. Kadiiiink. Kadiiiink ... idoooonk.

Table tennis!

I looked over, beyond the iron-railing fence, to the square within the square. A tree partially obscured my view but there *was* movement there. I wandered towards it and, sure enough, there on the paving stones, between the neatly tended flowerbeds and empty benches, overseen by the stone eyes of George II in statue form, were two Ping London table-tennis tables. And there was a game in progress.

Sort of.

I leaned against the railings and watched as a tall Indian man played a game of table tennis with, um, himself. He'd serve and then race round to the other side of the table to try and return the ball while racing back round to where he'd started ... and so on. He played every shot with as much height and as little speed as possible, ballooning the ball up and over the net, trying to give him enough time to position himself on the other side of the table.

If it sounds impressive, well – it wasn't. He did manage to return service a couple of times but that was as good as it got. On the whole, there was decidedly more ping than pong. But he was a tryer. He didn't give up. Every time he failed he simply scurried off to retrieve the ball and gave it another go.

Without taking my eyes off the solo spectacle, I reached my hand into the bag that hung over my shoulder. It was the same bag I'd carried with me the day I'd met Clive at White City and, sure enough, as I ferreted around amongst the newspapers, a novel, my iPod, the small case with my darts in and a couple of CDs that had been sent to me via the radio station, my hand soon came to rest on the wooden handle of the table-tennis bat I'd bought that day. I'm a terrible hoarder. I knew I'd left it in there.

As if on cue, the latest of his one-shot rallies ended and the ball shot off the table, heading vaguely in my direction. As our soloist scuttled after it, he turned in my direction also and our eyes met. He smiled shyly, as if embarrassed at being discovered in his strange solitary pursuit.

He didn't speak. Neither did I. Instead, I instinctively drew my hand out of the bag and held the bat aloft for him to see. It proved to be the opening line in what I think was my first ever conversation to be conducted in the silent medium of table-tennis bats. His smile changed, no longer embarrassed. I waved my bat from side to side. His bat beckoned me into the square.

As I passed through the gates I noticed for the first time that he wasn't wearing any shoes or socks. His bare feet poked out from the bottom of his dark blue jeans. Just under the edge of the table I could see a small collection of his belongings: his coat draped over a backpack and a pair of shiny, patent leather shoes arranged neatly to the side. There was no handshake. Instead, he held the flat surface of his bat out towards me and, without thinking, I used the thin edge of mine to tap it: the ping-pong world's version of an urban fist-bump greeting.

As our bats were getting on better than we were, I thought it was time for one of us to speak.

'Hi,' I said.

'Hi.'

'I'm Dave.'

'Bo.'

'Hi. Bo?'

'Yes. Bo. Hi.'

It wasn't the zippiest of chats.

'Do you want a game?' I asked.

'For sure.' Bo bowed from the waist, confirming his agreement. 'Yes.' He spoke with a slight accent but not one I could readily identify.

I approached the table, sliding my bag off my shoulder and placing it next to his shiny, shiny shoes as I did so. It had barely hit the ground when – *kadinkidonk* – the ball was fizzing my way. My right arm lashed out in reflex and I surprised myself when bat met ball. But ball didn't meet table. It spun off to the right and into a flowerbed.

'One nil,' said Bo, punching the air.

'Are we not knocking up then?'

'One nil.'

Hmm. Okay. It was like that then, was it?

I retrieved the ball and bounced it across the table to Bo, making sure that this time I immediately adopted the bent-kneed pose of table-tennis readiness.

Kadinkidonk, kadinkidonk, kadinkidonk. Kadink!

One all. Get in.

It had been impossible to tell if Bo was any good at the game when I'd watched him playing by himself, but I had assumed he probably would be simply by dint of the fact that, if nothing else, he was obviously particularly keen. I was wrong. Yes, he was keen. He was very, *very* keen. But he was also useless. Really, *really* useless. On his forehand he was vaguely competent but his backhand was cack-handed beyond belief, meaning that if ever I sent the ball to his wrong side, the point was almost certainly mine. I wish I could tell you I was good enough to direct the ball at will but the truth is that it often flies in the only direction I can manage at the time. As it happened, instead of trying to target Bo's backhand I spent more of the game trying to keep it on his forehand, in order to keep the rally going and the score dignified.

I still won 21 points to 12.

'Would you like to play again?' he asked.

It was by far the longest sentence he'd spoken and there-fore my best chance at unravelling his faint, oh so faint, accent. But I still couldn't work it out.

'Yeah, go on,' I said. 'By the way ... where are you from?'

'Me?' said Bo. (Who else could he think I meant?) 'I am from Sweden.'

Of course. I should have known.

Beep. The sound was faint. My phone was in my bag. But it reached my ears. It reached my heart. I knew what the text message was going to say. I was late.

'I'm sorry,' I said. 'I'm going to have to go ...'

'But we're playing!'

'I know,' I said. 'But I have to run ... I'm late ...'

'Then I win this game!'

I'd won the first four games – to 12, 9, 11 and 15 points respectively – and I was 7–2 up in this one! It was pretty obvious who was going to win. Again.

'Okay,' I said. 'You win this one.'

Rest of the World: **16**
Me: **10**
Beth: **Unimpressed**

CHAPTER 7

'So, what have you been up to?'

'Oh … nothing much, Mum,' I said, holding the phone against my shoulder with my chin. 'The wedding plans are rolling along, we've found a photographer we like …' and then, to try and make her laugh, I adopted an air of mock casualness and added, 'Oh … now that I think about it, I did bump into a Swedish Indian man called Bo on Sunday. He was playing table tennis by himself so I joined him for a few games.'

'That's nice,' she said, not skipping a beat.

It wasn't the response I was fishing for. She didn't sound the least bit surprised. You'd think I'd just revealed to her something as mundane as me defrosting the fridge. I decided that she obviously hadn't heard me properly and was just trying to politely respond to my *laissez-faire* tone of voice.

'I said,' I said, enunciating my words a little more carefully this time, 'I bumped into a Swedish Indian man called Bo on Sunday …'

'… and he was playing table tennis by himself,' she continued, 'so you joined in for a few games.'

'Yes,' I said. 'Yes. Sort of.' So she *had* heard. Hmm. 'Does that not, y'know, sound … a bit odd to you?'

'Well,' she said, with baffling simplicity, 'you can find anything you like in London, can't you?'

As it happened, I had found a fair few things that I liked in London recently. And there'd been a couple of things outside London, too. Just not very far outside. As this map shows:

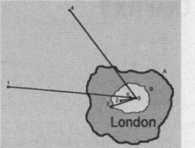

A = the M25
B = the inner ring road
1 = Didcot
2 = White City
3 = Twickenham
4 = Milton Keynes
5 = Liverpool Street
6 = Golden Square

No game had taken me more than sixty miles from home. It had been a very enjoyable series of distractions: an afternoon here or a morning there – sometimes it had been even less than that – and they'd all been welcome.

You could be forgiven for thinking I'd entered into all of this as some kind of professional project. But really, I hadn't. I'd just had some spare time on my hands and games had seemed as good a way as any to use it up. But Twitter didn't know that.

And because much of the communication between my various opponents and I had been conducted via Twitter, it meant that other people were able to look in on it. It wasn't hard for people to piece my movements together. And for some, the conclusion being reached was that I was ignoring most of the people I'd asked for a game in the first place.

'If you only wanted to play games with people near London,' said one tweeter, 'you should have made that clear when you asked!'

Oh. I suppose they had a point.

'You have a point,' I replied. 'I didn't really think it through.'

'Well, it's a bit late for that now, mister!'

I couldn't help feeling that I'd been a bit rude. Something had to be done.

CHAPTER 8

Liverpool is a vibrant city. It's lively, has plenty of culture – high and low – and a heritage it can rightly be proud of. It has a more clearly defined personality than most other cities, something of which it seems to be both proud and defensive by turns. If it was a member of the family it would be your slightly deranged-but-fun uncle. The one you always look forward to seeing because you know he'll be entertaining. The one your parents are a bit worried about you seeing because he's a bit, um, unpredictable. I love Liverpool. (Not as much as it loves itself, obviously. But then, who does?)

The day's game was poker. I mentioned before that I occasionally play at a friend's home game. Every now and then I play online too. And always for real money – the game doesn't make sense otherwise. Bear that in mind, because I am about to tell you the most ridiculous yet delicious thing there is to know about my forays into the poker world. Here goes …

I, David James Gorman, have made a profit out of poker.

Just look at those words! I enjoyed typing them so much I'm going to do it again. I'm not even going to cut and paste, I'm going to *actually* type each letter again:

I, David James Gorman, have made a profit out of poker.

It's true! I've *actually* made more money than I've lost. Gambling! On cards!

I know boasting isn't very nice, but please, please, just indulge me for a few seconds more. It's an unlikely fact, so just let it dance around your brainbuds a moment longer. Drink it in. Slosh it around. Now spit it out.

Because while it really is a true fact, I'm afraid it hides a far less impressive reality. Here's the thing: I don't play high-stakes poker. It's rare for me to risk more than a tenner on a game. The most I've ever risked is fifty pounds and frankly that was too much for my blood. It made my palms sweat. It didn't suit me at all.

Cumulatively, in all those low-stakes games I've comfortably lost money. Yes, I've won a few games here and there but I've lost many more, and I know full well that my winnings don't come close to covering my losses.

But I'm in a fortunate position. Because I make my living in the unfashionable fringes of show business I have, on occasion, been invited to play in a televised 'celebrity' game (y'know, when all the proper celebrities have turned them down). The remarkable thing about these games is that they're neither high-stakes nor low-stakes – they're no-stakes. Now how does that work? Well, instead of an appearance fee, the producers offer you free entry to the game, a game that is then played for real money. There is quite literally nothing to lose, but there can be a significant sum to win. I've played in four such games. And I've won one of them.

My opponents that day were a mixed bag. By the time it had been whittled down to three, I was sitting between Cleo Rocos, a woman whose curvaceous figure I had grown up with thanks to her career-defining role as a Miss Whiplash-sidekick (and so much more) to Kenny Everett, and Howard Marks, the world's most famous ex-drug-smuggler.

Neither of them had played the game before. I think the producers had invited Cleo thinking she would be kooky, and Howard on the grounds that it would be funny for a man who had once controlled ten per cent of the world's hashish trade to be called the dealer. They were right both times.

I played reasonably well in the endgame and built up a significant chip lead but I can't pretend the final hand – unusually, I knocked them both out at the same time – didn't involve a great deal of luck. My winnings, I'm almost embarrassed to tell you, totalled £5,000.

And, I'm afraid, *that's it*. That one game, ladies and gentlemen, boys and girls, explains why I, David James Gorman, have made a profit out of poker. An impressive statistic it might be, but I'm a singularly unimpressive player. Without that win I'd be a few hundred pounds down but with it, well, I reckon if I stick to my normal brand of occasional, low-stakes card play for the rest of my life, I'll still be in the black. And it's all down to one win: a win I didn't need to play especially well to secure, and one that involved no risk whatsoever. I love poker. (Not as much as it loves itself, obviously. But who does?)

You really can't separate money and poker. If you've never played the game you might think it's all about luck. It's not. Of course luck's involved. But so is skill. That's why there are professional poker players. There are people out there who make a profit out of the game year on year and have done for twenty, thirty, forty years or more. They do it by being good. Regularly.

You simply can't be *that* lucky. It's not just about the cards you're dealt: it's about the way you play them. It's about the bets you make. *And* the bets you don't make.

Your bets are about value – real, perceived and *projected* – and for that to make sense they simply have to have value outside the game, too. If they don't, if it's just played for tokens, then people play differently and the elastic that holds the game together snaps.

If you play a game of informal, jumpers-for-goalposts football in the park with your mates, you'll know the score is likely to end up being something ridiculous like 14–11 and, while you still compete – you still want to win – you also want to enjoy yourself. You try audacious moves. You sky it over the imaginary cross bar from thirty yards, you trip over your own feet trying a cheeky back-heel, and your mate goes for an overhead bicycle kick and misses the ball completely. You attempt to play Playstation football because when something does come off, when you do dribble round three people, dummy the keeper and knock it nonchalantly between the 'posts' it feels amazing. You do it because you're indulging your fantasies and because, deep down, you know the score doesn't *really* matter.

Well, that's sort of what poker becomes when there's no money involved. People make ludicrous bluffs and ridiculous bets, backing 50–1 shots even though they're only offering 2–1 rewards. Because if one of those things does come off, you become the George Best of the green baize card table. And if they don't come off, hell, it doesn't really matter.

For poker to make sense, it *has* to *really* matter.

You don't need a lot of money to make a difference. If a group of ten friends sits down to play a £10 tournament there's £100 at stake. That might be £70 for the winner and £30 for second place, with everyone else taking away nothing but an hour's worth of entertainment for their money. But that £70 is worth winning, so suddenly you stop taking the ridiculous long shots, you make more calculated bets and you bluff only when you think you can get away with it. When there's no money involved everyone just ends up betting into everything because you're always thinking, 'But what if …?'

With money involved the best player wins. Without money involved the best hand wins. *That's* when it becomes a game of luck.

In many ways poker was the most ridiculous game I could be playing that day. If I'd been heading to Liverpool to play almost anything else it would have made more sense, because the journey wouldn't have been about money; it would've been about a game. But if it was about poker then, by default, it was about money too. I knew it was going to be very low stakes. A fiver. I didn't know how many would be playing but even if there were as many as ten and it was winner takes all, the most I could make would be £50. Minus my own £5 stake. £45 wouldn't cover my train fare to Liverpool let alone my hotel. This was the opposite of my occasional no-lose televised games: this was a no-win situation.

With a small backpack hanging over one shoulder and a cap pulled down over my brow, I stepped out under the huge, Victorian, arching roof of Liverpool Lime Street station.

The height of the roof confuses the world. We know we're indoors but somebody needs to tell the pigeons. I enjoyed the tingly, metallic taste of train-station air on the tip of my tongue. And I enjoyed the sight of two bronze statues on the concourse welcoming me to Liverpool: Ken Dodd and Bessie Braddock. The most non-stop of all comedians and an old-school, firebrand socialist: a nice distillation of the city's self image.[5]

The last time I'd been in Liverpool I'd been performing a show at the Empire Theatre, right next door to the station. My Merseyside visits are too few and far between to feel like I know my way around but I thought the familiarity of the venue might help me get my bearings so I headed that way, turning right and leaving through the station's grotty, less-used side entrance, to look across the grotty alley at the Empire's grotty stage door. Theatres and train stations share a schizophrenic quality: beautiful out front – often gaudily so – but all peeling paint and decrepitude where the public doesn't see. I like the decrepitude. I feel at home there.

I'd printed a map from the hotel's website but I had a bit of time so I challenged myself to see if I could find my way there unassisted. I've no doubt that I went round the houses but I made it. From Lord Nelson Street – the posh name for

_____

5. Or a tax-dodger and a battle-axe if you prefer your Scouse clichés more in keeping with the Carla Lane sitcom, *Bread*.

the grotty alley that broadens out east of the station – I turned into Seymour Street. And from there every street I walked seemed to have a male first name: Seymour turned into Clarence, Clarence to Russell and Russell to Rodney. A posh girl's dance card if ever there was one. There were boarded-up shops and derelict pubs that were now just canvasses for fly posters. They'd been pasted one on top of another for so long I reckon the brickwork could crumble and a pub – or a *papier-mâché* pub-shaped shell – would be left standing. Those posters have been so compressed for so long I suspect the base layer will soon be forming a rich seam of coal.

There were stretches of 1980s housing and 1960s offices, next to a crumbling church with a stone pyramid tomb dominating its graveyard: a show-off's resting place for sure. And there were parades of grand Georgian townhouses, stretched tall like top hats. I'm told there are sixty Grade II listed buildings on Rodney Street alone. Most of these townhouses seem to now contain consulting rooms for doctors and the like. (And the not like: alternative medicine was well catered for, too.) But one of these old buildings was my home for the night: a fifteen-room hotel.

I'd booked it online through a website specialising in late deals and was feeling pretty smug about getting somewhere quite so fancy, quite so cheaply. It was a gorgeous building but sadly the stone steps leading up to the impossibly heavy and absurdly broad wooden front door, the beautifully preserved tiled floor in the hallway and the elegant, polished banister arching back on itself as the stairs carried me up to the first floor only served to raise my expectations and the room that followed simply couldn't deliver. It was like a long, anticipatory drum roll without a crash of cymbals to top it off.

It wasn't an unpleasant room. It was just rather drab and ordinary. From the front door to the first floor it had all been original features and late eighteenth-century ambience, but in my room it became obvious that the building had lived several lives before. Behind one door there was a space – too big to be called a cupboard, too small to be a room. Odd holes and cut pipes suggested it had once housed a boiler but now it was just an empty, unusable, windowless, purposeless space. It was as if they'd paid the same reverence to later refits as they had to the building's genuinely historic, original features: '... and this is where we've kept the stud-partition wall, put in during the 70s to hide the boiler – such a lovely touch!'

Not that any of that mattered. It wasn't like I was going to be spending much time in my room and besides, it was so cheap – I'd got it for roughly a quarter of the normal price – any annoyance at the boutique hotel not being quite boutique enough was simply churlish.

I freshened up with a shower (in a tiny cubicle that looked even tinier for being situated at the end of an enormous, expansive and completely empty, bathless bathroom) then headed off to play cards.

'Aigburth, please.'

My cabbie looked confused. Aigburth was the name of the suburb I was heading to, but from the way he narrowed his eyes it was obvious I'd pronounced it incorrectly.

That was my cover blown. When taking a taxi I always try to appear like a man with local knowledge. I can't shake the idea that if a cab driver catches the whiff of 'stranger-in-town' upon me, I'll suddenly be taken on an unnecessary forty-minute detour with the meter rigged to run at bank holiday rates. I don't know why I think it'll happen: I've been a stranger in many a town over the years and it's not happened yet. But no matter how much my real-world experiences tell me it's unnecessary, I can't stop myself instantly slipping into man-about-town bloke-mode the minute my arse hits taxi-cab upholstery.

'Do you mean Aigburth?' he asked.

It was my turn to be confused. He was definitely questioning my pronunciation ... but at the same time *his* pronunciation seemed identical to my own. I'd been unsure as to whether the A-I-G was supposed to rhyme with '*vague*' or not – I'd decided against but was then unsure as to whether it was, '*ig*', '*arg*', '*egg*' or '*eye-g*'. In the end I'd plumped for something *egg*-ish. And despite his schoolteacher-correcting-the-simpleton tone, so had my driver.

'Yeah ... Egg-burth,' I said, trying to correct myself but not knowing which bit of the word I'd got wrong in the first place.

'Egg-burth?'

'Yeah.'

'So, what you wanna go there for?'

'Um,' I tried to think of a good lie but none came to mind so I told him the truth instead. 'I'm playing a game of poker.'

I sounded like I was lying. *I* didn't believe myself and I knew it was true. The cab driver's eyes bounced off the rearview mirror and burrowed into mine while he weighed up my words. Was he escorting some mysterious high roller to a smoky den of iniquity?

It didn't take long for him to make his mind up. 'All right,' he said, 'you don't have to tell me if you don't want to. Each to their own.'

We rode in silence from there, only speaking again when he dropped me on the corner of the street.

'Just be careful, eh, mate?' he said as he handed me my change. 'Whatever it is you're up to ... be careful.'

I stood on the pavement and watched as he drove off, finding myself rooted to the spot, waiting for him to turn right and disappear from view. I looked around at the neat rows of red-brick terraced houses and the small cars – Metros, Micras and Corsas – parked bumper to bumper on either side of the street. It felt like a nice enough area to me. It certainly didn't feel threatening. But somehow the cabbie's well-intentioned words had induced a little bout of paranoia.

Did I have to be careful? More careful than normal? I suppose I *was* about to enter a stranger's house – I didn't know anything about them. That involves a risk of sorts. And I did once get a threatening email from a Scouser. But that was years ago. Nevertheless, thoughts of that encounter started to play on my mind. They'd taken offence at something I'd said on a radio show – I genuinely forget what – and their response had been to fire off an angry email. I don't remember much of their missive apart from the fact that it had started with polite restraint only to spend the next three or four paragraphs tumbling into uncontrollable spitting fury, coarse abuse and threats. The final words – the one phrase I could suddenly recollect with absolute clarity – were, 'If you ever come to Liverpool, I'll break your fucking legs.' Hmm.

I approached the front door. Maybe – just maybe – I was about to walk into a trap. A trap I wouldn't be able to walk out of. I raised my finger to the doorbell. The top bell. But I didn't press it. Not yet. Maybe I'd been invited to play poker by someone who'd spent the last five years trying to lure me to his leg-breaking salon. No. Surely not. I rang the bell. *But maybe.*

The door opened. I was greeted with a smile. A bad sign. Anyone who's ever watched a Bond film can tell you people who want to kill you *always* greet you with a smile. Why should leg-breakers be any different?

Fortunately, that was the nearest Andy got to Bond villainy all night.

'Dave!' he said. 'I wasn't expecting it to be *you*!'

You see? Bond villains are *always* expecting him.

'You must be Andy, yeah?'

'Yeah.'

'You did … you did know I was coming?' I said nervously. 'I mean, we emailed and …'

'Oh yeah, but … coming from London to play poker? I didn't think you would when it came down to it!' He paused. Then realising he was still in the doorway, continued, 'Anyway, come in … we're just up here.'

I followed Andy's broad, muscular frame up a couple of flights of stairs to the top of the building. It was a two-storey house but it had been converted into flats, and Andy's living room was in the attic space. There I was relieved to discover no leg-breaking equipment. What I did find was tatty carpet; mismatched, beaten up, second-hand furniture; and a collection of film posters and magazine covers hanging on the woodchip wallpapered walls. It was, basically, your typical student flat, only with far more DVDs than I remember from my own student days.[6] There were racks and racks of the things, hugging the walls wherever I looked. I don't think I've ever seen so many DVDs in one room before. Except in HMV. And to be honest, even then it was a close-run thing.

But this wasn't a flat full of just-cut-the-apron-strings freshers. They weren't second or third years, either. Andy and his mates were post-grad students. Academics. Trapped in the limbo between the grown-up and the student worlds.

The room formed a stubby 'L' shape and an old dining table – scratched and coffee-mug stained – stood in its neck. The other players were already gathered. They all had their evening's drinks with them: a can of lager on the table and a couple more wrapped up in a carrier bag at their feet, or a small bottle of vodka clutched to their side.

'Did you bring anything?' asked Andy, aware of where my eyes were falling.

I hadn't. And I felt guilty. I felt rude. I knew I was supposed to bring something – Andy had explained the form in our brief exchange of emails – but I'd forgotten to do so.

---

6. And not just because DVDs didn't exist when I was a student. I mean there were more DVDs than … oh, you know what I mean.

I suspect my liver had made me forget. It was in no mood to process more alcohol. Not after the weekend I'd just given it. I'd spent the weekend in Germany. Drinking beer. And playing darts.

Hang on. That needs explaining, doesn't it? Here I am telling you about the journeys I've made in the name of game-play and yet I have neglected to tell you about a flight to Germany! To play darts! Hmm. We can come back to Liverpool in a minute. Let's you and me go to Germany for a while.

The reason I haven't mentioned the trip before now is that it was, officially, work. And I've been thinking of this book as being about the things idleness – or my fear of idleness – drove me to when I *wasn't* working.

Dinslaken, a small town in the north-east of Germany – not too far from Dusseldorf (and, therefore, not too far from 1981) – had been playing host to the European Darts Championships. The tournament was covered by Bravo TV and someone who worked there must have known about my love of the game because, despite having done no sports[7] broad-casting of any kind, I received a phone call asking if I wanted to work on the production.

I did. Of course I did. It was a chance to spend four days at close quarters with some of my sporting heroes. I'd leapt at the chance.

But I don't have a lot to tell you about Dinslaken because I hardly saw the place. For four days I was trapped (having a ball, but still – trapped) inside the venue: a concert hall cunningly disguised to look like the type of anonymous, munic-ipal building you visit to pay a parking fine. I wasn't introducing the show – they had a professional for that – and I wasn't commentating, either – they had a team of professionals for that

---

7. Yes, it is a sport.

as well – I was simply doing pre- and post-match interviews, grabbing vox pops and filming silly features they could use to fill any spaces that might appear if some of the games ran short.

Pre-match interviews were never done immediately before the match – the players need time to focus – so instead we'd just try to grab them as soon as they arrived at the venue but before they entered the practice room: a place of brooding, silent intensity. (Well, silent but for the *thud*, *thud*, *thud* of dart hitting board over and over and over again.) This meant I had to be available at a moment's notice and was pretty much forbidden from leaving the building. In the whole four days I was only able to take one ten-minute stroll into town. It was very peaceful. I saw five ice cream parlours. I bought one ice cream.

I wasn't even staying in Dinslaken. Maybe it doesn't have any hotels. Maybe it does and they were all full. Maybe it was just cheaper to stay elsewhere. I don't know. All I know is that it takes thirty to forty people to film four days of darts and we were all staying about fifteen miles away in Oberhausen.

Each day the routine was the same. We'd go straight from a bleary-eyed breakfast to a coach that would take us mob-handed to Dinslaken. We'd swarm straight into the venue and straight to work. We'd finish some time close to midnight, at which point it was time to board the bus once more and head back to Oberhausen. Tired, but wired from a few solid hours of live broadcasting, we'd head straight to the pub behind the hotel for a few drinks.

Rinse and repeat. Four times.

I don't normally drink beer. I don't really like it all that much. I like a glass of wine. I love a rum and coke. But beer? I can take it or leave it. And I normally leave it. But in Oberhausen that wasn't really an option. Everyone was drinking lager. Lager was what you drank. Litres and litres of the stuff. Anything else would have complicated the system. In Oberhausen getting a round in was easy. You asked if anyone wanted a drink, you tried to count the number of yeses and then you ordered a slightly larger number of drinks just to be on the safe side. And every drink was the same. Nobody ever asked, 'What are you having?' It was only ever, 'Do you want one?' It was democratic. Sort of.

Of course, I didn't get to see Oberhausen either. But from the leaflets in the hotel lobby I can tell you there are three main points of interest in the town. The first of these is a large gasometer, 'the largest disc-type gas holder in all of Europe!' I don't think it holds gas any more, but it does look quite impressive in the photos. The second is Centro, 'the biggest shopping mall in all of Germany!' – how the spine tingles! But the final and perhaps the most intriguing thing in Oberhausen was the presence of a global superstar. He was only a couple of years old, had been born in Weymouth but had moved to Germany at a young age. He had risen to fame in the July of that year and was something of a worldwide phenomenon. In the UK certainly his antics had seen him grab headlines on the front *and* back pages of every newspaper.

I wonder if Paul the Octopus's fame will be remembered? Only time will tell. What had made Paul famous was his ability to predict the outcome of football games during that year's World Cup. Cynics were quick to point out that he wasn't actually *predicting* the results at all. He was just taking food from a small plastic box and he just happened to be choosing the box that just happened to be decorated with the flag of the nation that just happened to go on and win the game in question. But his track record of eight correct guesses out of eight is so statistically impressive I think it's rather pointless debating what he did or didn't know. I mean, he didn't know he was born in Weymouth or even that he was called Paul, but that doesn't make either of those facts less true.

I loved my long weekend in Germany. I loved being so close to the sport, meeting the players and getting a real sense of their emotional ups and downs as the tournament progressed. I also loved seeing the technical side of how it was filmed. I've never seen a television director work harder.

Darts is a quick game. Throwing three darts might take only twenty seconds. During that time, the player is not just lobbing lumps of tungsten at the board; he's also doing complex sums and making snap decisions. Say, for example, a player has left himself needing to score 111 to win. He's probably going to aim for the treble 20, the single 11 and then the double top. But if his first dart misses and hits the single 20 he'll change tack and go for treble 17 with his second dart and then double top. Of course, if he misses the treble 17 and only hits a single then he can no longer finish. So he'll use his final dart to leave himself as easy a double as possible for next time. Depending on the player he might choose to go treble 14 (leaving himself on double 16) or possibly treble 18 (leaving himself double 10). Or he might do something else.

If you didn't understand any of that, I wouldn't worry about it. The point is that there are lots of things that can happen and they tend to happen quickly. And yet, when the TV people get it right, the camera seems to know what the players are going to aim for *before* they do. It'll cut from a close-up of the treble 20 to a shot of the player's fevered brow, to a close-up of the treble 17 to a close-up of the double 20 – and somehow the director manages to cut to each of those close-ups moments before each dart is thrown. In football, the cameras follow the action; in darts they get there first.

They don't do this because the cameras are operated by Paul the Octopus. No, it's down to someone far more impressive than that: Eric the Bristow.

Eric Bristow was *the* player to beat when I was first watching the game as a kid in the 80s. He was the best in the world and he was blessed with a larger-than-life personality to boot.

He was loud, brash and funny. If he hadn't been brilliant he wouldn't have got away with it. But he was. So he did.

These days he works in TV, and he's the best spotter there is. A spotter's job is to watch the games on a monitor and call out what shots he thinks a player will go for. It's a remarkable thing to witness. He knows each player's quirks and foibles. He can think as them. And he can do it before they do. And he doesn't stop being loud, brash and funny while he's at it.

While his achievements in the game have been surpassed (most notably by the player he mentored, Phil Taylor), in that Oberhausen pub with the cast and crew, Eric was still the top dog. He hasn't lost his superstar aura. Everything revolved around Eric. I hadn't dared approach him, but on the last day he called me over to his corner of the bar. I'd been summoned to visit the Don.

'I'll be honest with you.' His huge arm had snaked round my shoulder and pulled me closer to him. 'When I saw you doing your stuff on day one, I thought, "Who's this bollocks?" But you know what … you're all right, you are. We like you. D'you know why? You don't take yourself too seriously, mate. I like that. We need that. You're a good lad.'

I squeezed him back.

'That means a lot, Eric,' I said – lager, emotion and pride all welling up inside me in equal measures. 'That really means a lot.'

'You're all right, you,' he said again. And then again. 'You're all right, you.'

Me! And Eric Bristow! Bloody hell. Before I packed my bag that night I wanted to call someone and tell them about me and Eric. Then I realised – the person I most wanted to tell was the ten-year-old me. So I left it.

Most of my bits were filmed in a corner of the players' lounge. Bravo had set up a dartboard in my corner, not for the players to use – they had the practice room for that – but to act as a backdrop for our interviews. In effect, this meant I had my own personal dartboard.

I might not have been allowed to go off anywhere in case I was suddenly called upon but there were still periods of inactivity. Thirty or forty minutes might pass by with nothing to do and nowhere to go. So I'd play darts. Just practising by myself; throwing hundreds and hundreds of arrows each day. I was in heaven.

At some point in the day, it wouldn't just be me kicking my heels and waiting for something to happen … I'd often find myself in company with my cameraman, Nick, or one of the various producers – Alex, Chris or Tony. They'd all readily pick up some darts and join in. We didn't play proper darts, however – not 501 down. Our games had to be easy, quick to start and quick to finish. So we stayed in the safe, amateur world of 'Round The Clock'.

RULES

Round The Clock

Players take it in turns to try and tick off each number on the board in order.

So you start by aiming at the 1 and only move on to the 2 once you've hit it. Then 3, then 4 and so on.

The winner is the first person to hit all the numbers in sequence and then the bullseye.

In the variation we played, hitting a double was like hitting two consecutive targets and hitting a treble, three.

So, if you were aiming at the 7, say, and you hit the double, you would count that as if you'd hit both the 7 and the 8 and move straight to the 9. If you'd hit the treble 7, you'd then move to the 10.

I'm proud to say that I emerged from the four days as the undefeated Bravo TV Round The Clock Champion. They weren't impressive wins, mind. No proper darts players were involved. Plus I was practising all day, and playing against people who had thrown their first darts just two weeks earlier. But a win is a win. And seven wins is seven wins.

Granted, I hadn't gone there with the specific intention of playing darts but hadn't that been the case with Bo, too? It was only right and proper to add these wins to my running total wasn't it? Of course it was.

In fact, before we head back to Liverpool, let's take a look at those scores:

Rest of the World:	**16**
Me:	**17**

Oh, yes. Gorman takes the lead! Take that, World!

'Did you bring anything?' asked Andy, aware of where my eyes were falling.

'I didn't,' I said. 'Sorry. I really should have thought … you see, I'm not drinking at the minute. Not since last weekend. Could I get a glass of water, instead?'

'Yeah. Of course. Where were you at the weekend?'

'Germany.'

'I saw a bit of that.' These words came from a new voice. From a softly spoken, slight young man with short hair and stubble that couldn't decide if it was a beard or not. Tim. 'It looked like you were having fun.'

'I was,' I said, feeling Eric's drunken embrace all over again. 'It was the stag-do I didn't know I wanted.'

'Are you getting married, then?' Another new voice.

'October.'

'Congratulations!' I don't remember which of them said that. I think they all did. Well, you would wouldn't you? It'd be weird not to.

We each put a five pound note in the kitty. That was it. That was our financial dealings for the night. In return for that we were given a pile of chips – small dull plastic discs, some black, some blue, some red, some white, with each colour being designated a nominal value. Everyone's stack added up to 1,500. Everyone's expression was serious. It was definitely time to don our poker faces. It was time to shuffle up and deal.[8]

I spent the first few hands concentrating more on taking in the company, trying to work out what they were like. Not as players, but as a social group. I wanted to fit in. I like a poker table where the game comes first. I want there to be a conversation but not if it means the deck hasn't been shuffled or the blinds haven't been posted. I don't want to have lots of long pauses followed by, 'Oh … is it my turn?' But this wasn't my game. Or my friend's game. I was in a stranger's house. I didn't want to be an arse. I felt obliged to play the game their way.

Andy was sitting to my left. Next to him was Lizzie. She was only 20 – the baby of the group. I'd been warned about Lizzie. She'd won their last six games. They weren't happy about that. Lizzie had to be stopped.

Next up was James. James didn't live in Liverpool. He'd driven over from his home in Manchester. Well, the east Manchester town of Stalybridge. (Or Staly Vegas as the locals know it, and not because it has a casino. There isn't a lot in Stalybridge, but it hasn't run out of its greatest natural

---

8. If you've never watched poker on TV – or played it yourself – there's an appendix at the back of the book that explains the basic structure of the game and some of the jargon.

resource: sarcasm.) It was obvious from early on that James was a player. He was used to playing elsewhere. He was used to risking more than a fiver. He knew what he was doing.

Here we turn a corner at the foot of the table and turn to our next player, Cec.[9] Cec was possessed of a lazy, nonchalant beauty. She had Audrey Hepburn eyes. She was Norwegian but smoked like she was French. She was constantly blowing cool smoke rings as if to amuse herself, but she was far too cool to be amused.

Travelling down the other side of the table, we continue with John. He really shouldn't have been sitting where he was. He was too tall and was hunching his shoulders to squeeze his mop of blond hair under the slope of the roof. When I first heard him speak I thought I detected a Northern Irish accent to his deep, rich voice, but the more I tuned in the more it became clear that he was from Scotland. He and Lizzie were a couple.

And finally the aforementioned Tim. Softly spoken but always alert, his eyes were constantly darting around the table assessing the mood of his friends. If he saw someone taking themselves too seriously, a wry smile would briefly play across his lips. He'd join in with friendly banter but back away the moment anyone looked close to getting upset. He was their barometer. He was my canary in the coalmine. If I kept an eye on Tim I'd be keeping an eye on the mood of the group.

The first few hands passed by with little incident and little of what I would call actual play. It was as if nobody knew they could raise. We were wrestlers at the start of a bout, patting and slapping away at each other's shoulders, not gripping, not holding, not throwing. There was no aggression. Poker really needs some aggression.

---

9. Pronounced 'Cess'.

I was just as guilty. I had an annoying succession of not-great-but-sort-of playable hands. Small pairs or suited connectors, the kind of cards that someone of my limited ability can do nothing with without a friendly flop. And I wasn't seeing any of those. I was slowly but surely losing chips.

I was actually relieved when James started to flex his poker muscles and make a few proper moves. It proved we were in a real game. It made me relax. Not everyone seemed to agree with me.

(As I'm aware that detailed descriptions of hands might be confusing to some I'm going to split the text into two columns for a while …)

If you'd like the detail, please stay in the left-hand lane	If you'd rather avoid the detail, this is the column for you
The first time James flexed his muscles came when he was on the big blind. Two or three players acting before him called, matching his 20 chips. But none of them raised.	The first time James showed us what he was made of was on a hand where two or three players had made the minimum bet.
When it came round to James, instead of checking, he raised, upping the ante with another 100. Lizzie actually gasped. So now the players who'd only been prepared to put in a measly 20 to see the flop had to put in another 100 or fold. All but one of them folded. Tim stayed in. Andy dealt the flop.	By making much larger bets James intimidated the other players into giving up the hand and cutting their losses.
James was first to act. He bet 200. Tim – who I presume hadn't hit anything on the flop – folded. James scooped up all the chips.	So James won a reasonable amount of chips. And nobody saw his cards. Somewhere in the middle of all this, Lizzie gasped in what I sensed was shocked disapproval.

'So what did you have?' asked Lizzie.

'I'm not telling you.'

'Wha–?' She looked disgusted by James's perfectly reasonable decision to withhold information. 'Oh, go on!'

Her cajoling prompted friendly chuckles all round.

'No.'

'*Jay*-ames!' she protested, her voice climbing high. 'That's so unfair!'

But of course it wasn't. It was entirely fair and it was an entirely unremarkable hand of poker. James was simply playing the game the way it's meant to be played. I don't know whether his cards were better than Tim's. And nor does Tim. But we do know that James won the hand and that's all that really matters.

There's an enjoyable poetry to the way conversations coalesce at the poker table. People don't even know they're doing it, but the chatter and the poker talk are always effortlessly interwoven: 'So I was in the pub on Friday – *I'll raise to* – and these three lads came in – *a hundred total* – that I used to know in school ...'

With the six of them all knowing each other well, there were inevitably times when the social side of the conversation involved references that were out of my reach. But whenever the friendly shorthand was approaching critical mass one of them – usually Tim – would lean in and offer a helpful explanation.

When Andy asked Cec about her next trip to Turkey I naturally assumed they were talking about a holiday. There was mention of the weather and what the camp would be like and it all seemed to stack up. But then there was talk of the 'dig' and some technical jargon that simply confused me but, just as I was about to ask, Tim saw my look of bemusement.

'Andy, John and myself,' he said, 'are paleoanthropologists ...'

'I see!'

'… and Cec is an archaeologist.'

'But,' Andy added, 'we don't hold that against her.'

It was a matey, almost jibeless jibe about an academic rivalry that clearly wasn't really there and Cec smile indulgently. The smoke ring that followed was smiling, too.

I was on the big blind. I looked at my hole cards. I had a 3 and a 7. A heart and a club. Bad. At least it wasn't a 2, 7 – the weakest starting hand available.

I looked at my cards. They were awful.

Andy folded. Lizzie called and put in 20 chips. James and Cec both folded. John joined Lizzie and me in the pot, adding another 20. Tim was on the small blind and decided to play, adding the 10 chips required to make 20 in total and then the action passed to me and my useless hand.

If anyone had raised I'd have folded – there'd be no point throwing chips after a hand as unlikely as this.

But they hadn't.

There was no point bluffing either – with three others in play, one of them was bound to have a decent hand. So I checked. There wasn't really much else I could do.

Lizzie, John and Tim all made the minimum bet meaning that I was effectively allowed to see the next three cards for free.

John dealt the flop. The first card was a 7, then a 3 and then another 7. Bloody hell. I'd just hit a full house.

When the three cards were dealt my hand was transformed. It went from being one of the weakest possible openings to being almost unbeatable.

This is why just calling had been a bad play on their part. This is why you need to be aggressive and make a raise. You always want information. You want to know what the other players think of their hands. By not raising the big blind they'd allowed me to stay in the hand without finding out any information. Yes, I'd got lucky. But they'd allowed me to.

Tim tapped the table to tell us he was making no bet. I did the same. I knew I had the best hand, and the chances of anyone getting a better hand out of this were so slim I wasn't troubled by it. But I didn't want to win the hand just yet. I wanted to induce some betting, and get some more money in the pot.

Lizzie looked at the flop. She picked up her hole cards and studied them briefly. She chewed her bottom lip. She eventually bet 50 chips. John sighed and then did the same. Tim folded. Back round to me. I knew I was going to bet – of course I was, I was definitely in front – but it was worth pretending I was making a tough decision.

I played with my chips. Then – eventually – with a bit of pantomime reluctance, I put in my 50.

John dealt the turn. It was a 5. With Tim no longer in the hand it was me to act first. I checked. I was deliberately trying

And the best thing was that, because I hadn't had to do anything yet, nobody at the table could possibly have known how good my hand was.

I'd got lucky. But they'd allowed me to.

Because I had a great hand – and nobody knew it yet – I deliberately hid how good my hand was.

to look like my hand was weak. I didn't want to scare anyone off.

Lizzie bet. 100 chips this time. John folded. I hemmed and I hawed, pretending to agonise over whether to hang on in there. And then I called the bet. The river came. It was a 10.

At each stage of the hand, Lizzie made a bet and each time I matched it with pretend reluctance.

From my point of view, the only hand to be scared of was a pocket pair of 10s. That would give Lizzie the best hand. That full house would beat mine. 10s full of 3s versus 7s full of 3s.

But how likely was that? Had she played like someone with a pair of 10s? I didn't think so.

With all the cards dealt I felt very confident that I still had the best hand so I waited for Lizzie to bet first ... and then made an even bigger bet to see if I could make even more out of the situation.

I wanted to maximise my winnings. I thought she was likely to bet again so I checked.

She did, putting in 100 chips. I raised, making it 300. It would cost her another 200 to see my cards.

'You fucking cunt!' she said.

I was shocked. Not by the bad language especially, but by the ferocity with which it was used. She was smiling at me. But I was sure there was some genuine upset behind it.

In return, Lizzie used some bad language towards me. It was difficult to tell whether it was used in jest or not. At the time it certainly felt like she was a bit upset with me.

'Mind your language, young lady,' I said, 'I'm old enough to be your father.'

I was trying to make light of it but as the last few words slipped out, I realised they were true. I was 39. She was 20. I was old enough to be her bloody father! What the hell was I doing there?

Lizzie didn't respond. She was just looking round the table to see if anyone else shared her sense of injustice. Her eyes seemed to say, 'What's wrong with just calling, why do you have to do that!?'

'What do I do?' she said, asking everybody and nobody.

'That depends on your cards,' said Tim, calmly. 'We don't know what your cards are.'

'It's just poker,' added John.

'Fine then,' said Lizzie. 'I call.'

We turned our cards over. She had an ace and a queen. I had a full house. I raked the chips my way.

'You cunt!' she said again. 'You only had a 3 and a 7!'

'I know,' I said, by now feeling genuinely concerned that I was upsetting the group dynamic. 'But that's why you shouldn't let the big blind play for free. If you'd bet more at the start I wouldn't have been in that hand.'

'You cunt.'

Eventually, Lizzie matched my bet.

We turned our cards over. I had the best hand and won a fairly sizeable pot.

Lizzie called me a cunt.

I really couldn't work out whether she was genuinely upset with me or not. I know that including the, um, choice language in the book will upset some people[10] and I sincerely apologise for any offence caused. But I've decided to leave it in precisely because I found it upsetting at the time. It really did cast a shadow over the rest of the evening. Don't get me wrong, I'm not pretending to be some delicate flower who's never heard such words before – and I have no truck with the old-fashioned, 'I'm-not-sexist-but-it's-just-not-right-coming-from-a-lady' point of view either. It's either fair game for all or it's not. But the word had been spat with venom each time and the one thing it isn't – at least, not in the company of someone you've only just met – is playful.

I wasn't upset because I was being called names. I was upset because I thought I'd upset someone. I thought I'd rocked the boat.

For a while it clouded my thoughts, nagging away at the back of my mind, making it harder to tune in to what was going on around me. Conversations whizzed by without me gaining a foothold because my head was elsewhere. Lizzie didn't help matters. Having uncaged the C-word she continued to use it with abandon. But only ever in my direction. Tim talked about his work in Zambia and Andy about the time he accidentally got caught up in the Israel–Lebanon war, but I couldn't focus on their tales because every time I made a bet that wasn't to you-know-who's liking she'd call me a you-know-what.

There's a problem when it comes to writing about poker. The game is suffused with a romantic machismo. Everyone who plays thinks they're good in the same way that everyone who drives thinks they can parallel park. It has its own language, a huge lexicon of slang, and using it makes you feel at least two

---

10. Hello Mum.

per cent cowboy. The trouble is, the moment you write about it you have to employ the jargon and that means a touch of cowboy swagger saunters onto the page whether you want it to or not.

I don't want to swagger in your direction. I don't want to claim any expertise I don't possess. Let me be clear – I didn't play well that night and I got what I deserved for it.

Andy was the first to exit the game, followed a short while later by John, Tim and Cec. James had done more winning than anyone else – or, more accurately, he'd done a lot less losing – and he had the chip lead to prove it. Lizzie was in a strong second place. I was bringing up the rear.

So that's how things were when the following hand was dealt:

Me: **10♣ Q♣**   Lizzie: **? ?**   James: **? ?**

The flop was good: **10♥ 3♦ 6♠**

The turn was okay: **9♦**

The river wasn't: **A♣**

Especially because Lizzie turned out to have **A♥ 6♣**, meaning her hand, two pairs: (**A♥ A♣ 6♣ 6♠ 10♥**) beat my one pair: (**10♣ 10♥ A♣ Q♣ 9♦**).

But what was annoying wasn't that I had a worse hand than Lizzie. It was that I *allowed* her to hit that ace: we shouldn't have even *seen* the ace. I should have made her fold long before that card was turned over. In essence, it was the same mistake that she'd made in allowing me to hit my full house earlier. My hand was strong after the flop, but it was vulnerable. If I'd pushed all in then, the likelihood was that Lizzie would have folded and the hand would have been over. As it was, I ended up putting more chips in at every stage and only committing all that I had left when it was too late. I was out. And it was entirely my own fault.

It wasn't a bad beat. I didn't get unlucky. I screwed up.

As Lizzie raked in the chips, a sheepish grin crept across her features. 'You can say it if you like,' she said. 'I know you want to.'

'No,' I said, not taking the bait. 'I don't like it.'

The rest of the game didn't take long. James aggressively raised every hand while Lizzie just folded and folded and folded, her stack of chips dwindling as she did so. With the end in sight, the Lizzie-must-be-stopped faction suddenly became her cheerleaders. Both Andy and John in particular were urging her to play some hands before it was too late. But she was having none of it. James wiped the floor with her. With all of us. The chips were all his. The £35 was his. A £30 profit for his efforts.

With the game over the tension between Lizzie and me dissipated and I found it easier to take in the chat. In a room full of post-grad students I suppose the talk of what-next – of funding opportunities, grants and the like – was inevitable.

John mentioned a friend who'd not long got his degree and was therefore now a fully fledged doctor, albeit only of the academic variety. 'And the coolest thing about it,' he added, his fruity not-Northern-Irish accent rolling around the words, 'is his surname. He's now Doctor Pepper.'

'I can do better than that,' said Andy. (The game might have been over but people were still raising the conversational stakes.) 'I know a Doctor Miracle.'

'You do not!' said Lizzie.

'I do,' insisted Andy. 'His first name's Preston.'

'Preston Miracle!' said James, incredulously.

Cec shrugged.

'Preston *Thor* Miracle, actually,' added Andy. 'Or Doctor Preston Thor Miracle to you.'

It's hard to imagine anyone having a name that improves quite so much with every additional element.

'So,' said a subject-changing Tim, 'are you into your darts then?'

'Yeah, of course,' I said. 'Love it.'

'Do you play as well?' asked John.

'When I can.'

'Do you want a game?'

He nodded his head, gesturing behind me. I turned and was surprised to see a dartboard hanging on the chimney breast of the far wall. I guess when I'd first arrived my attention had been drawn to the poker game and the gathering of folks at the table.

'Sure!'

We slid the tatty sofa back half a yard to make room for our improvised oche. It was obvious the board wasn't at regulation height but I figured we might as well do our best to get the throwing distance somewhere close.[11]

John took a practice round with the house darts and then offered them to me. They were as light as air. I've got used to darts with a bit of heft to them and find it impossible to throw anything else these days. I delved into my bag and produced my own familiar arrows.

'Do you always carry those with you?'

'Um … pretty much,' I nodded. I wonder what he'd think if he knew there was a table-tennis bat in there, too. 'You never know.' I took three practise darts. 'So … what do you want to play? 501 down? 301?'

'How about Round The Clock?'

'Can I play as well?' asked Lizzie.

---

11. The bull should be 5 foot 8 inches off the ground. The oche – or throw line – is 7 foot 9¼ inches from the board's face.

'Of course you can.'

'What is it?'

Lizzie had a unique approach to darts. She treated it more as a test-your-strength exercise than a game of accuracy. Instead of aiming, she'd pull her arm back behind her head like a javelin and then, using the whole of her upper body, she'd release the dart with such force that the board nearly came off the wall. Or at least it did when she hit the board. She also hit the wall a few times. On one occasion she managed to invent a new trick shot where the dart ricocheted off the board *and* the chimney breast before striking the TV with an ear-splitting *ska-thwhack*!

The whole room flinched. We waited to see if the TV would explode – it didn't – and then we marvelled at the amazing feat. The TV was tucked away in an alcove that should have offered it complete protection. What we'd just witnessed looked to be impossible. Lizzie just shrugged and threw another dart with the same wild fury.

With my own darts and four days of practice still fresh in my arm, I was aiming for the bull before John was into the teens. I'm not sure anyone was keeping tabs on Lizzie's score. It seemed she was more intent on trying to destroy the flat than the opposition.

I missed several shots at the bull, allowing John to close the gap to a much more respectable margin, but I was getting closer with every throw and eventually one slid in.

I turned and shook John's hand.

'Good game,' I said.

'Well played,' said John.

Rest of the World: 17
Me: 18

Lizzie shook her head in my direction. 'You c–'

'Until we meet again,' I said quickly. 'Farewell.'

CHAPTER 9

I felt a little foolish as I skulked away from Liverpool the next morning.

I'd bounced out of Didcot like I was walking away from a great first date but this was more like the morning after a regrettable one-night stand. It wasn't that I'd had a bad time – indeed, much of it had been fun – but had it been fun enough? Was that even possible?

If I want a treat on a weekday afternoon I sometimes pop out to my local café for a slice of cake. I like my local café. I love cake. It's a win–win situation. My investment in the cake – the couple of quid it costs *and* the few minutes it takes for me to walk to the caf – is easily outweighed by the niceness of the cake. But what if the cake cost more than a short walk and a couple of quid? What if I had to travel a few hundred miles on an expensive train to get my hands on that cakey goodness? What if the cake was so far away that I had to spend a night in a hotel, too? All that? Just for a slice of cake? I don't think there's a cake in the world tasty enough to justify that kind of effort. And I've tasted some pretty nice cakes in my time. Surely the same is true for a game of low-stakes poker?

Given the circumstances, there was nothing anyone could have done to make it fun *enough*. I shouldn't have booked a hotel. I shouldn't have got on the train. I should have just emailed Andy and suggested that I'd be in touch the next time I was going to be in Liverpool and left it at that.

Why had I expected it to be anything else? I had no idea. Like I say, I felt a little foolish that morning.

There were other reasons for feeling foolish: my trip to Liverpool was just the first in a three-day gaming series. I'd arranged to play others in Stockport and in London. Only not in that order.

Stockport is just 35 miles from Liverpool. Travelling from London to Liverpool to Stockport and *then* back to London would have been an almost sensible way to proceed. Indeed I *thought* that I'd arranged to do exactly that. That's certainly the way I'd scribbled it down in my diary.

But I'd made a bit of a cock-up on the organisational front. The dates in my diary weren't the dates I'd agreed in the emails I'd been sending back and forth with Nigel in London and Lou in Stockport. The fact that they were all about the same board game – something called 'Settlers of Catan'[12] – didn't help, but I'm not making any excuses. I'd just made a mistake. I'd thought about asking them to switch the dates around but I knew they'd both invited friends along so I decided the decent thing to do was to just take it on the chin. Oh well, London to Liverpool to London to Stockport to London it was.

*

---

12. I'd never heard of the game before I sent that first 'Who wants to play?' tweet, but within minutes I'd heard of it over and over and over again. It was easily the most mentioned game in all the replies I received. It was obviously a bit of a phenomenon.

In Wandsworth, south-west London, my first game of Settlers of Catan was at the Ship, a riverside pub that's been serving ale for over 220 years. From the outside, it was an uninspiring looking place. The three storeys of square brickwork had been painted beige and it was penned in by incongruous neighbours: a concrete manufacturer cast shadows over it from one side while on the other stood a modern development of yuppie flats – pale-brick structures with asymmetric balconies that looked big enough for a plant pot but not for a person. The developers had tried to give the buildings cosy, waterside names – Dolphin House, for example – but the nearby street names were far more evocative and they were there first. Smugglers Way and Jews Row, anyone? Can't see those getting planning permission today.

Once inside, however, the pub came to life. There was a lot of good, solid-wooden furniture – no doubt artfully arranged to look quite so unarranged – and the dark wood and oxblood-red walls made the large space feel intimate and private. The phrase 'gastro-pub' seems so rife with delusions of grandeur and misplaced aspirations that it never fails to make me blanch,[13] but I'm happy to concede that here was a pub that was gastro without being ghastly. It hadn't forgotten it was a pub. It was comfortable in its good-old-fashioned-boozer skin. It just happened to serve good food, too.

I was there a little early so I bought a drink, propped up the bar and waited. My liver was glad I'd stayed dry in Liverpool, but in Wandsworth it wanted a rum. Maybe it wanted one because I'd walked up Smugglers Way? 'Yo ho ho' and all that. I am very suggestible.

Nigel – the man who'd organised the game – was the first of my opponents to arrive. Late thirties, tall and blond, he

---

13. Which, I assume, is what most of them do to their asparagus.

looked to me like a Home Counties Kiefer Sutherland. He might not have been wearing chinos but he exuded the air of a man who was.

'We've got a private room booked,' he said after we'd exchanged pleasantries. 'Follow me.'

I did, only pausing momentarily when it looked like the only place he could possibly be leading me was the Gents. But a surprise jink to the left took us through to a room, dominated by a huge wooden dining table that could comfortably accommodate twenty or more. The lighting was low; the few candles that were dotted about the place were contributing almost as much as the dimly lit and heavily shaded wall lights. As the candles flickered, the dark fleur-de-lis wallpaper danced as if flirting with the sombre, timber panels that extended from dado rail to floor while in the middle of the far wall, above the dado rail, was a huge, ornate, gilt-framed circular mirror. We'd walked not into the Gents but into a gentleman's club from between the wars. It didn't feel like a game was about to commence. It felt like a will was about to be read. Or a duel announced.

'The others won't be long,' said Nigel and he was right. Before he'd put a full stop on the sentence the door swung open and in they came.

Marc and Sevitz. I was introduced to them simultaneously and for a short while I found myself unable to think of them as separate entities. I suppose the fact that Marc was Marc's first name and Sevitz was Sevitz's surname didn't help. I'd been given incomplete information for two people and sufficient for just one. I tried to separate them in my mind but, for the first twenty minutes or so, I couldn't do it. I didn't know who was who. They were a two-headed beast. They were a Marcansevitz.

But there was something else fusing the two of them together in my head. It wasn't that they looked like each other

– although there were similarities – it was more that they both reminded me of the same person but for different reasons.

Many years ago, while performing in Melbourne, I'd been introduced to a comic by the name of David Smiedt (or Smiedty, if you want to comply with Australia's nicknaming by-laws). The two of us hit it off instantly. With him living in Australia and me in the UK I can't pretend we have the most active of friendships but we have been able to meet up a few times over the years, and occasional emails still ping between the hemispheres from time to time.

To all intents and purposes I think of David as an Australian. I think he does too. But his family didn't actually move there until he was eighteen. He was born and raised in South Africa. His family are Jewish. In the 1980s his father – with his son growing more politically aware and active by the day, and with a sense that turbulent times were just around the corner – decided to get out of South Africa and so they emigrated.

Marc looked like Smiedty. He had the same high forehead and jet-black hair, the same tanned complexion and five o'clock-shadowed chin. They both wore dark-framed glasses and they both had the same I-know-something-you-don't-know semi-smile of half amusement.

Sevitz might have worn the same glasses but he didn't really look like Smiedty. He *sounded* like him. He had the same South African accent: one that's been worn away by years spent elsewhere. But he had Smiedty's mannerisms, too. The same eagerness to speak and brightness in his eyes. When I told them about my game of poker the night before ('I got on a train and paid for a hotel so that I could spend the evening being insulted by a girl half my age …'), Sevitz picked up the conversational thread and went off on a rapid-fire reminiscence of his father's crazy home game and its made-up rules.

'It's all deuces wild unless there's a six on the board when queens and jacks swap places and hearts can be diamonds unless it's a Thursday …' His improvised rant paused, but only so he could take a breath. 'They just make stuff up! It doesn't make *any* sense. The thing is, I don't think they're playing poker to play poker. It's more a social thing. You know what it's like – it's the most clichéd, South African, Jewish, suburban life …'

His assumption – that I'd know what *that* was like – amused me. If the South African, Jewish, suburban life was indeed a cliché, surely it was a fairly exotic one to bandy about in a Wandsworth pub.

But ridiculously, I *did* know what it was like. Smiedty has told me enough tales of his pre-Australian, clichéd, South African, Jewish, suburban life to make sure of that.

When I was looking at Marc I was looking at Smiedty, and when Sevitz was talking – which was often – I was listening to him, too. It only served to fuse them together more firmly in my consciousness.

Incidentally, when I say their glasses were the same as Smiedty's I only mean that they were of a type; that their frames were stylistically similar to his. But I can be much more precise when I say that the two of them had the same glasses as each other. They were 100 per cent identical.

'I got them first,' said Sevitz[14] when I remarked upon it. 'This is the first step in his *Single White Female* process. He wants to be me!'

'No, I don't,' said Marc.[15] 'You know damn well I didn't know you had these frames.'

'Boys, boys, boys,' said Nigel, calming down the play-bickering. He reached into his shoulder bag and produced the game box. 'Gentlemen,' he announced, 'Settlers of Catan.'

*

---

14. Or was it Marc?
15. Or was it Sevitz?

Twenty-four hours later and someone else was placing an identical box on a table in Stockport, where there was a very different, but equally affable, atmosphere.

The busiest bus route in the whole of Britain is the 192 in Greater Manchester. It travels between Piccadilly Gardens in the centre of the city through Ardwick, Longsight, Levenshulme, Heaton Chapel, Heaton Norris and Stockport, before continuing on through Heaviley, Davenport and Great Moor to the end of the line, Hazel Grove.

It must also be one of the only bus routes to have been celebrated musically[16]: a few years ago singer–songwriter, Dave Hulston, released an album called *The Willow and the 192*.

Dave Hulston was born in Longsight. The 192 was *his* bus. For a few years during my early twenties I, too, lived in Longsight. The 192 was my bus, too. I think the hundreds, possibly thousands, of trips I took on the 192 during my years in Manchester have left me with a residual feeling of familiarity for the places along its route. Of course, I felt like I knew Stockport: it was only five or six miles away from my Longsight bus stop, after all. How different could it be?

I lived in Manchester for ten years. But during that time I think I only visited Stockport twice, and both of those were fleeting, hit-and-run visits. Stockport – or Stocky as we called it – had one important function to me back then: it was a sign that I was nearly home. Returning from late-night gigs I'd always find comfort in Stockport's twin landmarks. There was the viaduct, with its twenty-seven arches of Victorian magnificence carrying the railway more than 100 feet above the valley of the River Mersey; and there was the Pyramid: a ludicrous office building with blue glass walls that stood unused for many a year, a sacrifice to late-80s pomp and optimism gone

---

16. When Nat King Cole sang about getting his kicks on Route 66 he wasn't referring to the bus from Romford to Leytonstone.

wrong. One was triumphant, the other risible, but they both set off the same feelings of not-long-now warmth on those night drives of my past.

It was only when I stepped out of Stockport station that I realised how little I actually knew of the place. It didn't feel like Manchester at all.

I walked through a pedestrianised precinct. I passed a bowling alley and a nightclub and I breathed in the chlorine-scented air of the local baths and the sickly-sweet odour of multiplex popcorn from the cinema. Everyone I saw – *literally* everyone – was wearing grey sweat pants: a bunch of twelve-year-old kids were smoking in a doorway. They had that strange defiant-yet-furtive look in their eyes as if they wanted to not be seen but would relish it if they were challenged. A couple of older lads were cycling aimlessly round on their BMX bikes occasionally kicking out at – but always missing – the pigeons. A grey-haired old man sat on a bench, feeding those pigeons bread, tempting them back towards the BMX wheels, and a young mum and dad walked their two toddlers hand in hand towards the station. And each and every one of them was in matching, baggy, grey sweat pants.[17]

It was oddly unsettling. Did Stockport really have its own dress code? How had I not known? Was I really this obviously an outsider? I can't tell you how quietly overjoyed I was to step onto the main road and see the first pair of jeans. Phew.

It was a bit early to head to my game just yet but there wasn't enough time to make it to my hotel and back, so I took a little stroll around. I stood for a while on Wellington Road Bridge just watching the River Mersey flow beneath it. I

---

17. I say 'matching', but it's only fair to point out that the pigeon feeder had personalised his with a few highly visible stains. Some from himself. Some from the pigeons. At least I hope they were from the pigeons.

looked across to the viaduct as it glowed a burnt umber colour in the slowly setting sun. It was easy to see why Lowry liked it so much, but there weren't many matchstalk men or match-stalk cats and dogs to be seen sprawling around it any more. There were plenty of people with meat on their bones in Stockport that day. The people of Stocky looked stocky. Ack. So did I.

On the other side of the bridge the river disappears under the city, unseen for a good stretch as it threads its way beneath roads and through culverts, under a 60s shopping centre and then on. That a river runs unseen beneath it is probably the most interesting thing there is about the Merseyway shopping precinct. It's not exactly a glamorous affair: not old enough to be charming, not new enough to be exciting … it simply refuses to make a statement of any kind. Not even an apology.

The same can't be said for the Plaza, a glorious 1930s Art Deco palace of delights that stands to one side overlooking the same square. It was a 'Super Cinema and Variety Theatre' in its day, one of the grandest, but after more than three decades of service it was transformed into, horror of horrors, a bingo hall. Oh, to be in Stockport in 1965! The year they covered the river with a shopping centre and turned the most beautiful building in town into a home for fag-ash Lils! What on earth were they thinking?

Fortunately the bingo stopped in 1999. It was then a full ten years before the Plaza's doors were thrown open to the public once more. It's a proper venue again now. Shows are staged and films are screened. The white, terracotta, angular front of the building stands tall and proud staring out defi-antly in the hope that nobody noticed the bingo blip. It really is a beauty.

Wandering a little further up the road my eye was drawn, through a pub window, to a lonely, unused dartboard. It's always nice when you spot one in its natural habitat. The Unity was a robust, stoic-looking pub, unfussy and all the better for it. It was a proper old man's pub, only it seemed to be missing the old men. I thought about popping in and giving my darts arm a bit of a workout but a quick glance at my watch confirmed it was time for me to be moving on. Maybe I'll look in later, I thought. There might be someone in there by then. I might get a game.

At Stockport bus depot I stood and waited. There were maybe fifteen fellow travellers at the same bus stand, all eyeing each other up carefully. No queue had been formed but we'd all made a mental note of the order in which we'd arrived. We all knew our place. Nobody spoke. Even the people in groups or couples seemed to fall under the silent spell of pre-bus tension.

Fifty yards away, however, there was no such spell. Fifty yards away, there was a conversation going on at an impressively high volume. I suppose that was the other reason we were remaining silent. We were all listening in. We were all fascinated. This was our pre-bus soap opera.

The cast looked interesting: a man and a woman both in their mid twenties. The plot involved them having just bumped into one another for the first time in many years. It was her shriek of surprise that first alerted us to their presence. I think we all expected the volume to subside after that but instead they both continued to broadcast to the world. I imagine it was partly to do with the large headphones that stayed glued to his ears like a couple of terrapins making love through his empty head.

He was a large lad. He wore three-quarter-length board shorts and a tracksuit top. She was slim, attractive with striking cheekbones and an even more striking gold lamé tracky top that clashed with her fake tan.

It soon became clear that he was on the pull, but I don't think many of us gave him much of a chance. He was the

Merseyway shopping precinct and she was the Plaza (during its bingo hall years).

'Eh, how are you?' he asked loudly, competing with the noise in his headphones.

'I'm all right, ta.' She wasn't being unfriendly but she was keeping her distance. 'You?'

'Yeah. Hey. I saw your mam the other day.'

'Me mam?' She shook her head. She chewed her gum. She didn't believe him. 'You never!'

'I did. Your mam, Carol!'

'Carol?' she squealed. 'That's not me mam. That's me sister!'

'No way?'

'Way!'

'No way! I thought she was looking good.'

All around me, bodies were turning slowly, satellite dishes tracking round in search of a clearer signal. He'd insulted her sister but he wasn't giving up.

'So, what y'up to?'

'Me? Nowt. Just working and being a mum really, you know,' she said, without a hint of a moan. 'It's knackering.' She smiled to herself. But not at him. She folded her arms at him.

'Aw, wow,' he said with a solemn, I-understand-your-situation shake of the head. He leaned in close and tried to slide his arm round her shoulders. His attempt at tenderness was rendered ridiculous by the shouting: 'It must be really hard for you,' he yelled.

She shrugged herself out of his half-embrace. She'd had enough.

'Anyway,' she screamed, 'I've gotta go. It's, um, good to see you, Kyle.'

'Kyle?' He laughed. 'I'm not Kyle!'

'What d'y'mean?'

'I'm not Kyle!' he said again. 'I'm Darren!'

'No way?'

'Way! I'm Darren. Who the fuck is Kyle?'

'I got you confused!' Her hoots of laughter bounced round the bus station's canopy. 'With Kyle!' More roars of laughter. 'You're not Kyle, are you? You're Darren!'

'I know!' said Darren.

'Aw, gizza hug, Daz!' She threw her arms open. 'I haven't seen you for ages!'

He hugged her. The lad had won an unlikely reprieve.

'What you doing later?' he asked.

'Nowt. You can come round if you like. When I've put me daughter to bed?'

Just then our bus pulled up, its rumbling, burping diesel engine drowning out the rest of the dialogue. We filed on – in strictly adhered-to arrival order, obviously – and then spread ourselves about the bus; all glad our chariot had arrived but secretly a little bit miffed that we'd missed the end of the story. Except we hadn't missed it at all. As the bus pulled away, those of us who thought to look back saw the two of them already locking lips.

Somehow, the fact that the pretty-girl-who-wasn't-Carol's-daughter-but-was-her-sister was now snogging Darren-the-boy-who-wasn't-Kyle seemed genuinely touching. I'm not sure why. I think I just liked the idea of the unseen character, Kyle. I liked the idea of a man whose behaviour was so reprehensible that the rest of us menfolk were deemed sexually attractive simply by dint of not being him. There was something to comfort the soul there.

Or maybe I just needed to eat.

Thirty minutes later, having arrived in the cosy suburb of Heald Green, bought a bottle of wine from the supermarket on the main drag (I was getting better at this) and found my way to my host's front door I was, for the second time that day, worrying that I'd misjudged the dress code.

This time it had nothing to do with grey sweat pants. Lou, the woman who'd invited me to play, was dressed for a sophisticated soirée. Her bright red dress was a stark contrast to my lounging-around T-shirt and jeans. She'd made an effort and I hadn't. Well, I suppose I had travelled up from London and she was in her own hallway, but you know what I mean.

We bumbled our way through the traditional I-brought-this/Oh-you-shouldn't-have introductions and then she showed me through to the front room where, for the second time that day, a pair of legs in blue jeans brought quiet joy. Such a relief. The dress code extended from smart-casual to casual-casual after all. I wasn't just a visiting scruff.

Lou introduced me to her husband, Tim; their friend, Katherine; and another couple, Lisa and Andy. Handshakes all round. How-was-your-journey? all round. Niceness all round.

'Now, I've made a paella,' said Lou. 'There's one for the meat eaters and one for those who don't, but I thought it'd be easier if you all just served yourself so come on through ...'

This serve-yourself system is all very well in principle, but I'm not sure Lou had taken into account the crippling polite-ness of her guests that evening. We found ourselves at a kitchen impasse, nobody prepared to pick up a ladle and go for it, all of us cursed by good manners: 'After you ...' 'No, after you.' 'No, no, really, after you.' 'Ladies first ...' 'But you're a visitor.' 'Please, after you?' 'I insist ...'

How did this country ever get anything done when we were raised to be this way? Somehow – presumably through some synchronised ladling – we got the paella on our plates and returned to the living room where there weren't quite enough comfy chairs for everyone and another bout of over-polite bartering took place: 'No, please, you take it.' 'No, you.' 'I wouldn't dream of it.' 'Please.' 'I insist.' 'But I've already insisted.'

I don't remember who sat down first but I'm happy to confirm that no independent adjudicators were called upon. I do know that I ended up in one of the comfy armchairs. I was a guest. And, as the other guests pointed out, I was a stranger who'd never been there before and that made me the guestiest guest of all. Crikey, this politeness was exhausting.

While we ate our good, hearty, healthy paella, the conversation bounced from game-playing (naturally) to other hobbies and pastimes. Both Tim and Lisa were really into photography and as that's a passion of mine too, we easily slipped into a nerdy conversation about preferred cameras and lenses and our shared love for a photography website, flickr.com. Katherine surprised her friends by revealing she liked darts so I was on safe ground there too, but when it came to Lou's love of crafting I had rather less to say. Which pleased me. Stuff I don't know about is always more interesting.

There didn't seem to be an area of crafting that wasn't on Lou's radar. If you could make it, she seemed to have made it. If it involved sewing, stitching, cutting or sticking it made Lou happy. She was doing a City and Guilds course in fashion design at the time but her work was for a local church. I knew it was a modern church when she told me it was called 'C3 Stockport'.

'That sounds like a nightclub,' I said. 'Y'know, in Stockport obviously.'

Lou grinned. 'Yeah. I suppose it does. We've been going for five years. The emphasis is on trying to reintroduce some creativity and fun to Christianity.'

'Sounds nice,' I said. I meant it too. I hoped my words hadn't sounded hollow. I feared they did. 'I mean it,' I added with a bit too much emphasis. 'I mean, I'm not a Christian, but I am in favour of creativity and fun and stuff.'

I was trying a bit too hard.

'I'm not, either,' added Tim, making me feel just as relaxed about my atheism as his jeans had made me feel about my jeans. (Not that anyone else was anxious, mind. Nobody was preaching. Nobody was looking at me and expecting revelation to strike. The insecurity was all mine.)

With the food settling in our bellies and our wine glasses topped up, it was time to play. We shuffled over to the dining table we hadn't used for dining, and with the lack of fuss and bother that only having exactly the right number of chairs can bring you, we all took a seat.

The words *With God all shall be well and all manner of things shall be well* looked over us from a frame on the wall. All manner of things did feel well there. With or without Him.

'Right,' said Lou, lifting the box on to the table, 'Settlers of Catan.'

So, Settlers of Catan. Let me tell you what I can about the game and how it works.

The first thing I had to do was lose my preconceptions. The board games I grew up with – from 'Snakes and Ladders' to 'Monopoly' – all had certain elements in common. As diverse as they are, they always share some essential board-game DNA: they all have a fixed board on which there's a prescribed route for the pieces to move; when it's your turn you roll one or more dice; and the result of that roll dictates how many spaces you can move. That's how board games work, right?

Wrong. Not for this game.

In Settlers of Catan the board isn't fixed. The first thing you do when playing is construct it. The board represents an island, Catan. It's made up of hexagonal pieces that fit together within a cardboard frame that represents the surrounding sea. Each of these hexagonal pieces, or hexes, represents a different kind of terrain, be it pasture, woods, fields, hills, mountains or desert. The hexes are shuffled face down and then placed within the frame at random, meaning that every time you play the game the island is configured differently. It's like starting Monopoly by creating a new, random route around London.

Monopoly theorists – they exist! – have actually worked out the best way to play the game on a standard board. For example, they'll tell you that the most powerful set to accumulate is the orangey-coloured Bow, Marlborough and Vine Streets[18] trio: the set immediately before Free Parking (it's because they're six, eight and nine spaces respectively after the In Jail/Just visiting square, and that means statistically that they're more likely to be hit).

Monopoly can be distilled into a list of simple dos and don'ts that will ensure you're most likely to win. But with Settlers of Catan there's no such thing. The board is different every time and so the winning strategy might be different each time, too.

As the name of the game suggests, the task in Settlers is to, um, settle. You're trying to establish communities on Catan – more precisely, you are trying to build settlements, cities and roads. To do this you need resources. Which is where the different terrains come in.

In the first round of play, each player gets to place two settlements on the board. They're placed on hex intersections, which, as you can see, means they sit between three different hexes.[19]

---

18. That would be St James Place, Tennessee Avenue and New York Avenue on the classic American board based on Atlantic City NJ.
19. Unless they're at the edge of the frame when they connect with two hexes and the 'sea'.

Before you locate your settlements, numbered discs are placed in the centre of each hex: I've used 2, 11 and 4 for my illustration. Now, let's say that you've created the settlement that sits between these three hexes. And let's say that the top hex represents pasture, the bottom left is woods and the bottom right is mountains. Now, when it's your go, you get to roll two dice. If you happen to roll a double one – the only possible way of scoring 2 – then your top hex would yield some resources to you. In this case, as it's pasture, you would earn sheep – or at least a small card with a picture of a sheep on it. If your roll had scored 4, the mountains would have given you some iron ore, and if it had been 11 the woods would yield wood. Wouldn't they? Yes. They would. Wouldn't you? I would. Yes. Wood.

But it's not just you that gets to act. You roll the dice. You collect any resources that your throw might yield and so does everyone else who might also have a settlement on a hex carrying that number. Then, if you have enough resources you get to build. The different resources combine to build different things so it takes, say, one brick and one wood to build a road, whereas you need to add sheep and grain to that combination to make a settlement.

Crucially, if you don't have enough resources to build you can always trade with other people, passing them two of your ore cards for one of their brick or whatever other deal you can negotiate.

To complicate matters further, there are other factors to think about too, like a robber, knights, trading with the bank, trading with harbours and more although, in truth, they don't seem all that complicated when you're actually playing. But the gist of it is there. Instead of moving a character around a board, the roll of the dice dictates what resources you have and you decide what you do with them. And, unlike Monopoly, where the goal is to obliterate your opponents, you're forced into cooperating with them. The game simply doesn't function if you don't.

The winner is the first person to score ten points. Points are awarded for settlements, cities, the longest road, the largest army and probably some other things I can't remember. It means there are several different ways of winning the game and most players feel in contention for a large part of the game. Results tend to be close.

It's fair to say I had a degree of cynicism about the way the game worked and how different it could be from game to game. In Wandsworth, the game was won by Marc, who managed to create a small but fertile enclave in a corner of the island. But when I tried a similar strategy the next day in Stockport, the game was won by Lisa, who built a long, spindly, winding road that seemed to reach all corners.

I enjoyed the company on both occasions but in truth I never really locked into the game. I never really felt like I was making decisions based on my own understanding and my own judgement. Maybe this kind of cooperative, hippy game wasn't really for me.

Rest of the World: **19**
Me: **18**

CHAPTER 10

Standing at a cold, dark bus stop in Heald Green, waiting for the cold, dark and lonely bus that would take me back to the heart of Stockport, I started to question what I was doing. In three days I'd travelled over 600 miles on Britain's railways and buses and for what? A game of poker – with a side salad of abuse – and two games of Settlers of Catan? That didn't make a lot of sense, did it?

The doubts I'd felt as I left Liverpool had only been underlined by the full seventy-two-hour experience. It hadn't been the grand folly I'd hoped. It was just folly plain and simple. It had all been fun but it hadn't been more fun than the train rides had been dreary. I was definitely looking at a three-day fun deficit. Travelling all that way to play a game with strangers – no matter how nice they were – well, that was just a bit needy, wasn't it?

I fancied a nightcap and a ponder. I warmed myself up by thinking of the Unity. The old-man pub without any old men. I'd head there. I'd throw some darts and have a rum. Everything feels a bit better when I've thrown some darts and had a rum.

THUD-THUD-THUD-THUD-WOOP-WOOP-WOOP-WOOP-THUD-THUD-THUD-THUD-WOOP-WOOP-WOOP-WOOP-THUD!

The noise coming out of the Unity was immense. I didn't get as far as the door. I didn't have to. From across the street I could see the tacky disco lights flashing – red, green, yellow, blue, red, green, yellow, blue – as the windows shook and the walls appeared to swell in time with the thudding bass-led beat and high-pitched beeps and whoops. The old men – and through the window they genuinely did appear to all be silver foxes – had turned up and were now raving, pogo-ing, bouncing and flailing to house music. In the corner, the lonely dartboard seemed to peer out onto the street, a forlorn look in its bullseye, as if begging me to rescue it from this hard house hell. Sorry, dartboard, this was every man for himself … I turned on my heel and headed for my hotel.

On the twenty-minute walk north I ran the last three days round and round in my head, trying to unravel the deep-lying sense of discontent in my gut. (It wasn't the paella. That had been delicious.)

In Liverpool I'd visited a life I used to live: the shared house, the student lifestyle limbo of my mid twenties – the life I'd lived just up the road in Longsight, Manchester. In Wandsworth, I'd visited a more recent life. Nigel and his friends were the geeks who'd inherited the earth. They all worked in online businesses; Nigel and Sevitz had met during their eBay years. They were smart, funny and confident about the world and their place in it. I hadn't spotted any wedding rings around the table: did they represent the carefree, I'm-all-right-Jack life of my early thirties? And in Heald Green, were Lou, Tim and their friends sent to show me my future? It had cropped up mid game that Lou and Tim had an imminent anniversary.

'Congratulations,' I'd trilled. 'How many years?'

'Fourteen,' had come the reply. Fourteen! I'd been sure they were younger than me and I'd been expecting to hear 'Three' or 'Four', not anything-teen! Blimey! Was that cosy, living-room life what I had in store? (In many ways I hoped so. It was bloody lovely, after all.) But was that what this was all about? Was I Ebenezer Scrooge? Only with ghosts so lazy I was left having to do all the work? Was I taking the train to meet the ghosts of Gorman past, present and future?

It felt like I was back on tour. But having not long finished a pretty intense period of work, what I needed was a holiday.

As it happened, Beth and I *had* been planning to take a holiday around this time, but a change in circumstances had made that impossible.

I should tell you a little about Beth. She's tall and slim. Her eyes are grey with a hint of green, although she prefers to think of them as green with a hint of grey. It matters not. Most of the time they're hidden behind her fringe of raven hair. She is beautiful. She is clumsy. Both those things make me smile. The tops of her ears are small and seem to contain less cartilage than normal ears. She will kill me for typing that last sentence.

She works behind the scenes in TV and radio. We've only worked together on two occasions. One of those was the day we met. The other, a year later, was the day we first flirted. I'm not a fast mover.

Since we'd been a couple our working lives had never intersected, and around this time we were struggling to make our free time intersect as well. In fact, there was precious little intersecting of any kind.

It had looked like we were both going to be free during the summer, which was why we'd put loose holiday plans in place. It would have meant going away a couple of months before our wedding but that suited us just fine: we were both more than happy to treat it as a cart-before-the-horse honeymoon, especially as it looked like we were only going to be able to take a short, four-day break immediately after the big day.

But then a spanner was thrown in the works. Beth had signed up to work on a TV show that had a last-minute change of schedule. They went into production much sooner than initially planned, meaning we were no longer able to take our summer break. We weren't complaining. It also meant they would finish sooner, so we going to be able to take a more conventionally scheduled honeymoon instead. It was a good change for us. It put the horse back in front of the cart.

But now it was Beth's turn to be working seven days a week, a lot of it away from home, and most of it filming in various fields in Shropshire.

'Why don't you still go away?' she'd asked. 'Maybe go off for a week and get some sun with a couple of mates. You need the break.'

'I don't want to go on a holiday without you,' I'd replied. Because I didn't. 'And besides, if I take a couple of weeks off the radio show I won't be able to take the time off for a honeymoon. And I think that's more important.'

And I did.

CHAPTER 11

I had decided to wind down my game-playing activity and chalk the whole thing up to experience but then a few days later, as I checked my emails, I found a couple of things that helped to persuade me otherwise.

The first one was just lovely ...

From: Andy
To: Dave Gorman
Subject: Kubb

Hi Dave,

I just wanted to say thanks for the game of Kubb we played. I've been trying to do more activities outside my comfort zone and I saw your tweet at just the right time. I think it becomes very easy to sit still and not stray from your normal activities, locked up in a bubble behind the security of our front doors. Thanks for providing me with an opportunity to say yes to something that involved meeting a stranger, feeling nervous and not being 100% comfortable – it turned out to be a really enjoyable and fun morning. I also found somebody else who plays Kubb at the Truck music festival I went to that evening!! She pronounces it with an accent on the 'u' so 'Koobb' (or something like that) but we still knew what we were talking about and we've made plans to play a game soon. I don't

think that would have happened if you and I
hadn't played our game that morning. Thanks!
   Andy

While the second was more intriguing ...

From: Biggles
To: Dave Gorman
Subject: Rod Hull's Emu Game!

Dave,
What are you doing this afternoon?
Would you like to play Rod Hull's Emu Game?
I live in Greenwich.
   Biggles

Not only was it intriguing ... it was in London!

Rod Hull was a highly successful British entertainer whose
heyday lasted through the 1970s and 80s. He was born in
Kent but his professional life began in Australia, which no
doubt explains why his act involved a puppet emu.[19]

For those unfamiliar with his work, Rod's right arm filled
the puppet while a fake arm looped over the top of it, creating

---

19. The emu is a large flightless bird native to Australia. It's the largest of all
Australia's birds and the second-largest bird in the world by height. Only the
ostrich is able to look down its beak at the emu, but they're family members
so I doubt they make a song and dance about it.

I once dated a girl who had reached adulthood without knowing emus
were real birds: she just thought 'Emu' was the made-up name for Rod
Hull's puppet. This gap in her knowledge came to light one day when I
mentioned having seen a nature documentary with some emus in it. 'What?'
she scoffed. 'And if they'd been frogs would you have told me you'd seen
some Kermits? Diddums!' She didn't believe me when I insisted emus
existed. Thank heavens for the internet.

the illusion that he was carrying the bird with its big, blue-ish body and bright orange beak. It's fair to say the illusion wasn't especially convincing. The fake arm was *obviously* a fake arm and Emu was *obviously* a puppet. His body looked like it was made out of tinsel that had been taken from a goth's Christmas tree and the only moving feature was his neck and beak.

But therein lay Rod Hull's genius. He took the most unbelievable conceit and with an utterly convincing perform-ance turned it into something people believed in. He gave his right arm a life of its own. It seemed to act independently of him; indeed, most of the time it appeared to be acting against his wishes. It wreaked havoc.

In truth, much of his kids' TV work did little for me. It was his forays into grown-up telly that were exciting. Emu would violently attack people, viciously going for the throat and even the crotch, and all the time Rod would try in vain to control his avian charge. Of course, everyone knew it was Rod's right arm that was pecking at their tackle but his performance was so skilful they never seemed to blame him. Even those who genuinely resented the invasion seemed to believe that Rod was on their side and that the bird alone should carry the blame. Once, after a Royal Variety Perform-ance, Emu grabbed and then 'ate' the Queen Mother's bouquet. I simply can't imagine any other performer taking the same kind of liberty and getting away with it.

His most fondly remembered appearance was on Michael Parkinson's chat show. The interview starts with Parky asking Rod whether Emu is a male or female emu. The split person-ality is immediately evident. Rod replies, 'Why don't you have a look for yourself?' while at the same time Emu reacts aggres-sively, scrunching his beak and straightening his neck in a gesture that clearly means, '*If you do, I'll peck your bleedin' eyes out, mate*.' The bird never actually spoke. It didn't have to.

Parkinson doesn't even complete his next question before Emu's beak has a vice-like grip on his knee. This is just the first stage in a performance of escalating physicality that eventually sees the host bundled out of his chair and onto the studio floor. He loses a shoe – and an ounce of his composure – in the process.

But it's before we reach this dizzying peak that I think we witness the most beautiful part of Hull's performance. When asked the not unreasonable question, 'Why is he so aggressive?' Hull protests, 'He's *not* aggressive!' I genuinely adore this moment. There's a hell of a lot of character in those three words. His tone of voice is eager to please and yet it carries more hope than belief. Emu is holding him to ransom. Say nice things about the bird and he *might* behave. Say bad things about him and he definitely won't. Hull's tone of voice is the one you hear harassed mothers using on trains when their feral children are clambering over your table: 'It's okay, he's just playing, aren't you, George? He won't kick or anything, look, no, George, don't kick …' But in the split second it takes him to utter those three simple words – 'He's not aggressive!' – Hull also produces two, no, make that three, beautiful moments of physical comedy. Of course Emu is aggressive. First, he takes a peck at Parkinson, who naturally flinches, but then the bird pecks at Hull, and then comes my favourite moment: *Hull flinches too*. It is a flawless performance. In one moment of improvised genius, he says one thing and does *three* others, reinforcing two quite distinct and fully rounded personalities as he does so. It's remarkable.[21]

These days it's common to dismiss the light entertainers of previous generations as being too twee, too cosy, too soft and lacking in edge, but for the best part of two decades, Rod

---

21. The clip is online so do watch it when you get a moment. At the time of writing it can be found here: http://bit.ly/emuHull

Hull was a truly anarchic spirit in mainstream TV, and I don't think anyone who's come along since has been anywhere near as dangerous. And if that's not reason enough to love him, then consider this: in the late 70s Rod Hull was invited to perform in Las Vegas, opening for Frank Sinatra. He turned the offer down because he wanted to tend to his potatoes.

Unfortunately, his life was to end in inglorious fashion. In 1994 the former millionaire was declared bankrupt and in 1999, while trying to adjust his TV aerial, he fell from his roof and died. He was 63.

As a child I'd owned an Emu glove puppet. It was just a disembodied neck and head so when left on the bedroom floor it rather looked as though Michael Parkinson had finally taken his revenge. But I had no idea a game about him existed. Until now.

Traffic puts a lot of people off cycling in London. They look out from their seat on the bus and think, 'I wouldn't want to be in the middle of that!' And they're right. They wouldn't. But there are other ways to go. My eight-mile ride from Bethnal Green to Greenwich involved almost no roads, the bulk of it being on the tow path of the Grand Union Canal and then the path beside the River Thames. But the best bit doesn't follow the river; it tunnels beneath it.

The Greenwich foot tunnel is one of my favourite things in London. Fifty feet below ground lies a foot tunnel lined with glazed white tiles. Walking into it is like entering a giant CAT-scan machine. It goes beneath the River Thames, connecting Greenwich to the south with the Isle of Dogs to the north. (The Isle of Dogs isn't actually an island. It's the sticky-out bit of land contained within the horseshoe-shaped bend in the Thames that you see in the opening titles of *EastEnders*.)

I probably go through that tunnel four or five times a year. I always find it exciting. For a start it's impossible not to contemplate the weight of the water above you. Just imagining a crack appearing in those beautiful white circular walls is enough. It's not so frightening that I avoid using it, but it's enough to make me quicken my pace when I reach the halfway point. You know ... just in case. But it's exciting also because it feels like it shouldn't be there. Using it makes me feel like an insider: as if I alone am privy to some secret knowledge. It's like leaning on a candlestick in a stately home and discovering it's the trigger that opens up a secret passage connecting the study to the kitchen.

The tunnel was opened in 1902 having been campaigned for by left-wing politicians who wanted to make it easier for the poor on the south of the Thames to get to work in the docks and shipyards to the north. Both entrances are housed inside brick rotundas with glass cupolas on top. If you ever take an overseas visitor there I recommend telling them they were modelled on Queen Victoria's breasts. The lifts are especially attractive. The wood-panelled walls make them feel like the TARDIS as re-imagined by H.G. Wells. If I had my way, both lift attendants would have to have an extravagant moustache of some kind just to look the part.[22]

The tunnel is regarded as a public highway so it remains open twenty-four hours a day by law. When the lifts aren't running there are spiral staircases instead, although they do require some huff and puff to get up – especially if you're carrying a bicycle on your back.

Having emerged from the tunnel I only had to cycle a half a mile or so to find the right address: a terraced house in Greenwich that had been converted into flats. I rang the middle bell as per my instructions, but there was no sound and no sign of any movement on the other side of the front door's stained-glass panels. I waited a while and then rang the

---

22. Two Khet-playing magicians spring to mind.

bell again. Still nothing. I was about to ring the bell for a third time when someone spoke.

'Hello. Are you Dave?'

The voice – a female voice – hadn't come from inside the house … it was behind me. I turned to find a woman in her mid fifties. Beneath a bouncy mop of ash-grey hair was a round face with ruby-red lips. She was panting. As she swayed from foot to foot, sunlight glinted in the thin film of sweat on her brow.

'Yes,' I said, 'I'm Dave. Are you …?'

'Biggles.'

'Biggles?'

'Yes,' she said with a wheeze. 'Biggles.'

'Of course!' I shook the confusion out of my brain. 'Sorry … you threw me for a moment, there. I thought you must be someone else seeing as you weren't in and … and … you weren't … um … well, I was expecting a man … because … um …'

'Don't worry,' said Biggles with a throaty chuckle, which then became a hacking cough. 'It happens all the time. "Biggles" is a bit "What-ho" and "Chocks away" and all that.' She inhaled deeply, throwing her shoulders back as her chest expanded with air and then, with a mighty *phwhoosh*, she let it all out. 'The thing is,' she continued. 'I've been called Biggles for so long now I can hardly remember what my real name is.'

'Ha! Really? Go on … what is it?'

'So,' she said, ignoring my question, 'shall we go?'

'Huh? Go? Where to?'

'Back to mine.'

'But … but …' I was very confused. 'But, this *is* yours … isn't it?'

'Oh God, no!' Biggles fanned herself furiously, her left hand flapping so fast it was a blur. 'I never give *anyone* my home address!'

'What? Well ... who lives *here* then?'

'I've no idea. Did you ring the middle bell?'

'Yeah.'

'Good. They're never in.'

'What?'

'I think it's empty.'

'I'm *really* confused.'

Biggles sighed an isn't-it-obvious? sigh before explaining herself with a this-is-the-last-time-I-tell-you tone of voice. 'I don't give strangers – especially male strangers – my home address.' She turned and started to walk, gesturing for me to follow. I wheeled my bike alongside her. 'I give people *this* address because a: it's empty and b: I can see it from my place. So I wait and when I see someone approaching I leave mine and walk over here. Usually I do a walk-by, y'know, just to see if they look okay. *Comprendê?*'

'Yes,' I said. 'Yes. Sort of.'

I understood what I'd been told but I wasn't close to understanding the whys and wherefores behind it. I wasn't sure I really wanted to, either. Just how often did she arrange to meet strangers 'at home', anyway? Why not just meet them somewhere else in the first place? It didn't make a lot of sense to me but, rational or not, I figured anyone that paranoid had to have reasons of their own and I didn't really want to find out what hers were.

While Biggles busied herself making tea, I stood in her front room feeling not quite sure where to put myself. With my weight on one hip and my head at 45 degrees I studied her bookcase. It was something of a shrine to Jackie Collins. *Poor Little Bitch Girl, Deadly Embrace, Lethal Seduction, Lovers and Gamblers, Lady Boss, Sinners, Thrill, Dangerous Kiss.* Stiletto heels, high-gloss lipstick, glamour, lust and sex dripped from the shelves. She's written a lot of books, has Jackie, and I reckoned Biggles owned pretty much all of them. She even had multiple copies of some, with as many as four or five different editions of the same title sitting side by side. Jackie's older sister, Joan, got a look-in too, with five or six of her novels filling out the shelf.

I moved over to the bay window. A couple of hundred yards to the left was the doorstep where we'd met. I smiled at the oddness of it all.

'I couldn't remember if you wanted sugar or not so I brought some through.' Biggles came back into the room carrying a tray of tea and biscuits. She entered elbow first, crabwalking sideways – pace-together, pace-together – until she was safely out of the door frame's orbit.

'Help yourself,' she said, placing the tray down on the table. 'I'm just going to slip into something more comfortable.'

I froze. The bookcase full of bonkbusters winked at me. Biggles giggled. 'Not like that!' she squealed. 'I mean for my feet. I'm a martyr to my feet, and these boots are killing me!'

When she returned a few moments later she was wearing a pair of fluffy pink slippers. She was also carrying the game. The box was about a foot square and three or four inches deep. Its bright colours had been faded by the years.

'Now,' she said, 'we need to get this thing set up, don't we!'

The top of the box was dominated by a large illustration of the game: a plastic version of Emu's head, his beak ajar with a green disc resting in it. In a small panel there was a watercolour of the game being played by a boy, a girl and, of course, a grown man called Rod Hull. The only photos of the game were on the side of the box and none of them featured Rod. I wondered if he'd actually *seen* the game before it had hit the shops. You'd think they'd have photographed him with it if they could. Then again, he did look a little frightening at times. His face appears kindly in the illustration, whereas I remember the flesh-and-bones version as being vaguely haggard and lost looking. His hair had always looked brittle and straw-like, but in the painted version it looked like, well, hair.

Biggles lifted the lid. The plastic contents hadn't faded with age: after thirty years the reds, yellows and blues were vibrant still. It took us a minute or two to slot the pieces together and there it was: *Rod Hull's Emu Game*!

At the centre of it was a red plastic circular base upon which was placed a yellow plastic Emu's head complete with bulbous, stick-on eyes and a blue, fake-fur crop of, um, well, if you squinted, feathers. Attached to the base were four blue arms and at the end of each arm, a small sprung lever. There was a motor inside the base and at the flick of a switch the head would rotate, slowly opening and closing its beak as it did so. The aim of the game was for each player to use one of the sprung levers to catapult small plastic discs into the mouth. It required delicate flicks and good timing.

Ten counters each. Biggles was blue, I was red, and the winner was the first to get all their discs into Emu's gob.

It was frantic and silly and oddly compelling because no matter how well you did, you always felt you could do better. The machine whirred and clicked as the motor turned and the two of us howled and shrieked as we boinged the counters towards the hungry beak. We celebrated every hit. We bemoaned every miss: 'Yes!' 'Arse!' 'Get in!' 'Ooof!'

The first game ended in a 10–8 win to Biggles.

'It's fun, isn't it?' she said, wiping a tear of hilarity from her eye.

'Yes,' I said. 'It is. Sort of.' I *was* enjoying it … just not as much as she was. But I was enjoying how much she was enjoying it. 'It's very silly.'

'Do you want another?'

'Of course!' And so … 'Arse!' 'Arggghh!' 'Ayyy!' 'Ack!'

'Go on,' I said. I thought the ice was sufficiently broken now. 'Why are you called Biggles?'

'It's because I'm scared of flying.'

I laughed …

'Beauty!' 'Bugger!' 'Bosh!' 'Balls!'

'And what *is* your real name?'

'I don't know,' she lied. 'But that's ten! I win. Another?'

'Go for it.'

We played another and then another and then another. And then, because there was still tea in the pot, another.

How anyone could own a share of this game and still end up bankrupt was beyond me.

Rest of the World: **21**
Me: **22**

CHAPTER 12

Playing games is a nice thing to do. Playing games is a nice way to meet people. Playing people is a nice way to meet games. But the more I played, the more my experience was telling me that these things were best undertaken close to home. Travelling for a game simply added to the burden of expectation; a burden the game – or its hosts – couldn't reasonably be expected to bear. So when I received an email that contained the following words: 'I live in London so it would probably be easiest to come round and play me at home, but I'm going to be in the Lake District for a week in August if you'd rather?', I knew exactly what I was going to do with it.

I stepped off the train feeling rested and relaxed. The sun was shining, the air was fresh. I had no appointment that evening … once I'd checked into my hotel the rest of the day was mine to wile away.

I was spending two days in the Lake District. I was in heaven.

I needed a holiday and this was going to be it. Or rather, this was going to be a *part* of it. I had five days free each week … but they were never going to be consecutive days so I could only ever get away for two or three at a time. So why not use my big pile of game-vitations to inspire me? Yes, it was silly travelling all the way to Liverpool *just* to play a game of low-stakes poker, but if I'd spent a couple of days enjoying the city *and* played the game, then it wouldn't have mattered all that much. I wouldn't go to Liverpool to buy a slice of cake … but I'd buy a slice of cake if I was in Liverpool.

This was my new plan. I'd still take on whatever came my way in and around the capital, but I'd use the invitations from further afield to create a series of little trips for myself. I would have my holiday after all. I'd just be taking it in instalments.

I took a taxi from the station in Windermere to my hotel in Bowness. Nominally they're separate places, but there's no clear moment where one stops and the other starts: they just melt seamlessly into one another. Like Ant and Dec.

They're pretty towns with a distinctly Cumbrian aesthetic and yet, looking through the taxi windows the place they most reminded me of was, oddly, Rome. It wasn't because of any classical architecture. (There wasn't any.) Nor was it because Windermere or Bowness had once been the seat of power for an all-conquering empire. (They hadn't.) And it definitely wasn't because all roads lead there. (There are only really three: the A591, the A592 and, of course, the A5074.) But they did share one defining characteristic with the Italian capital: tourists.

The place was overrun with tourists. Walkers yomped, sightseers gawped and wherever I turned a new coachload of daytrippers could be seen pouring forth. I wasn't surprised. The higgledy-piggledy streets that spread out from Windermere's banks are lined with chocolate-box cottages and proud, old, characterful houses – all stone walls, galleried upper floors, interesting turrets and slate roofs. But if you try to take a photograph of any of it, the chances are you'll find twenty-five cagouled strangers in the frame, just as they'll find you lurking in their photos, too.

That's not a complaint, by the way. If it were, it would be shot through with hypocrisy: I was a tourist too, after all. There's no point trying to separate tourism from the Windermere and Bowness experience – it was the Victorian tourism boom that made them in the first place. It was tourism that built these Siamese twin towns and it's tourism that sustains them.

In 1847, a new railway line opened to carry people from Oxenholme, via Kendal, to a small village known as Birthwaite. Birthwaite was chosen because it was about half a mile from Lake Windermere, England's largest lake. Now, what would you have named the station after – the tiny village or the enormous lake? The lake was the draw. So Windermere station it was. Birthwaite grew. Birthwaite became Windermere: a town named after a train station named after a lake.

Nowadays we look at Windermere and Bowness and see quaint, old-fashioned, rural towns but back then, their rapid growth was seen by some as an act of vandalism. No less a man than William Wordsworth was opposed to the new railway. He thought the sudden influx of visitors would spoil the natural character of the area. (Well, what would you expect from a man who liked wandering lonely as a cloud?) Incidentally, 1847 was also the year Wordsworth stopped producing poems. Scholars say he stopped after the death of his daughter, Dora, who passed away in the July of that year, but maybe he simply downed his quill in protest at the railway? Or maybe the crowds – hosts of people, not of golden daffodils – simply killed his mojo? People certainly came. The rich industrialists of the North West, the men who owned the mines and the mills; they came and grand hotels sprang up to meet their needs.

I was staying in one such establishment. It had originally been a 'water cure' hotel. Sitting on the hillside not much more than a hundred yards above the town, it offered glorious views of the lake and the deep green sea of trees beyond. Inside the white walls, the glory had faded a little. Flocked wallpaper, frilly curtains and unnecessary chintz were the order of the day. A portrait of the Queen hung above a radiator in the corridor. I watched as a couple of British guests offered it a wry smile, but most just ignored it. The same could not be said for the Japanese and American visitors – a significant majority. They all seemed to be awestruck, verging on worshipful in its presence. Which no doubt explains why it was there. I wasn't the target market for this hotel. They were selling an old-fashioned England to old-aged foreign visitors. I loved it.

I dumped my bag in my room and went out to join the tourist fray taking a stroll down to the lake's edge to watch swans glide and ducks flap. Toddlers skittered around chasing pigeons, their squeals of excitement cutting through the late afternoon breeze. I dread to think what noise a child would make if they actually caught one.

As the sun started to descend, the temperature dropped, the water turned to inky blackness and slowly but surely the number of people diminished. I stayed where I was, pulling my coat up round my shoulders and pulling its sleeves down over my hands. It was worth it, because for one brief moment – for no more than twenty seconds – I found myself alone on the promenade, the only sounds being the water gently lapping against the fleet of wooden rowing boats tethered to the jetty, and my own slow heartbeat. The bliss of solitude.

It was brief. The late-shift tourists were clocking on. Couples approached, strolling arm in arm; an old lady stood patiently on the pebbled shore waiting for her poodle to scamper back from the water's edge; and a few teenagers gathered in the shadows. Everybody spoke in hushed tones – even the dog's pants and growls were like library whispers. Nobody wanted to be louder than the lake.

After a bite to eat in a nearby restaurant, I headed back up the hill to the hotel for a nightcap and an early night. In the bar, I found an empty armchair and snuggled into its plump cushions with a rum and coke and a novel I wasn't reading.

From my seat in the corner I had a view of the whole bar. It was a good spot for people-watching, and a gaggle of elderly Americans was more than entertaining enough. There were ten or twelve of them in total. They wore loose-fitting slacks with elasticated waists; the men drank whisky on ice and the ladies gin and tonic. Or, '… just a soda.'

'You're gonna have to help me out here,' said one of the old boys, as he paid for a small round at the bar. He held out a meaty palm for the barman to inspect his enormous collection of English coins. 'I'm struggling with your money,' he confessed. 'Please, take what I owe you.'

The callow youth behind the bar counted out the money, starting with the largest denomination he could ferret out – a £2 coin – and making his way through a few pounds, fifties, twenties and tens until he'd made the right change.

'There you go, sir,' he said with a smile. 'That's perfect.'

The American gent furrowed his brow. 'You haven't taken a tip.'

'There's no need for a tip, sir.'

'No, no, you gotta take a tip.' He started fishing through the coins himself, 'Now here, let me …'

'Honestly, sir, it won't be necessary,' said the barman with impressive resolve. 'Now you enjoy your evening.'

I watched as the old man carefully delivered the drinks to his table before equally carefully delivering a monologue to his friends about the English bar tender who hadn't required a tip. A debate ensued. The non-tipper's wife argued quite fiercely that her husband simply shouldn't have taken no for an answer and should have just tipped anyway. Other members of the group confessed that they'd heard a rumour tipping wasn't necessary in English bars, but hadn't been sure whether or not to believe it 'til now.

'I can't wait to get home and tell Jack about this,' said one. 'He won't believe it! He. Just. Won't. Believe. It!'

I wanted to join their coach party. They were obviously having a whale of a time. They'd been in Stratford the day before and they were heading to Glasgow in the morning, but they didn't *need* to be visiting these cultural hubs – they could have been going anywhere, because the fun for them was simply in being somewhere different. Their itinerary was full of country houses, castles and museums but the strongest memory they'd take home from that day wasn't of Wordsworth's cottage or The World of Beatrix Potter: it was of the barman who refused a tip. Lovely.

My attention turned to a married couple sitting on the fringes of the group. He had a huge digital camera resting on his lap and the two of them were attempting to review the photos they'd shot that day. The camera was almost as big as his head. And he had a big head. He had big thumbs too, which meant he struggled to deal with the giant camera's tiny buttons. They weren't just viewing the photos, either: they were laboriously cataloguing them. The routine went as follows: he'd look at a photo twice, once without his glasses and once with. Then he'd tilt the camera so that she could take a look. She was judge and jury. If she didn't like the picture she'd say, 'Delete,' and if she liked it, she'd say, 'Keep.' If it was a keeper she'd then pick up her notepad and write down a brief description of the photo's contents, occasionally muttering under her breath as she did so: 'John at lunch,' or 'Bus by hotel,' or what have you. And so it went on. Look-glasses-show-verdict-note, look-glasses-show-verdict-note, look-glasses-show-verdict-note … It was hypnotic.

'Hey, does anyone want to join us for "Bluke"?'

The question, addressed to the whole bar, came from a woman at the other end of their party, one-third of a more animated splinter group.

'Not tonight, Joyce,' said the non-tipper's wife. 'I'm bushed.'

'What about you?' asked Joyce.

I looked up from the pages I hadn't really been looking at.

'Who, me?'

'Yeah … do you know Bluke?'

I didn't really understand the question. Bluke? Was it a nearby village?

'I'm sorry, I'm not from around here,' I said.

'No,' she said, waving a deck of playing cards in the air. '*Bluke!*'

'Oh … no. I mean, I don't know it.'

'Wanna learn?'

I think you already know where this is going …

Bluke

Bluke is a trick-taking card game.

It's played with all fifty-four cards – that's every card in the deck, including the two jokers.

The number of cards you get in each hand varies. In the first hand, the dealer deals thirteen cards to each player, but in the second hand it's twelve cards, and in the third it's eleven and so on. For the thirteenth hand you all get just one card but this is only the game's halfway point. Now the number of cards increases with each hand so for the fourteenth round you get two cards, for the fifteenth you get three and so on, until you're back to a hand of thirteen cards each. In total, you play twenty-five hands.

Once the cards have been dealt, the top card of the remainder is turned over to decide trumps. As in other games, a trump will beat any card of another suit. So, for example, in a hand where clubs are trumps, the 2 of clubs beats, say, the ace of diamonds. If the card that's turned over is a joker – or as Joyce and her pals called it, a 'bluke' – then there are no trumps for that hand.

The play starts to the dealer's left. Each player lays down a card and the highest card wins the trick.

If you can follow suit you have to do so. Unless you have a bluke. Blukes can be played at any time. Blukes are like supertrumps. They beat **any** other card. In our deck we had a colour joker and a black and white joker. These were deemed the Low Bluke and the High Bluke respectively. The High Bluke is the most powerful card in the deck. High Bluke beats Low Bluke.

But what makes the game is the bidding. When your hand has been dealt and the trump suit has been declared, you all make a bid as to how many tricks you think you'll win.

The important thing here is to not overbid. If you fail to make your target you lose ten points for every number bid. It doesn't matter how close you come. If you bid seven tricks and make six, you still get minus seventy points, just as you would for winning none. For some inexplicable reason, the term used to describe not making your bid is 'going set'. Going set is a very costly thing.

If you make your bid, you score ten points for every number bid, plus one point for every extra trick you win. So if you bid five and make seven, you would score fifty-two points: fifty for the five you predicted plus two for the two you didn't.

Bluke is a good game. It's certainly been added to the Gorman family card-game repertoire. It's best with four players, works well with three and is playable, but a little less fun, with just two.

My fellow Bluke players were, like the rest of their coachmates, from Ohio. Specifically, Joyce and Vic were from Lorain, about thirty miles west of Cleveland, whereas Carl was from Akron.

'Tyre city,' he told me, and then to explain he added, 'we make a lot of tyres there.' He shook his head ruefully. 'Least we used to.' For a slim man he had impressive jowls. They kept on shaking long after his head had stopped.

'I like Cleveland,' I told them. 'I spent a week there a while back.'

They looked shocked at this revelation.

'Really?' asked Joyce.

'No!' said Vic.

'Yeah, it was nice,' I said.

'You went to Cleveland on vacation?' Joyce was incredulous.

I wasn't quite sure how to answer. If I told them I'd been there on tour they were bound to ask what kind of show it was and if I told them *that*, they'd want to know more, and the last time I'd been involved with a group of Ohioan pensioners who travelled together by bus, it really hadn't gone well ...

I'd performed in Cleveland for a week. The evening shows didn't exactly break box-office records but they did okay. The problem was with the unwisely scheduled matinees. With tickets not selling I think the promoters ended up trying to manufacture an afternoon crowd by giving free tickets to a couple of nearby old folks' homes.

Don't get me wrong, I like it when an older generation come to see my shows, but there's a big difference between people choosing to buy tickets and a busload of people coming not because they want to but because it's free. Some of them struggled with my accent. They were the lucky ones. Many of those that did understand me didn't like what they were hearing. It was a story-telling show and it involved me discussing an encounter I'd had with one of America's leading creationists: the senior vice president of the Institute for Creation Research. My, um, *analysis* of his beliefs clearly wasn't to their liking.[23] Two or three people left in disgust.

It's rare to see someone storm out of a theatre in disgust. Rarer still to see it happen in slow motion. One of my Cleveland walk-outs had a tank of oxygen piped up to his nose at all times. He wheeled it along on a small trolley with a

---

23. That particular part of that particular stage show led to a few odd moments on the tour. I'll tell you about another one, later.

squeaky wheel. He travelled at half a mile an hour. Step, squeak, pause for breath, step, squeak, pause for breath. It took him five minutes to get to the back of the auditorium.

I had no idea how Joyce, Vic and Carl felt about such matters but I was enjoying the game and didn't want to find out, just in case. So I skirted the issue with a white lie.

'Yeah,' I said. 'It was a vacation. Nice. The Rock and Roll Hall of Fame was interesting, and I saw a baseball game ... it was great.'

'That's cool,' Vic nodded his approval.

'You can't be very impressed with Lake Windermere,' I added. 'If you're used to Lake Erie, Windermere's just a puddle!'[24]

They chuckled but wouldn't admit to being unimpressed.

'Oh, come on!' I cajoled them. 'You can tell me.'

'No!' cried Joyce vehemently. 'It's just so pretty! We loved it, didn't we, Vic?'

'Sure did.'

'Now,' Joyce changed the subject, 'what's a young man like you doing out alone? You must have a young woman in your life?'

'Are you trying to pick me up, Joyce?'

'Ha!' Carl's jowls wobbled some more. 'Vic won't like that. Will ya, Vic?'

'What's that?' asked Vic.

'I'm thinking,' Joyce joked, 'of trading you in for a younger model!'

'Actually, I'm engaged,' I said. 'Her name's Beth. We're getting married in the autumn ... the, er, *fall*.'

'Aw!' said Joyce. 'Congratulations!'

---

24. Windermere is a ribbon lake, about 11 miles long and up to a mile wide. Lake Erie is 240 miles long and up to 57 miles wide. In terms of surface area, Erie is roughly 1,750 times bigger.

'Good luck,' said Vic.

'I hope you two … I hope you two … I hope you two …' Carl was going to keep saying it until everyone was looking his way – which we now were – 'I hope you two are as happy as me and my first wife *thought* we were going to be!'

Carl sent himself into spasms of laughter at that and I found myself laughing too, more at the sight of Carl's hilarity than at the line itself, but he took it as a sign of approval and so he roared, hooted, whistled and wheezed some more.

'Is this your first marriage?' asked Vic.

It was the first time anyone had asked me that question and it took me by surprise.

'Yes,' I said, trying not to snort rum and coke through my nose. 'Yes, it is.'

'Well, you're young next to us,' said Vic, defensively, 'but you're no spring chicken.'

'It doesn't matter *when* you find that person,' added Joyce, soothingly. 'What matters is that you find them.'

She reached out a hand to Vic's knee and he rested his hand tenderly on hers.

'So how long have you two lovebirds been together?' I asked.

Vic beamed from ear to ear. 'Two days,' he said.

'We sat next to each other on the coach out of Oxford,' added Joyce, coyly. 'He's a smooth talker. Aren't you, Vic?'

'I do all right,' he said. 'I do all right.'

Vic was having the holiday of his life. He'd won Joyce's affection. He won our game of Bluke, too. He was a winner. But what do you expect from a man named Victor?

Rest of the World:	22
Me:	22

CHAPTER 13

I woke the next day with something of a hangover. It was my own fault. I shouldn't have tried to keep up with Joyce, Vic and Carl. Blimey. I looked at the time. They were more than an hour into their trip to Glasgow already. I wondered how they were coping.

I skipped breakfast and spent an hour in the pool instead. I counted the lengths as I swam them. I don't normally but the pool was tiny and thirty-five lengths sounded impressive. It did the job, too. As I washed the chlorine out of my hair, the last remnants of my hangover chased the soapsuds down the drain.

I put my walking boots on – don't look so surprised, yes, I do own a pair of walking boots – and headed into town for sustenance. On a little side street dominated by shops selling reclaimed furniture, antiques and bric-a-brac, I found a small, unassuming café and ordered a jacket potato with cheese and beans. I didn't especially *want* a potato with cheese and beans – I ordered it more by reflex than anything else. It had been my carb-heavy lunch almost every other day during my coast to coast to coast to coast bike ride. Most of those days I'd cycled sixty miles or more, and while I wasn't planning a walk that would come close to that in terms of exertion, the simple fact that *any* outdoorsman activity was on the agenda had rewound my brain to old habits.

'Do you want salad with that?' asked the teenaged girl behind the counter.

'Yes,' I said. 'Yes, please.'

I'm glad I did. When I received my plate, it was a sight to behold. Next to the potato, with bright yellow cheese melting into the luminous orange baked-bean lava, sat two tiny lettuce leaves with three ready-salted crisps, a slice of watery tomato and spoonful of potato salad. Wow. A baked potato with three slithers of deep-fried potato and some boiled potato mixed up in mayo on the side!

I confess that the sight of my three-potato dish led to an unpleasant moment of snobbishness on my part. I'm not proud of myself. And I do realise that nobody who's ordered a baked potato with cheese and beans is entitled to any form of snobbishness. But it happened. I sat there thinking superior thoughts about how provincial it was of them to partner potato with potato and more potato. Oh no, you'd never get anything that unsophisticated back in that-there fancy London! But do you know what? It was lovely! It was absolutely spuddy delicious! Who knew? They did, that's who. Snobbishness noted. Snobbishness discarded. I told myself off, scoffed the rest of my nosh and then paid for my lunch, making sure I left a guilt tip just in case the girl working there had been able to detect any of my earlier attitude and then headed off for a constitutional.

I chose a three-and-a-half-mile loop over Brant Fell, a route that took me from road to lane to track to nothingness, through fields and woods, over peaks and through valleys but, most importantly, a route that took me away from the crowds, filled my lungs with air and made me feel like I was using my time off wisely. If I filled my two days in the Lake District with swimming, walking and a bonus game of Bluke it didn't really matter how my scheduled game panned out. The trip was already more than worth it.

I'd played poker against a Tim in Liverpool and Settlers of Catan against a Tim in Stockport. Tonight, I'd play against my third Tim. Like the other Tims, he would also be mild mannered and softly spoken. (I don't think I've ever met a

Tim who wasn't. Do any exist, or is timidity a part of every Tim's id?)

I'd actually met tonight's Tim once before. This Tim, Tim Harford, hosts a Radio 4 show called *More or Less*. The show's noble aim is to explain how numbers are presented – and sometimes *mis*represented – in the news, and for some reason I'd been invited on to the show a couple of years earlier.[25]

When Tim swung by to pick me up at the hotel I nearly went to greet him with a bear hug, as if we were dear pals of old, but at the last minute I realised we'd only met that one time. I managed to swerve my swinging shoulder and turn it into a far more appropriate firm handshake. The thing is I felt like I knew Tim better than I did because I'd read so much of his writing. Tim's an economist. He writes for the *Financial Times* and has written two or three best-selling books, too. I occasionally read his stuff online and had not long finished reading one of those books. A million other people have done the same.

'How's the hotel?'

It could have been a simple, polite enquiry but Tim's sly grin suggested there was more to it than that.

'It's fine …' I offered warily as we walked out to his car. 'Why do you ask?'

'My wife used to work there.' We pulled out of the car park. 'She told me some stories, that's all.'

'Go on.'

'Well … let's just say that when *we* stay in a hotel she always washes any glasses before she'll drink from them … I think all ex-chambermaids are the same.'

---

25. The reason, I suppose, is that I studied mathematics at university. I dropped out but I guess I still feel comfortable around numbers and have even written some stand-up about the subject in the past, as this video confirms: http://bit.ly/DGMaths (It does contain some swearing – sorry, Mum.)

'Then I guess we all ought to be doing it ...?'

'Yeah, I guess so.'

'Or maybe it was just your wife?'

'That is a possibility ... but why take chances?'

We made our way through Bowness, through the invisible border to Windermere and out the other side, hugging the water's edge until we'd reached its northern tip. Here we left Lake Windermere, continuing north through a few tiny villages, and skirting one or two more lakes before pulling off the main road beside Dove Cottage – the former home of one William Wordsworth.

It looked no different to dozens of other houses we'd already passed in our ten-mile drive, but I still felt compelled to give it an appreciative 'Oo!', simply because I knew he'd lived there. But it was just a drive-by oo-ing. We weren't stopping to take tea with Wordsworth's ghosts. We were heading to a large house nestled on the hillside behind.

I hadn't yet grown bored with stunning lake views, and when I stepped out of Tim's car it was impossible not to stand and stare. Lake Grasmere twinkled back at me. Show off.

'Is this ... um ... yours?' I asked, with a nod towards the large stone house.

'Oh, no ... it's just a holiday let.'

'Well, you've definitely found a great spot here!'

'Yeah. Do y'know The Landmark Trust?'

'No.'

'It's a really great organisation,' said Tim, opening the boot and lifting out some groceries, 'I think you'd like them.'

He was right. I do.

The Landmark Trust was set up in the 1960s by the philanthropist Sir John Smith. The charity finds minor historic buildings, restores them and then turns them into holiday lets. Without it, many of our nation's beautiful buildings: gate-houses, lock-keeper's cottages, windmills, lighthouses and other homes of interest and character would be ruins, while many others would have been swallowed up by crass, insensitive developments.

Most people credit Sir John with purely altruistic intent. They say he was motivated by a passion for both architecture and education. Personally, I can't help thinking there was something more selfish at the root of it all. I reckon he created this network of nice places to stay because he hated hotels.

I'm sure all John Smiths hate hotels. If you want to look like a man and his mistress out for a dirty weekend, just check into a hotel as 'Mr and Mrs John Smith'. Nobody will ever believe you. Check in as 'Sir John and Lady Smith' and you look like a pair of dirty weekenders angling for an upgrade.

It's just a theory.

'My wife was brought up near here,' explained Tim, as he nudged the front door open with his shoulder. 'She's at her parents this evening with the kids – they're having a movie night – so we've got the place to ourselves for a while.'

'You don't stay with the in-laws?' I asked, following him into the echoey hall.

'No, well, we've got some friends coming to stay with us tomorrow ... That's the great thing about this place: the flexibility. It sleeps eight ...' Tim was already in the kitchen and, as he began putting the groceries away, his voice disappeared behind cupboard doors.

The thick stone walls and high ceilings meant the atmosphere inside was cool and airy. By the time I'd made it through to the kitchen, Tim was beginning to prepare food and pour wine. I enjoyed watching him dance the holiday-let two-step. You know the one: you want a corkscrew, say, so you instinctively reach for the top drawer on the right but then you remember this isn't your usual kitchen and in *this* house – two, three, four – the corkscrew is in the second drawer on the left.

There were wooden floors, loose rugs and furniture that simply belonged in a house of this era. Farmhouse chairs were arranged around a huge wooden table. Tonight's game board was already sitting upon it. Or rather game boards, plural. It was all one game ... there just seemed to be an awful lot of it. This one looked complicated.

'I saw on Twitter the other day that you'd played Settlers of Catan.' Tim passed me a glass of red. 'What did you make of it?'

'Hmm. Well ... um ... I think so many people had suggested it to me that I sort of built it up in my mind too much. I thought it was going to be the most mind-blowingly brilliant game but ... well, it just didn't really do it for me.'

'That's a shame,' said Tim, 'it *is* a good game.'

'That's the thing,' I said, 'I met nice people, I had nice evenings and I *think* it probably *is* a good game ... but something about it just didn't quite connect.'

'How do you mean?'

'Well ... have you ever been walking somewhere and you get to a bus stop and you think about staying there and getting the bus but you also think about walking on and seeing if you can get to the next stop before the bus comes?'

'Um ... yeah?'

'Well, it's a judgement call, isn't it? You decide to stay put or walk on, based on your knowledge of how far the next bus stop is and how frequent the buses tend to be and how you feel in your waters and stuff. But if you don't know where you are or what the service is like you're just *guessing*; you have nothing to base your decision on ...'

'Uh huh ...'

'Well, it felt like that with Settlers. It felt like everyone else was making judgement calls: Do I hold onto my wood or build a road now? Do I trade with them or the bank? Should I trade for this or for that? They were backing hunches, making informed decisions, while I was just making it up ... guessing. I never really understood the consequences of anything I did, so I never knew if I'd made a good decision or a bad decision.'

'It's definitely a game you need to play a few times, yeah.'

'It made me feel guilty,' I added. 'I don't think I'm patient enough. I want to get it immediately.'

'So what games have you liked?'

'Khet,' I said, 'I loved Khet.'

'Is that the one with lasers?'

'Yes!' I was impressed. 'And Kensington surprised me too. We used to have that when I was a kid ... I liked that.'

'Hexagons? Red and blue discs?'

'That's the one!' He was good. 'And Kubb. Completely different kind of game ...'

'Sort of skittles-y?'

'Yes. Yes! Khet, Kensington, Kubb ... all the Ks, really – they obviously spelled Catan wrong. The thing with something like Khet is that it's got levels to it, there are things you need to get your head round ... but two strangers can buy it, open the box and be playing it well within twenty minutes. I don't think you can say the same for Settlers of Catan.'

'I see what you mean,' said Tim, 'but this style of game – the games coming out of Germany – they're very rewarding if you invest time in them.'

Tim was clearly something of games connoisseur. He had his finger on the pulse of the games world in the same way other people do the music industry. He knew about the new releases, the hits and the misses. Apparently Germany is now leading the way in board games just as Britain ruled 60s pop. In the game-world, people talk about 'German-style games' in the way they used to talk about the Mersey beat.

'So how come Germany is coming up with all the big new games?' I asked.

'I wrote an article about this recently ...'

'Really? Go on.'

'Well, the Germans say it's because they have a superior education system.' Tim sipped his drink. 'But in Britain the feeling is that it's because their TV is shite.'

'Ha! So,' I turned my attention back to the game laid out before us, 'I'm guessing this is one of the German-style games ... yes?'

'Yep ... this is "Agricola" ...'

The word wasn't pronounced the way I expected it to be. I'd expected the word to be broken into two distinct parts: *agri* and *cola* (which, if it does exist, is surely a soft drink for farmers), but the emphasis is actually on the *ick* sound in the middle, making it more *uh-grick*uller.

It is about agriculture. It's not about fizzy pop.

Farming might not seem like the most exciting subject for a board game but in a world where millions of people tend virtual farms online,[26] it's obvious that not everyone sees crop rotation and animal husbandry in quite the same light.

> **RULES**
>
> The idea of Agricola is to build up a diverse and well-balanced farm. Each player starts with two farmers – a husband and wife, perhaps[27] – and a two-room hut on a small plot of land. Over the

---

26. The 'real-time farm simulation game' 'Farmville' has more than eighty million players on Facebook alone. It's the most popular application on Facebook by some margin: about fifteen per cent of the people who log on to the site in any given day play Farmville.

I have a blind spot when it comes to computer games and I find myself completely confused by Farmville's popularity. To make matters worse, my mum is one of the people playing it. She shows signs of addiction. When planning a day trip she worries not just about who will feed her cat but also who will tend her farm. It's a real cat. It's a fictional farm. I simply don't understand what there is to be gained by playing it or in what way it is actually a 'game'. (I've asked Mum. She doesn't know either.)

27. Or maybe they're living in sin. There's nothing in the rules to say either way.

course of the game you can plough fields and plant crops, or fence off pasture and keep livestock. You can extend your home. You can upgrade from a wooden hut to a clay hut and from a clay hut to a stone house. If you've got enough room you can have kids but you will have to feed them. To help do so you can even install an oven. I kid you not.

The game takes up a lot of space. (There were four boards in the middle of the table.) You don't play **on** these boards as you would a traditional board game – instead, they act as a sort of central store, the place where resources are amassed, and they also act as a timeline of sorts, making sure everyone can always see what stage of the game has been reached. Each player also has their own personal board to represent their farm. It's a little larger than the cover for this book and it's broken up into fifteen square plots of land. Your wooden hut occupies two of these squares but the thirteen that remain start off fallow. If you're able to change their use as the game progresses – either by ploughing it or building on it or whatever – you represent that by covering the square with an appropriately designed piece of card.

As you've probably gathered, it's another game with no specified path to follow. This one has no dice either. You just take it in turns to make decisions about what you're going to do with your farm for a total of fourteen rounds.

I'd love to give you a more detailed run-down of the game's structure but the truth is that it was far too complicated for me to take in. I can't really imagine anyone's first game of Agricola approaches real playability. It just couldn't. Once again, I was the stranger at a bus stop trying to work out whether or not to walk on but with no information, not even gut instinct, to help me decide. Throughout our game Tim was the teacher and I was the pupil. But I felt like the sickly school kid who's missed most of the term and is now feverishly trying to cram all the learning in before the end of year exams. We wouldn't have had a game at all if Tim had sat there waiting for me to make my own decisions. When it came to my turn I'd stare at the various boards in front of me with tokens dotted all over the place and try my hardest to discern first what I *could* do and then what I *should* do. I had very little success in this endeavour.

Sometimes I'd have no choice but to ask Tim to explain what my options were. He'd normally spell it out with something like, 'Well, you could pick up wood or reed but if I were you I'd take a sheep because ...' and that's what I'd do. At other times I'd manage to take in the options and say something like, 'So, I think I'm going to fence in this field ...' which would usually prompt a raised eyebrow and a 'Really? Why are you doing that?' from Tim. I'd explain myself: 'Well, I thought I might want to put some cattle in there next round,' and Tim would gently explain the error of my ways: 'Hmm, but there's a harvest coming and you haven't got a way of turning cattle into food yet, so why don't you ...'

In essence, I don't think I made one completely solo decision all game. One way or another, Tim was steering me to my best course of action ... which must have been tricky because on a couple of occasions he was doing so against his best interest: 'Well, you can see that I need reed, so if I were you I'd take this now, because you could do with it and I'm bound to take it in the next round if you don't ...' and so on.

Just after our first 'harvest', we fed not only our Agricola farmers but also our real selves, with real pizza fresh from the real oven in the real stone house. The wine was good and there was an excellent cheese board, too. But I was very aware that it wasn't really Tim versus Dave. It was Tim versus Tim. I was just representing the Tim Harford 'B' team. If I had won, it would have been dishonest to chalk it up to myself. Not that there was any danger of that happening. As you'd expect, Tim

Harford 'A' beat Tim Harford 'B'. The final score was 43 points to 34.

'That's very respectable for your first game,' said Tim, kindly.

'Thanks,' I said. 'But I don't think I really earned any of those points. I don't think I really played the game. I feel like a bit of a fraud, really.'

'Why?'

'Well, I think of myself as someone who *likes* games,' I said. 'Only games have moved on while I wasn't looking. I'm not sure I'll ever get on with these German-style games. So maybe I don't really like games at all – if these represent the pinnacle of game development, maybe I'm not really a games kind of person, after all?'

'Nah. You were getting it,' said Tim, encouragingly. 'It's like learning a new language. Once someone gets Agricola, say, they pick up things like "Carcassone", "Puerto Rico" and "Tikal" quite easily.[28] There's a lot in them. They're very tactical.'

'Hmmm?' I didn't know whether to believe him. But I was prepared to give it a go. 'Do you want another game, then?'

Tim looked at his watch. Then at the clock on the wall, as if it might reveal something different. 'Sorry,' he said, 'I'd love to. You could play without me now, I know you could. But I have to go and pick up the family. We have to get the girls to bed. But let's do it again in London some time. Bring Khet. I want to play that, too. Deal?'

'Deal.'

We shook hands.

---

28. These are all examples of this new breed of German-style board games. In Puerto Rico, players take on the role of colonial governors trying to ship goods from the Caribbean to the Old World; in Tikal you are Indiana Jones-style adventurers discovering lost temples in a Central American jungle; while Carcassone is about establishing mediaeval cities. Many people see Carcassone as the best way in to this kind of gaming. It's probably the easiest to grasp and quickest to play out. It's the gateway drug of the German board-game world.

Rest of the World: **23**
Me: **22**

'How was the game?' asked Beth when I called her from the hotel that night.

'Well, it was brilliant to see Tim, but I'm not sure about the game,' I told her. 'How was your shoot?'

'It was good … But what do you mean, you're not sure?'

'Well, I don't know whether *I* played it or not. I don't really know whether I understood it or not. But I had an ace time. It's lovely up here. We ought to come up here when we get a bit of time off. Have you ever heard of the Landmark Trust?'

'No …'

'We need to look them up; they sound great. We'd stay in some cool places.'

'You sound pretty upbeat …'

'I am,' I said. 'It's been a great couple of days. This is a great way to holiday.'

'So what does the game matter?'

'It doesn't,' I said. 'It doesn't.'

And it didn't.

CHAPTER 14

'Tickets, please!'

I looked up from my book to be quite startled by how much my surroundings had changed. It looked like an entirely different train.

A party of four were now sitting at the table to my left. The two men were wearing dinner jackets and dickie-bows, while the women were dressed in sumptuous, satin ball gowns. They had an empty bottle of champagne on the table and from the redness in their cheeks I surmised it probably wasn't their first. They also had a full-blown picnic on the go. It involved caviar. My eyes drifted up and down the carriage. There were more of them. Dinner jackets and ball gowns were everywhere, outnumbering the jeans-wearers by at least five to one.

It hadn't looked like this when I had boarded the train at London Bridge. Was I being pranked by a hidden-camera TV show? Had everyone changed clothes while I'd had my nose in a book? Or had people got off and new people boarded? *Invasion of the Bolly Hatchers?* (Sorry.)

My book was obviously quite an engaging read for all this change to have gone on about me undetected. The novel in question was *American Star* by Jackie Collins. I was enjoying it far more than I thought I would.

Hang on. I hadn't booked a first-class ticket: it hadn't seemed worth it for a journey of just over an hour. Damn. I must have sat down in the wrong carriage. I was going to look like a fare dodger if I stood up and moved down the train now. Arse.

Hang on. I looked around me. This *was* standard class. Blimey. If penguins and shuttlecocks were downing champagne and caviar in standard, what did first class look like? What the hell was going on?

At Lewes station, a leaflet advertising opera at Glyndebourne solved the riddle. I don't know where I thought Glyndebourne was but it was news to me that it was down that way.

The only thing I knew about Lewes in advance was that its Bonfire Night celebrations were both flammable and inflammatory. It is the town where they burn an effigy of Pope Paul V alongside their Guy Fawkes. They also burn other, more up-to-date effigies, too. Assorted *bêtes noir du jour* go up in flames, be they local figures or people in the national news. In 2008, for example, with the global economic meltdown the story of the moment, an effigy of Barack Obama was burned alongside the Chancellor of the Exchequer of the day, Alistair Darling. Photos of America's first black president being burned in effigy made excellent kindling for sensationalist headlines. Indeed, the Lewes Bonfire Night finds its way into the tabloids every couple of years, generally with stories that paint the town as a place of Royston Vasey-like oddness.[29]

But I've always found the stories to be a little less than convincing: I always feel like I'm being manipulated when a red top adopts shocked tones and cries: *They Burn A Pope!* in its headlines. I can never decide whether it's genuinely virulent anti-Catholic sentiment being expressed or just a pantomime version of anti-seventeenth-century-Catholicism.

---

29. Royston Vasey is the fictional town in the TV show, *The League of Gentlemen*. It is also the real name of controversial comedian Roy 'Chubby' Brown, who also appears in the show as the Mayor of Royston Vasey, Larry Vaughn. When I wrote, ' ... paint the town as a place of Royston Vasey-like oddness', I was thinking of the fictional town. But actually the sentence works just as well if you take it to be the man, too.

I don't know about you, but I can't find it in me to afford Pope Paul V any more respect than I do old Guido Fawkes, just because he held high office. We can't go around respecting every man that was ever Pope any more than we can respect every king or queen of England that ever lived. Particularly as it turns out that some of them, Popes included, were – whisper it – not very nice people. Mister Fawkes might have been the man with the box of matches and the barrels of gunpowder, but he was essentially a mercenary: the plot – an attempt to assassinate the king and install a Catholic head of state to Britain once more – was hatched by the Catholic hierarchy. And I don't doubt they had their reasons. I'm sure Protestants and Catholics were taking turns to persecute one another back then. Even so, Paul V publicly expressed his disappointment that the Gunpowder Plot had failed and it's hard to imagine a modern Pope doing the same. Times – and people – have changed. Being a Pope now isn't like being a Pope then. The same is true for lots of jobs. Doctors, teachers, soldiers, web designers – they've all seen radical changes over the last 400 years ...

Knowing about the Gunpowder Plot's religious background didn't turn the Fifth of November bonfires of my youth into sinister affairs. I must have watched a dozen guys burn without once stopping to think about who or what it represented. I'm pretty sure they could have made the guy a lot more lifelike and chucked in a Pope Paul V and it wouldn't have made much difference to me. Bonfire night was a jamboree. It was about seeing how close I could get to the fire before my cheeks became uncomfortably hot, writing my name in the air with a sparkler, oo-ing and ah-ing at the fireworks and then having a baked potato. (With cheese and beans, naturally.)

If the rest of Britain is able to watch human effigies burn without feeling drunk on hate and religious intolerance I couldn't see any reason to assume Lewes was any different, no matter what the headlines told me. But what did I know? I'd never been after all. I made a mental note to ask about it.

Lewes is definitely a place that makes a good first impression. The station is a beautifully preserved example of Victorian architecture.

If you ever meet one of those men with miles and miles of incredibly detailed model railway laid out in his attic – the kind of man who wears an authentic signalman's hat to stand in the middle of his chipboard island and operate it all – the chances are his model train station will look like Lewes station. The yellow brickwork is stout but the white wooden canopies, and even the royal-blue iron latticework on the footbridges, lend it a certain daintiness.

The beautiful station was a good prelude to the main feature. Lewes looks like a toy town that's been oh so carefully arranged between the chalk hills of the South Downs. It feels as though each building has been set down temporarily, studied from every conceivable angle and only allowed to remain once the overlord model maker has convinced himself that it aids the elegant balance of the whole. I can't think that I've ever visited a more attractive – and archetypally British – town centre.

I hadn't booked a hotel in advance and I only had a small backpack with me so I went for a wander around the ancient buildings, looping around the castle that stands at the heart of the town, weaving through various little alleyways and ginnels – or twittens as they call them there – and just breathing in the rarefied, genteel air.

There are other British towns and cities steeped in history – the Chesters and Yorks of this land – but there was something about Lewes that set it apart. Or was it the absence of something? There was no McDonalds or Burger King. No

Starbucks or Pizza Hut. It wasn't that the place was devoid of high street chains but it certainly seemed to be without the most invidious examples – those brightly coloured litter magnets, the standard bearers for standardisation.

Lewes seems to revel in its independent spirit while simultaneously being the epitome of a middle-class English market town: it's quite a trick to pull off. I imagine this plays especially well to the American tourists who long for that old-fashioned English charm but lustily cherish their own free-spirited republicanism.

One of the Founding Fathers of the United States, Thomas Paine, once lived in Lewes. Every building he visited seems to have a plaque telling you all about it. Lewes is proud of Tom Paine. No detail is too trivial to mention.

It was during his time there that he first began politicking: printing pamphlets and campaigning for better pay and conditions for his fellow Excise officers. He met Benjamin Franklin in London (you know, the way you do), and decided to emigrate to the New World (you know, the way you do). He arrived in Philadelphia in 1774 and went on to play a pivotal part in the American Revolution. His pamphlet, *Common Sense*, helped to spread revolutionary zeal throughout the emerging nation. The ideas he espoused weren't especially new but his writing had a common touch that carried them to the streets and to the taverns, not just to the educated elite. In a population of roughly two million free inhabitants – many of them illiterate – he sold 100,000 copies in three months. The common man enjoyed Paine's *Common Sense*: he was an eighteenth-century bestseller.

How could American tourists fail to love Lewes? It has an eleventh-century castle, several fifteenth-century timber-framed houses (including the one given to Anne of Cleves as part of her divorce settlement from Henry VIII) and, to cap it all, the Thomas Paine connection means it's a part of *their* history, too. Thomas Paine helped define what it means to be an American.

I was a little early for our meeting at the Lewes Arms, so I tucked myself away in the corner, with Jackie Collins and a rum and coke for company. I hid the book inside that day's *Guardian*, not because I was embarrassed[30] you understand … I just didn't want to spoil the atmosphere.

It's a lovely pub. I say that, but I guess most people don't share my view as to what qualities make a pub lovely. If they did, more pubs would be serving up a nice bit of peace and quiet. There was no jukebox at the Lewes Arms, just the sound of restrained chitter-chatter flowing through the air. It wasn't a big pub by any means, but it felt even more intimate because it was broken into three distinct rooms, each one smaller than many a modest living room. It felt more like a private house enterprisingly selling drinks than a full-steam-ahead commercial enterprise, and it was all the better for it.

I sat with my back to the dartboard and the Toad In The Hole table. The Toad In The Hole table? Ah, yes. 'Toad In The Hole' was the game I'd come to play.

I knew very little about it, only that it was a traditional Sussex (or maybe just Lewesian?) pub game. The table was a couple of feet tall. It was essentially a beaten-up wooden box with metal legs at the bottom and a battered, contoured sheet of lead on top: if you gave a twelve-year-old boy a two-foot-square sheet of lead, a lump hammer and a Stanley knife and asked him to try and shape it into a scale model of a volcano … well, that's what it looked like. The lead rose a couple of inches to a peak in the middle, where there was a circular hole about two or three inches in diameter. Intriguing.

'Hi, Dave.'

---

30. I was embarrassed.

I lowered my newspaper, folding it around the novel as I did so. I looked up to see Ben's smiling, impish features.

'Do you want another drink?' he asked.

It'd been a long time since I'd seen Ben, but he didn't appear to have aged. (Perhaps he was a little grey around the temples. Just a little.) We'd first met many years ago, when I was a nineteen year old starting out in the world of stand-up, and Ben was also starting out as one-sixth of a sketch group called The Cheese Shop.

The comedy circuit was – and still is – an unforgiving place for an act with more than one person. The pub and club gigs that were once my bread and butter used to pay somewhere between £50 and £100 per act: a self-defeating exercise for any group that had to split the money six ways. So our paths crossed less often than they might have done, but for some reason that didn't really matter on the comedy circuit. It's a transient world that incubates a particular kind of friendship. There's a kinship – a shared understanding of what the job entails – that somehow enables people to put friendships down and pick them up again years later as if no time has elapsed.

I was once in a dressing room in Newcastle when a comic I hadn't seen in over two years walked in. His first words were, 'Hey, remember I was telling you about that cactus… ?' It sounded for all the world as though he was picking up a story from the night before. (Perhaps the oddest thing about it was that it didn't strike me as odd at the time. I *did* know exactly what he was talking about. I slipped back into the two-year-old conversation just as easily as he had restarted it.)

In the late 90s, The Cheese Shop starred in several Radio 4 series and three of their number – Ben included – also popped up on Saturday morning TV doing sketches for children (and hungover adults) for two or three series of

BBC1's *Live & Kicking*. I knew the group had gone their separate ways shortly after that but what those ways were I didn't really know. I was pretty sure they were all still writing and/or acting in some capacity, but without dressing-room chats and backstage gossip to top me up, I'd more or less lost track.[31]

A mutual friend was responsible for putting us back in touch. 'If you're playing games with people,' she'd said, 'you need to go and see Ben Ward. He's the two-time European Masters Champion at Toad In The Hole.'

'The two-time what-what at *what*?'

'I've no idea what it means either,' she'd shrugged. 'It's some game he plays. I'll send you his email address.'

Which was how Ben and I came to be in the Lewes Arms that night.

'Sorry I'm late,' he said, placing the drinks on the table between us. 'I was in a meeting that went on a bit longer than I expected.'

'Work?'

'Not really, no.' He smirked a secretive smirk ... and then decided it wasn't really a secret: 'A couple of weeks ago we, um ... bought the local football club.'

'You *bought* a football club!'

'Yeah. Not *just* me ... some friends ... do you know Patrick Marber?'

'The writer? Yeah. I mean, well ... I don't know him but I know who he is ... I saw him doing stand-up when I was at university.'

'Small world. He's involved ...'

---

31. The easiest to follow has been Dave Lamb. He's an actor who has cropped up in several big TV shows. He also provides the brilliantly sarcastic voice-over on Channel 4's hugely successful and much copied *Come Dine With Me*.

'What league are they – um, *you* – in?'

'Blue Square Bet South,' said Ben.

I tried to nod bloke-ily. I hoped it was a nod that said, 'Ah yes, the good old Blue Square Bet South. You always know where you are with the Blue Square Bet South. South. That's where,' but I don't think I pulled it off.

'If you think of the Premier League as being Division One,' explained Ben, with the patient tone of a man who'd grown used to explaining the same thing many times over, 'then we're in Division Six. It's non-league football. It's great. If you only ever watch Premier League football you should come and see a game. It's a very different experience. The Dripping Pan's a great ground ...'

'The what?'

'The ground. It's called the Dripping Pan. It used to be used for salt panning.'

'Hang on. I think we need to go back a bit. How do you end up owning, or part-owning, a football club? That's serious stuff!'

'Oh, you know what it's like ...' Ben took a sip of his beer. 'You're in the pub one night and someone says, "The local football club's in trouble ... we should do something about that," and you agree because it seems like a good idea at the time ... but you never do, right?'

'Right.'

'Well, it was like that. Only we did.'

'That's amazing.'

'The club's been on a bit of a rollercoaster ride. In the last ten years we were promoted four times. We used to be in Ryman 3!'

'Tch! Ryman 3, eh?!'

'We ended up in the Blue Square Bet Premier League. That's the top of the National League: above that it's the Football League and then the Premier League, obviously.'

'Obviously.'[32]

'It means we got to play teams like Oxford United. We beat *Oxford United* at the Pan!'

'Heady days, indeed.'

'Yeah … trouble is, we didn't beat many other teams in the Premier. It was a bit of a disaster. So we went down again …'

'Still, four steps forward, one step back … that's pretty respectable stuff.'

'I know. But it wasn't sustainable. It was fuelled by over-spending. The club's finances collapsed and it was looking pretty bleak. It's amazing they didn't go under last year, really.'

'So you stepped in?'

'Yeah, there are six of us. Thing is, clubs are going bust all over the place … It's always the same, overspending and bad planning. We want to break the cycle of private ownership. The club's been here for 125 years. Really we want the whole town to own it.'

'Is that possible?'

'If it's possible anywhere it's here. Lewes is different. Some people have put money into it not because they're fans of the club but because they're fans of the town. The plan is that next year or the year after – once we've stabilised things – people will be able to buy shares for an annual payment of £25. One man, one vote.'

---

32. I find the nomenclature of England's football leagues more than a little confusing these days. It used to be simple. Division One then Two, Three and Four.

Nowadays, the top tier is the Premier League. Then there's the Championship and the third tier has been rebranded League One. That's three leagues that are all named to suggest they're at the pinnacle. Maybe the person responsible used to work for a coffee company? In a world where 'tall' means 'small' and 'grande' means 'medium', anything is possible.

The fourth tier is called League Two. Beneath that is the National League System which starts with the Conference National, which is fine except that, thanks to sponsorship, it's also called the Blue Square Bet Premier League. Blimey.

'Bloody hell,' I smiled. 'I'm impressed. It *is* different here, isn't it? There's a sort of quiet revolutionary spirit in Lewes ...'

Ben chuckled. He didn't say anything. He didn't need to. He had the perfect response under his jacket. He unzipped it slowly and then held the lapels apart with pride. At first glance the image on his T-shirt appeared to be the classic two-tone print of a beret-clad Che Guevara, an image now so universal as to be rendered almost meaningless. It's worn by hard-line anarchists and middle-class pretenders alike, in much the same way that Ramones T-shirts are worn by grizzled New York punks and twenty-year-old trust-fund Charlies who wouldn't know 'Blitzkrieg Bop' if it bit them. But on closer inspection I realised it wasn't Che at all. It was Thomas Paine.

Ben had a revolutionary on his chest and another revolutionary tale on the tip of his tongue: 'Have you heard of the Lewes Arms boycott?' he asked.

'No.' I looked around me. Every seat was occupied. 'A boycott? Here?'

'There *was*,' said Ben. 'Have you had a look around town?'

'Yeah.'

'You probably saw the brewery. Harveys? Down by the river?'

'Uh huh.'

'It's the oldest independent brewery in Sussex.' Ben raised his glass and sampled some of its output – Harveys Best.[33] 'It's a Lewes institution. Greene King bought this pub in the 90s. They used to sell Harveys alongside their own beers. But Harveys Best was outselling Greene King by about four to one. So in 2006 they stopped selling it.'

---

33. The lack of an apostrophe in Harveys Best or, indeed, in Harveys anything, is intentional – that's just how they do it. (It's Harveys Best Bitter, not Harvey's Best Grammar.)

'What happened?' I asked. I already knew the answer.

'There was a boycott. There was a vigil outside every night explaining what was going on. They lost about ninety per cent of their trade.'

'And they caved in.'

'After 133 days, yeah.'

'After 133 days! That's more than three months!'

'I know. But the Lewes Arms has been here for 220 years. So has Harveys. People care about that sort of thing here. It was written up in the *Independent*, the *Guardian*, the *Observer*, the *Mail on Sunday* ... it was on Radio 4 ... Greene King made themselves look pretty stupid.'

'Wow ... But if I was in business and I was selling a lot of something, I think I'd keep stocking it.'

'Yeah. And hopefully it's had a knock-on effect across the chain. There's no reason why they shouldn't all be able to stock local ales. Mind you, this isn't Greene King any more. It's Fuller's now.'

With perfect synchronicity we raised our glasses. Ben supped his pint. I sipped my rum. Both glasses were returned to the table with a satisfied, and satisfying, *bang*.

'Have you heard of the Lewes pound?' asked Ben.

'No,' I said. 'Is that where they lock up non-Harveys drinkers?'

'No. It's our own currency.'

'Really?'

'Yeah. Let me see if I've got any.' Ben opened up his wallet and started fishing around. 'Here we are,' he said, holding out a green and blue sort-of-banknote for me to examine.

I held it in my hands. It felt more authentic than some of the foreign currencies I've dealt with. On one side there was an image of Lewes Castle and on the other an image of the South Downs. Where my brain was telling me there ought to be a portrait of the Queen there was instead, surprise surprise, a picture of Thomas Paine. He was quoted on the note, too: 'We have it in our power to build the world anew.'

'Is it legit?' I asked.

'Of course. It's a Lewes pound. It's worth one pound sterling. There are around a hundred or more shops that accept them and it's growing. The idea is that if you spend a Lewes pound it stays in the local economy … But if you spend a pound in a national chain, it doesn't.'

'It's basically a gift voucher, isn't it?'

'Effectively, yeah. It's nothing new. Lewes used to have a currency of its own in the 1800s, too.'

'Of course it did …! Does it work?'

'Yeah.' Sip. 'And no. The problem is people want them. As souvenirs. People take them away with them, sell them on eBay.'[34]

'Which takes them out of circulation …'

'Exactly, but I think that'll settle down. Now, seeing as I've got my wallet out … do you want a drink?'

When Ben returned he didn't just bring drinks. He also brought four chunky brass discs. They weren't a part of the Lewes currency system – he hadn't got small change from his Lewes pound – they were our toads. I don't know where the name came from. They weren't very toadlike.

Ben started to explain the game: 'You stand behind this line,' he said, taking his position seven or eight feet from the table, 'and then you try and throw the toads into the hole,' – he readied himself – 'like this …'

With a gentle underarm toss he let go of the brass disc. It turned slowly through the air, not all the way over, just a quarter rotation, so that by the time it reached the hole it was almost vertical. It dropped through without touching the sides.

---

34. At the time of writing you can buy a Lewes pound – worth £1 sterling – for £3.99.

'Bloody hell!'

'Ha! I don't *normally* get it first time,' Ben chuckled. 'Here, you have a go.'

He passed me a toad. Copying him, I rested the disc in the curve of my index finger and on the back of my thumb as if I was going to flip it heads-or-tails fashion, but instead of using my thumb to spin it I tried to release it with the movement of my whole hand. It wobbled in the air before landing with a metallic clank on the far-right corner of the table. It bounced off the curving, leaden molehill and clattered noisily onto the wooden floor, spinning under the feet of a group of twenty-something girls sitting nearby.

'Sorry,' I said, although they didn't seem remotely put out by the brass intrusion. Hardly anyone else in the room had looked up from their pints, either.

'That wasn't bad,' said Ben encouragingly. 'I mean it wasn't good, obviously. But it wasn't bad. Good technique. You hit the table. You get two points if it lands in the hole and one point if it stays on the tabletop – but not if it hits the backboard. Anything that touches the backboard doesn't score, whether it goes in the hole or not.'

'How's it meant to stay on the table?' I asked. 'There isn't a flat bit for it to land on!'

'Yeah, this table is a bit bent out of shape ...'

'You mean it's not supposed to be like that?'

'No, that's just wear and tear.'

'What? So it's meant to be flat?'

'It was once, yeah.'

'And it's now shaped like a small volcano simply because it's been hit over and over again by these?' I held up one of the discs.

They were heavy, but it was hard to believe they'd push the centre of a sheet of lead up like that.

'Yeah. It's weird isn't it? In theory I think you're meant to melt the lead down every five years and resurface them, but in practice …'

'They look like this?'

'Some of the old ones do, yeah. But every table's different. On this one the hole's quite big so it's easier to score two points. This is a high-scoring table. But you're right; scoring one is tricky. There's a table in Hailsham with an even bigger hole. It's the easiest I've seen for scoring two. They say it's like chucking a pea up West Street.'

'Ha! I expect they do *that* here as well!'

'What?'

'Chuck peas up West Street.'

Ben laughed. 'We do, actually.'

'What?'

'Every October Lewes hosts the World Pea Throwing Championships.' He wasn't joking. They do.[35] 'Anyway, we'll walk over to another pub in a bit and I'll show you a table with a flatter surface … Go on, have another throw.'

I tried again but this time my toad skewed off to the right, missing the table completely and landing straight at the feet of the same girls. Oops. I skulked over and with another apology went down on my haunches to gather the toads I'd skittered in their direction. I had to look the other way and find them by touch alone; it was the only gentlemanly way, given the shortness of their skirts.

While I was pit-patting the floorboards in search of brass, Ben picked up a tiny nub of chalk and drew a vertical line down the middle of the blackboard. He scrawled a 'D' and a 'B' on either side of the line and then beneath each of our initials the number 31.

---

35. The world record for pea throwing is 38.7 metres.

'It's a bit like darts,' he explained, 'we're counting down, first to zero. And you have to get exactly zero – if you go over you bust, and that's the end of your go.'

'Uh huh.'

'Now, to stop the first player having too big an advantage there's a staggered start.'

'Which means …?'

'Which means the first player throws two toads then the second player throws three and then after that it becomes four toads each turn. Until the end … but I'll explain that when we get there. You can start if you like.'

I did like. I did start. I didn't score. But at least both my toads hit the table on their way to the floor so it wasn't completely humiliating.

Then Ben stepped up. I was fully expecting him to nail all three of his toads.[36] But I was wrong. He only got two of them. But somehow even his miss seemed more artful than either of mine. It hit the table as if carried on a cushion of air and then slid gracefully to the floor with no more than a dull *thud*. How it was possible for my duds to announce their failure with three times as much noise as his is beyond me, but that's exactly what they did.

On my next go, I tossed all four toads and, remarkably, one landed plum in the hole. It turned somersaults all the way but I didn't care about that. It landed with a satisfying *thonk!* and I hissed a 'Yesss!' in celebration, pumping my fist like I was Andy Murray breaking serve at Wimbledon.

'Well played,' said Ben as he chalked up my new score: 29.

We chatted and we played, we played and we chatted, filling in the blanks about what had happened in the years since we'd last seen each other.

---

36. Of all the sentences I've ever written, I think this one might well be my favourite.

'After I did the *Live & Kicking* stuff with Gez and Rich,' said Ben, pausing to score yet another two points, 'I got offered work writing for Ant and Dec on *SM:TV*.'

'You're the king of Saturday morning kids' telly,' I said. '*Live & Kicking* and *SM:TV*! They were massive shows!'

'The Ant and Dec stuff went well and I started doing more and more writing,' said Ben, with a self-effacing shrug. 'Most of it for kids' TV. Sitcoms and sketches. So I've written episodes of *The Basil Brush Show*, something called *M.I. High*, and sketches for *Horrible Histories*.'

'Oh, I *love* that,' I said, genuinely pleased that I'd seen one of the shows and was able to offer a heartfelt compliment. '*Horrible Histories* is brilliant stuff. I think people probably underestimate writing for kids – I wouldn't know where to start.'

'It's like anything else,' said Ben, smiling. 'You work it out as you go along. It's a good discipline. It's a different challenge but, well, it's a challenge I like. So, what about yourself … What's this game thing about?'

'It's honestly not *about* anything,' I said. 'I wouldn't even call it a "thing" … I'm just giving myself a holiday. I mean, if I'd emailed you and said, "Hi Ben, remember me, I'm thinking of coming down to Lewes for a day out so would you like to meet for a drink?", it probably would have seemed a bit intense, a bit weird. But, "Hi Ben, can you show me this Toad In The Hole game?" Well, that sort of makes a bit more sense. Doesn't it?'

'Sort of.' Ben didn't sound entirely convinced. But he gave it another go. 'Yeah … sort of.'

'I also have a theory,' I added, 'that it'll lead me to a nicer class of pub. I think any pub where two men can play dominoes without feeling out of place is a pub where you're far less likely to get head-butted. I like the kind of pubs where men can play dominoes. I like the kind of pubs where nobody gets head-butted.'

'Have you played dominoes then?'

'Not yet. I've had offers though, and I'm sure I will.'

'So you're playing games against *anyone* who asks?'

'When I can,' I said.

'Nice ... Now, we're near the end of the game ...'

'Are we?'

'Yeah. I only need three points. So now I don't get four toads. I get three. When you get below four, you get as many toads as you have points left.'

I looked up at the blackboard. While Ben had scored 28, I'd scored just 11.

'So my only hope now is that you fail to finish. If you put two of these in the hole you'll score four points and go bust, yeah?'

'Exactly.'

'Well, if you could keep going bust while I scored another twenty points, that'd be dandy.'

'Let's see,' said Ben. His first toss hit the table and bounced to the backboard. His second one hit the table gently, so gently that it didn't bounce – it just slid back towards us and caught on a curled-up lip of lead that was peeling back from the table-top. 'This for the game,' said Ben, before lobbing his final toad in a perfect parabola – *thonk!* – into the hole.

'Well played,' I said as we shook hands.

'Thanks, and that was honestly quite good for your first game.'

I wasn't convinced by the compliment but I decided to roll with it. 'I do play darts,' I said. 'Got a board at home. I guess the distance and weight are similar. I mean this is under-arm and all that but there's got to be some kind of transferable skill. I'll bet Phil Taylor would be a bloody good Toad In The Holer if he put his mind to it.'

'You're probably right,' said Ben, polishing off his pint. He looked at the empty glass. 'Do you want another?'

'I do,' I smiled. 'But it's definitely my round.'

From my position at the bar I looked back and saw that Ben wasn't sitting alone waiting for my return. As soon as I had left, people from other groups had started drifting towards him. He was holding court. A couple of men, one in his forties, the other his fifties, were hanging on Ben's every word. I watched as he dipped into his bag and handed them both envelopes. It could have been a sneaky drug deal, but I could see that it was actually just people collecting their Lewes FC season tickets. You know, in the same way most football fans pop down to the local and pick up their season tickets from a member of the board ... For a split second I felt an unfamiliar emotion dance lightly from the left-hand side of my brain to the right and back again. The moment I became aware of it, it disappeared, melting away, falling back through the crevices of my brain to nothingness. But not before I'd recognised it for what it was.

It was envy.

I wanted to live in Lewes. I wanted to write for kids' TV. I wanted to part-own a football club and be one of the best Toad In The Holers in the world. Beth and I could live in a fifteenth-century cottage. I could write in the attic by day and boycott a pub or two by night. If we moved here now and put some work in, maybe we could get our feet under the table in time for Bonfire Night! Maybe we could burn an effigy of Simon Cowell or something!

Hmm. There was something infectious about Lewes. It all seemed so very appealing. But deep down I knew it wouldn't suit me at all. I didn't *really* want all that. But maybe I wanted to want it.

*

Carefully negotiating the small knot of people around Ben, I placed the drinks on the table. 'So a little bird tells me,' I said, 'that you're the two-time winner of the European Masters?'

'Yeah.' Ben took a sip and then stood to take his place at the toe-line and begin game two. 'But,' he added, 'the European Masters is basically a drinks party at my place.' The toad arced through the air and landed – *thonk!* – in the hole. 'It's an invitational tournament. About twenty people. But the standard's high. That's why it's the Masters.' He lined up his next throw. 'We did hold it in the pub one year but that was the European Open.' He let the toad go. 'But,' – *thonk!* – 'I'm also the reigning World Champion.'

'Really?'

'Well, my team is.' Ben chalked up his four points. 'The European Masters is a singles tournament but the Worlds, well, that's for teams of four. Like the league.'

'And are they held round your flat as well?'

'No, no ... nothing to do with me. They're organised by the Lions Club.'

'The lion cub?'

'No. The Lions Club. It's a volunteer ... thing ...'

'Like the Round Table?'

'I guess. Anyway, they organise the Worlds and they have sixty-four teams of four competing. Something like 100 teams apply every year. That's a proper international tournament.'

'Really?'

'Well ... no. Not really.' He paused. 'But there is a team from Holland.'

'Really?'

'Well ... no. Not really.'

'Oh.'

'There's a team *called* Holland, though,' said Ben, turning the dial to let a tiny bit more truth seep into the conversation. 'But I think only one of them has ever been to Holland. That's

Ron.' He took a sip from his drink. 'We call him Dutch Ron.' And another. 'Because he's Dutch.' When Ben talked about the world of organised Toad In The Hole, his features grew more impish and the glint in his eye brightened. He liked talking about it. He liked knowing too much about it. He liked confusing me. And because he was entertaining I liked being confused.

'The World Championships is what started it all ... there's been a real revival in it since they started in '95. I'd say back then there were probably no more than ... ooo ...' – his eyes darted up and to the left, to the invisible blackboard in the sky people use for counting – ' ... ummm ... no more than fifteen tables actually active in the world. These days there must be, ooo ...' – eyes up, eyes left – 'at least thirty-five in pubs and clubs ... and more in private homes.'

'So the game's been rescued from the brink of extinction?' I asked. 'That means the World Championships is like a really successful breeding programme for pandas.'

'It is,' Ben agreed. 'That's *exactly* what it's like.' (I think we were both a bit tipsy by now.) 'Some pubs had tables knocking about unused. Sometimes they didn't know what they were but it's become a bit of a Sussex thing. Especially here in Lewes. Pubs want to have a bit of tradition.'

'So where did you get *your* table?'

'I asked the Lions if I could buy one and this lovely old man agreed to make one for me. Of course, once I had one, friends wanted one so I went back and ordered four more. Then more people started saying, "Well, of course you've won the European Masters; you've got your own table," so *they* wanted tables and I had to go back and asked for eight more and this guy was like, "Look, I'm a seventy-year-old man. I didn't mind making you one but ...!" So then my dad started making them – it's his kind of thing – although he's stopped now as well. But there are people making them again now.'

I looked up at the blackboard. We'd been taking our turns as we chatted. I was languishing behind on 16. Ben needed just two points. He had two toads to get them. He only had to use one. *Thonk!* First time.

'Well done,' he said, 'that's an improvement. I beat you to 20 on the first game; you got to 16 on this one.' He drained his pint. 'Come on ... let's go to the Elephant and Castle. There's another table there ... you should definitely play more than one table.'

As we strolled through the cool night air, Ben asked me about the games I'd played so far.

'D'y'know what ...' I wobbled drunkenly. 'I played something recently that was like a kid's version of Toad. Flicking plastic discs into a hole.'

'Really?'

'Sort of. Not so much a hole, though – more Emu's beak: Rod Hull's Emu Game.'

'Did I tell you I've written for Emu?' asked Ben.

'Sod off!'

'I have.'

'No way!'

'Yeah.'

'You've written for Rod Hull! I *love* Rod Hull.'

'No, no ... no ... it wasn't Rod. It was his son, Toby. He did a kid's sitcom for ITV.'

'Hang on.' A startling thought had just landed. So startling I needed to stop and hold on to a lamppost for support. 'That means you've written for Basil Brush *and* Emu!'

'I know ... I only need to do Sooty and I've got the set.'

'Bloody hell!' My tone of voice was three parts admiration to two parts envy. The slur of my words was five parts rum. 'So, go on then ... what was he like? Toby?'

'I don't know. I worked on it from home. It was weird because Emu is obviously just a pit bull with feathers. But we had to give him a sense of justice. He was allowed to be violent but only if – according to Emu logic – he was on the side of the righteous.'

'How do you mean?'

'Well, we had one scene where Toby goes to show him how a *piñata* works. He takes one swing at the paper donkey and Emu goes nuts.'

'So Emu was allowed to be violent as long as he was defending a paper donkey?'

'Yeah. That's about the size of it.'

'It's definitely harder writing for kids, then,' I said, stepping into the warm glow of the Elephant and Castle. 'I'll get 'em in. Same again?'

The Elly's table was very different to the one at the Lewes Arms. The lead top was covered in nicks and dents where the toads had clipped it edge on, but it was pretty much level.

'It's a lower-scoring table,' explained Ben. 'Twos are harder to come by but ones are easier … The best technique here is to get the toad to land flat. Instead of landing straight in the hole, you really want to land just in front of it, with a bit of momentum.'

'You sound like a golfer explaining the way the green plays at St Andrews compared to … um … compared to … er …' I tried to think of another golf course but nothing came to mind, '… to a course that isn't St Andrews.'

'Well, you do get to know the tables,' said Ben. 'There's this one in Eastbourne with a little nail under the lead in the bottom-left corner. It's a volcano-shaped table like the one at the Arms, but that nail means there's a barely perceptible little lump in the lead. If you get the toad to land just right, so that it slides towards the nail, that's where you score your one.'

'Aaah!' I said, a penny (not a toad) dropping. 'And you can't win with twos alone because you have to get from 31 to zero!'

'Exactly. That's why in my team we keep all the stats on every player. We know who's best on which table. We always field our strongest team.'

'So what do the stats say about this table?' I asked. 'Does this suit your style?'

'Yeah. This is my kind of table, for sure. This is like the one I have at home.'

'I guess I'm screwed then,' I said, taking a large slug of rum. 'You're a world champion, you've already thrashed me and now we're moving to your preferred kind of table. I don't stand a chance!'

'Let's see,' said Ben placing the toads in my palm. 'Your turn to start.'

To my amazement both of my first two toads stayed on the table. That felt good. They also both slid all the way to the backboard meaning neither scored. That felt bad.

Ben took his three throws. On the table. In the hole. In the hole. Five points. Back to me.

I let my right hand hang limply by my side. I tried to use no muscles. I tried to do nothing. I wanted to get a pure sense of the toad's weight. I tuned in to what gravity and brass were telling me. Only when I was truly at one with the toad did I start to use my arm. I was a computer-operated toading machine. I swung it gently, resting the metal disc on my finger and thumb, and then let go. The toad hopped gracefully through the alcohol-soaked air and landed with a solid *whooomph!*

I'd missed the table completely. Straight on the floor.

So much for science. I shuffled the next toad into my hand and without any thought just lobbed it in roughly the right direction. It landed at the front of the table – *clank* – it slid a few inches – *schhhwp* – and then it dropped through the hole – *dahbonk!*

Bloody hell ... so *that* was how you did it.

My third toad of the round landed on its edge and skipped to the backboard. No score. My fourth did a little spinny jig on the tabletop but came to rest in a place of safety. One point. A three-point round. Hmm. I was getting better.

While Ben tossed his toads[37] I scanned the room and took in these new surroundings. The Elephant and Castle was a different kind of pub. It was far bigger than the Lewes Arms. It had more of the things you expect to see in pubs these days: there were big plasma screens on the wall, music was playing and the fruit machines were blinking, beeping and buzzing away. But there was still evidence of its Lewes-ness, and I don't just mean that there was Harveys Best Bitter and Toad In The Hole.

The Elly was also the headquarters for the Commercial Square Bonfire Society. There were photos on the wall alongside black and gold stripy jumpers and other more mysterious bits of bonfire paraphernalia.

I knew there was something I'd meant to ask, but for some reason I felt oddly nervous about broaching the subject. I was having such a good time. But what if the sensational stories were right and Lewes really was a hotbed of rabid anti-Catholic prejudice? What if I asked the question and Ben said, 'Oh, yeah – the papers are spot on. We hate Catholics here. Can't stand 'em. We'd burn real ones if we were allowed'? What would I do then? That would take the shine off the evening.

Of course I *knew* it wasn't going to happen. Didn't I ...? Of course I did.

'So, do you do the bonfire thing?' I asked.

'Oh, yeah. Of course! It's a great night. There's nothing else like it.'

---

37. See previous footnote

'Some people ... um ... some people think it's a bit, y'know ... dodgy.'

Ben just laughed, threw another toad into the hole and then set about explaining the Lewes Bonfire to me.

I'm not sure it's something that can be adequately explained in the course of one evening. We talked about it for the rest of the night. We talked about it all through our third game of Toad, all through our one and only game of darts[38] and all through the walk we shared through the Castle Precincts to the high street, and we hardly scratched the surface of it.

There are, I learned, six bonfire societies who all parade on the same day, joining forces at times but all doing their own things and running their own bonfires. Ben was a member of one of the societies. He assured me that he'd never once witnessed any genuine anti-Catholic sentiment.

'The thing is,' he said, 'it doesn't matter what effigy goes past, people just want to see it burn. So when Pope Paul V goes past them in the parade, of course they're shouting, "Burn the Pope." But one year there was a Donald Duck and everyone was shouting, "Burn the duck," at that. They don't hate ducks.'

'What about the Catholics in Lewes? Do they take part?'

'Some do, for sure. Absolutely they do.' He took a reflective sip of his beer. 'There *is* a banner that goes up every year saying "No Popery". We were talking about it one year and someone suggested we should hang another banner on the Catholic church saying "Popery" and then halfway between the two of them, another banner saying "Some Popery", so that the three

---

38. This game provided me with my only win of the night. It was, however, far from a foregone conclusion. We played 501 down and Ben – a non-darts player – comfortably outscored me at the start. He only lost because he failed to hit his doubles at the end. All of which proves that when it comes to throwing a lump of metal at a target over a distance of around eight feet, he's really very good, no matter what shape the metal lump or on what axis the target lies.

of them just became a measure of how much "Popery" was at each location.' Ben pulled a face. 'Don't get me wrong,' he continued, 'there *have* been situations with Orangemen coming over to watch it and sort of use it for their own ends. Ian Paisley came over one year – there's a church of his order in Lewes. I don't know what he said but some people thought he was trying to align himself with it ... or it with him.'

'So what happened?'

'The next year they burned an Ian Paisley.'

I laughed. 'It sounds like it's more anti-authoritarian than anything else.'

'Yeah. I guess so. And you know ... burning stuff is fun! And anyone who opposes it becomes an enemy of the bonfire and that becomes a part of the fun, too. You only have to look at the place – we're seven miles from Brighton. The people of Lewes don't just *read* the *Guardian* and the *Independent* – they write them. When the Lewes Arms boycott was on, it wasn't people with pitchforks, it was people with laptops.'

'There are clowns in native American culture,' I began, with the misplaced profundity so often found in drunks, 'who play a very important role in society. So, for instance, with the Hopi, their sacred clowns have the right to break all of society's rules. They ridicule authority; they mock anyone who misbehaves ... It sounds to me like your bonfire night does something similar here. It's a release. A night of madness and the leaders of it ... they're your sacred clowns.'

'It's not just one night,' added Ben, wisely skipping past my bar-room philosophising. 'It's a big commitment. D'you know about the out-meetings?'

'The what?'

'Every year the societies go to other towns and villages and join their parades. Every weekend from early September to the end of November.'

'People celebrate Bonfire Night in September?'

'Yeah. They all have different characters. There are two villages – Rotherfield and Mark Cross – they do it on the same night. If you go to the first one it's odd because they're letting off fireworks and it's still daylight. So you all get on a bus, have a drink in one village, march down to the other village, have a drink there and then walk back to where you started and get the bus back to Lewes. They go all over East Sussex. Mayfield, Hailsham, Hastings, Battle, Rye … everywhere really. And there's much more to it on the night than people expect. It's not just some effigies and a bonfire.'

'Go on.'

'Well, each of the bonfire societies is different but, for example, they'll probably start around five o'clock with a march round their part of town. Each society will have between 500 and 2,000 people in its march – they all have different costumes, say Vikings or Tudor period or whatever – and they carry flaming torches. The march is followed by a barrel race –

'Is that what I think it is?'

'It depends on what you think it is.'

'A race with barrels?'

'Yeah. They put the spent torches in these half-barrels and then race them down the road. I say "spent torches"… there's actually a lot of wood around so there's always a lot of fire around, too. Anyway, then they throw some crosses in the river and then they head back to their base before the main procession where they meet all the other societies. There are bands, and every society has "smugglers".'

'Smugglers?'

'People wearing the stripy jumpers. Each society has its own colour scheme. There are blue and white stripes, red and black stripes …'

'Black and gold stripes …'

'Very good,' said Ben. I smiled like the class swot that I

was. 'This is where the effigies come into it. There are the big effigies – the Guy Fawkes and the Pope …'

'Pope Paul V.' I was showing off now.

' … and smaller effigies, the enemies of bonfire. Normally local figures. Anyway, the grand procession goes through town and then each society heads off to their own fire site. I don't know if they all do this but there's one where there's a sort of sermon from a fake priest. And the crowd throw fireworks at him.'

'Fake fireworks?'

'No, real ones. It ends with someone asking, "What shall we do with him?" and everyone shouts, "Burn him!"'

'Like a panto *Wicker Man*?'

'Yeah. This is when the effigies go up. They've got fireworks all over them so it might start with, say, Catherine wheels on the hands, and it ends with the heads being blown sky high.'

'It definitely sounds like more fun than watching a normal guy go up on a normal bonfire,' I said reflectively. 'When I was a kid, our guys weren't good enough to be a scarecrow. We just used to have an old pair of cords and a rugby shirt stuffed full of rags …'

'Then,' said Ben, hitting his stride, 'the whole thing reforms and they go back into town. There'll be costume competitions and that sort of thing. Then there's another march where they light flares and everyone's letting off bangers and there are hog roasts and things like that … then they all throw their torches and crosses in the road and make a bonfire.'

'Haven't they already had a bonfire?' I asked, struggling to keep up with the running order.

'There's always more fire,' said Ben. 'This is when they say the bonfire prayer …'

'There's a bonfire prayer?'

'Yeah,' said Ben. 'Keep up. You know the first line.'

'Do I?'

'*Remember, remember the fifth of November ...*'

'Is that where that comes from? Bloody hell.'

'*Remember, remember the fifth of November / Gunpowder, treason and plot / I see no reason ...*' He stopped. 'Hang on ...'

'What?'

'Well, there's a rhythm to it. Normally the crowd responds with a "plot-plot" at the end of that line. It doesn't sound right without it.'

'I'll throw in some "plot-plots" if you like,' I offered.

'Okay.' Ben took a deep breath and then went at the verse with pace. '*Remember, remember the fifth of November / Gunpowder, treason and plot ...*'

'Plot, plot!'

'*I see no reason why gunpowder, treason / Should ever be forgot ...*'

'Got, got!'

'Good work! Anyway, that goes on and then people run backwards and forwards through the fire.'

'You must be making some of this up now?'

'No. People run through the fire ... I think the key there is that you don't want to bump into someone running the other way. Then – and this is just one of the societies – you hear a bell ringing, *ding ding, ding ding*, and a replica of a Victorian fire engine comes out of a side street and puts the fire out.'

'Wow.'

'Did I mention the blazing hogs' heads or the amazing tableaux?'

'I don't think so.'

'Then I missed some bits out. But, well, the point is there's a lot to it. It definitely isn't, "We-hate-the-Pope".'

'No.' I said. 'No further questions, m'lud.'

We paused for a moment outside the hotel.

'Thanks for coming down,' said Ben.

'Not at all ... thanks for showing me around, and for showing me Toad In The Hole. I really appreciate it.'

'Come down again some time.'

'I will,' I said. 'I will. I'll come and see a football game. I'll bring Beth.'

'Beth?'

'My fiancée.'

'You're getting married?!'

'Yeah,' I smiled, 'and don't sound so bloody surprised!'

'It's not that,' chuckled Ben. 'It's more ... well ... you're travelling all over and playing games with whoever ... It just feels more like a single man thing to do.'

'Ha. I suppose you're right. I'll stop when we get married.' I paused. 'Not in a the-old-ball-and-chain'll-soon-put-a-stop-to-that! way,' I clarified. 'It's just, well, she's working all hours at the minute, and I've got loads of free time at the moment. But, I'm going to get busy again in a bit, so I'll have to stop then. But this, right now – this is my holiday. Sort of.'

'And she doesn't mind?'

'Nah,' I scoffed. 'She pretends to worry when I'm meeting a girl and ...'

'"Pretends"?'

'Yeah. I'm playing. And I'm away from home. But she knows I'd never play away from home. I think she gets a bit more worried when I'm meeting a bloke to be honest. Y'know, in case they're weird or violent or something.'

'So is she worried about me?'

'Nah ... she knows we know each other from way back. Besides, she knows it's all right, really. She knows I'm safe.'

'With the girls?'

'Of course. And with the blokes. She knows nothing bad's going to happen. I paused. Nothing bad happened. 'Y'see? I told you.'

CHAPTER 15

When I woke the next morning, confusion reigned. I understood why I was ravenous: I'd forgotten to eat the day before. But I didn't understand why I wasn't hungover: a boozy night out on an empty stomach is usually a recipe for disaster. Odd. Maybe I wasn't really awake. Maybe I was still asleep and I was just dreaming about waking up. What a peculiarly mundane dream that would be: getting up, having a shower and brushing my teeth. I rarely remember dreams but I'd like to think my subconscious would come up with something more active than that. Still, just in case it was a dream I made the walk to breakfast on tiptoes so as not to wake myself up.

I remained suspicious of my sober, healthy, bright-eyed and bushy-tailed state for quite a while. Even as I checked out of the hotel it didn't quite seem possible. But then a spit of rain fell and then a little more and then … well, that was definitely real. I made a quick dash across the road for cover, heading straight into the small gift shop and museum attached to the castle.

I feigned interest in some of the Roman artefacts in their glass cases but found myself more genuinely excited by the room that contained a highly detailed model of the whole town. Given that the 1:1 scale version already looked like a model, the model was, well, pretty much spot on.

As soon as the rain passed I left and headed into the castle itself. I climbed a zigzagging staircase up to the top of the motte where, within the ancient outer walls, I was surprised to find a small, secluded garden. I had it all to myself, too. There didn't appear to be another soul in the castle grounds.

I used my sleeve to wipe the edge of a bench dry and perched my bum in the driest patch. I used my mobile to take a quick snap of the pretty circular lawn. In the background, a large doorway built into the castle wall was framed by pink roses. I attached the picture to a text message:

To: Beth
Wish you were here. It's lovely. D x

As my thumb hit the send button I heard a small cough to my left. I looked up. There was a young woman standing in the ill-defined space at the entrance to the garden – the no-man's land that was no longer the zigzag stairway but not yet the garden.

It sounded like a 'Can-I-come-in?' cough but I imagined all it really meant was, 'Phew-I-made-it-up-the-stairs.' We acknowledged each other's presence with a smile and a quick eyebrow-hello. But then we both realised that we'd seen each other the night before in the Lewes Arms, which made our simple eyebrow-hellos seem a bit inadequate. So we repeated the eyebrow manoeuvre but threw in a few extra touches – a bounce of the head, a smile with just a touch of '*Tsk!*' – changing them from simple hellos into something far more complex: 'I-don't-actually-know-you-but-fancy-running-into-you-again!' greetings.

She was one of the short-skirted girls whose night I'd constantly interrupted with my poor toading skills. She started walking towards me with a series of awkward shrugs and a 'Hello'.

I shielded my eyes from the sun. 'Hi.'

'You were in the ...'

'Yeah ... and you were one of the ...'

'That's right. Yeah.'

Her blonde hair was tied back in a ponytail. She wore a bolero jacket made of black leather and decorated with dozens of badges. On the right-hand side of the jacket band names, slogans and various cartoon faces were jostling for position, while on the left there was just one badge: *I ♥ Troy.* A boy? A pop star? Or the ancient city? Looking at her, it was hard to tell.

'I'm sorry I kept throwing my toads at you.'

'I bet you say that to all the girls.'

'Ha. Not really.'

'It's Dave, isn't it?'

'Uh huh.'

'I'm Lou.'

'Hi, Lou.'

'Um … this might sound a bit weird but … um … well, I heard you saying that you're playing games with people?'

'Yeah …'

'You said you play games with anyone who asks …?'

'Um … yeah.' There was a pause. 'Do you want to play a game?'

'No.' There was another pause. 'But, um, I have some friends who I think would like to play a game with you.'

'In Lewes?' I asked, with an involuntary glance at my watch.

'No.' She glanced at her watch, too. Perhaps I'd given her the impression that our watches were important. 'No. They live in Portsmouth. I live in Portsmouth, too. I'm just visiting a friend. You live in London, don't you?'

'Yes.'

'Can I give you their email address? It's not mine. I'm not …' The words tailed off. She delved into her handbag and pulled out a pen and some paper and began scribbling. 'They'll play a game with you,' she said, passing the paper my way. 'If you like.'

'Thanks,' I said. 'I'll email them.'

'That would be good.' She paused. She looked like she was about to add something else but before she did my phone beeped. 'Bye then,' she said.

'Bye.'

I looked at my phone. It was a message from Beth. It had a photo attached. The inside of a Portakabin.

```
To: Dave
This is my view. You win! See you at home
tonight. B x
```

From: Dave Gorman
To: Steve
Subject: Game

Hi Steve,

I bumped into a friend of yours called Lou
the other day. She says you wanted to play a
game. What did you have in mind?

Dave

From: Steve
To: Dave Gorman
Subject: Re: Game

Hi Dave,

I contacted you on Twitter about this some
time ago but you didn't reply. What's up with
that? Lou told me she saw you. Thanks for the
email. Friends and I play a board game called
'IDVE'. I'd love to play it with you. I live near
Portsmouth. You could stay at mine if you like.

Steve

From: Dave Gorman

To: Steve
Subject: Re: Re: Game

Hi Steve,

The offer of a place to stay is very nice of you, but if I can make it to Portsmouth I'll probably get a hotel. I don't like to impose!

I'm sorry I didn't reply to you on Twitter. I had a lot of tweets in a short space of time. It wasn't really possible to read all of them, let alone reply. Sorry! No offence intended.

I've never heard of DIVE. I've played a couple of the modern German-style board games recently (Agricola, Settlers of Catan) but I find them quite tricky to get into first time … is it that kind of thing or is it more traditional?

Cheers,
Dave

From: Steve
To: Dave Gorman
Subject: Re: Re: Re: Game

Hi Dave,

The game isn't called DIVE. It's IDVE. You probably won't have heard of it but I can assure you it's very easy to play.

I live some distance outside Portsmouth itself but I can pick you up in town and drop you back if you like. I can play any night of the week that suits you. When can you come down?

Steve

From: Dave Gorman
To: Steve
Subject: Re: Re: Re: Re: Game

Hi Steve,

    I can probably make it up in three or four weeks. Maybe. I've got a few games to play between now and then. I'll be in touch nearer the time if that's okay?

    Cheers,

    Dave

From: Steve
To: Dave Gorman
Subject: Re: Re: Re: Re: Re: Game

Okay.

CHAPTER 16

It had taken me a while but I'd finally made sense of what I was doing. The Liverpool-London-Stockport-London jaunt had simply been a ridiculous thing to do. It had turned three games into staging posts of a tightly run tour. It was as if an imaginary sergeant major had been at my side yelling orders: 'Eat, travel, eat, travel, game, game, sleep, travel, eat, travel, game, travel, sleep, eat, game … attt-hennnnnnn-shunnnnn!'

Why had I done it? I knew why. I recognised habits of old. I have in the past allowed whimsical, playful distractions to overtake me. There's an unhealthy part of my personality that tends to obsess and collect; that will take things to extremes. I can be a dog with a bone at times. But I didn't want to let it happen again. Not with this. It wasn't a treasure hunt. There wasn't a prize for playing the most games in the shortest amount of time.

My trips to Windermere and Lewes had shown me the right way to enjoy this experience. So I settled happily into a nice rhythm of short trips in and around London, and longer jaunts further afield. I spent a morning playing skittles in Hyde Park and used an invitation to play boules to justify a couple of days' sea air in Llandudno. I played Zombies!!! and Ticket to Ride in Twickenham one Sunday afternoon, and then spent three days drifting between Norwich and Lowestoft playing Blokus and Bananagrams. I played Scrabble in Carlisle, Ingenious in Glasgow and Ker-Plunk! in Oxford. I played Tikal in Enfield, Werewolf in Shoreditch, Blood Bowl in Aldershot and an unconventional game of Monopoly in Windsor …

*

'It's a good job my husband didn't see you on the way over,' squealed Caroline, my Windsor play-date. 'He'd run you over as soon as look at you!' She snorted with laughter at the idea. 'He *hates* cyclists!' The snort turned into a bray. 'Come in, come in,' she said, still wheezing from her laughing fit. 'You said you were going to cycle, but I didn't think you really would! You must be *knackered*!'

I was. A bit. I wasn't a horrible sweaty wreck, and I'd done okay for time, too. But I knew my muscles were going to tighten. The return leg wasn't going to be quite so quick.

Before undertaking my 1,600-mile bike ride I'd obviously done some training rides. My most frequently used practice route was a journey from East London out west to the royal town of Windsor and then back again. It's a round trip of about sixty miles – a distance I knew I had to get comfortable with – and it gave me a taste of both city traffic and country lanes. After a while, as my fitness and my navigational skills improved, I found myself able to get to Windsor in less than three hours. I knew I'd be slower now – I'd lost most of my fitness in the eleven months since the big ride – but the moment I'd read Caroline's email inviting me that way, I knew I was going to put myself back in the saddle. And back in Lycra – a sixty-mile round trip would have to involve Lycra.

I leaned my bike up against the side of the porch and unhooked my pannier bag from the back. The driveway was long and curved. I couldn't see the road from the doorway so I was sure nobody could see my bike from the road. For the first time in my life I left my bike outside and unlocked.

Caroline had an extraordinarily large home. The three-car garage was as big as a house while the house … well, it was big enough to make the three-car garage look like a normal, one-car garage. It was huge. But it was well proportioned. It looked like a normal house that had been bulking up at the gym. (In reality, of course, it was just a bulky house with a gym.)

Inside it was much less traditional than I was expecting. If you're the director of a sci-fi film and you're looking for a staircase for your cold, calculating, alien emperor to sweep down, then I can recommend Caroline's hallway. It's an expansive floor-to-ceiling open space and it's all white. The walls are white. The floor is white. The staircase is white. Caroline's trousers and plimsolls were white too, so at first glance the lower half of her body seemed to disappear into the background. It was like being welcomed in by a floating torso. Caroline was wearing a navy blue T-shirt and a *lot* of jewellery. She was in her fifties although I wouldn't have been surprised to learn that bits of her were newer than that.

For a moment we stood in the hallway in silence, me watching the top half of her body floating in space while she watched my lycra-clad form glowing in self-consciousness. I know most people think all cycling gear will always look utterly ridiculous but I'm inclined to disagree. I think it looks more than reasonable when you're on your bike, okay when you're standing within two or three yards of your bike and only becomes risible when you and the bike have well and truly parted company.

'I, um, brought a change of clothes,' I said, waving my pannier bag in the air as proof. 'Would it be okay if I ducked out and got changed somewhere …?'

'Of course,' she said. 'Do you want to shower as well?'

'Nah … I'll be all right,' I said. 'I didn't work too hard so I'm not sweating.'

'No, go on … have a shower, you'll feel better.'

'I feel fine, honestly …'

'Go on.'

'There's really no need.'

Caroline wasn't taking no for an answer.

'Come with me,' she said, leading me through one door to the kitchen and then through another to their sizeable indoor swimming pool. From there I could see through another door to the gym.

'If you go through here,' she said, opening a little side door, 'you can have a quick shower while I set up the board and make some tea.' She reached her arm through the doorway and pulled a cord. A bright neon light flickered into life and the low hum of an extractor fan kicked in.

I stepped inside the tiny room and closed the door behind me. To my left was a white, plastic, standard-issue garden chair upon which was sitting a pile of neatly folded, fluffy, white towels. In front of me was a shower. A lone bottle of bright blue shower gel stood in the corner of the cubicle. And that was pretty much it.

I had a quick sniff of my armpits. They were fine. I got undressed. It didn't feel right. Not in a stranger's house. We'd barely said hello and here I was completely naked within her walls – in a few minutes' time I'd be drying my doodahs with one of her towels. That's not right. Not right at all.

I put my cycle wear in a pile on the floor and then arranged my fresh clothes on the chair, with one of the towels on top. I made sure they were all stacked in the right order: towel, pants, T-shirt, jeans, socks. Perfect. I turned the shower on, waited for the water to heat up, stepped in and pulled the thin, yellow plastic curtain behind me. I aimed to make it quick: I wanted to be naked for as short a time as possible. I squirted a bit of shower gel into my hand and got busy … top left, top right, down below.

You know what it's like when you're naked and taking a shower at a stranger's house and then all of a sudden they walk in without any warning? No? I do.

Both hands down below. Freeze. There was barely three feet of air and a flimsy sheet of yellow plastic between us.

'Hello?' I gulped nervously.

'Knock, knock,' said Caroline, ignoring the fact that she'd already opened the door and stepped inside. 'It's only me,' she added. Oh, so that's all right then! I mean it *would* have been weird if she'd brought some friends along but seeing as it was *only* her ...! 'I brought you a cup of tea,' she said. 'I'm just going to leave it here ... under the chair.'

'Thanks,' I said weakly as the door closed.

As I dried and dressed myself I played a game of 'Don't Take Your Eyes Off The Door Handle Not Even For A Second'. It turns out I'm quite good at it when I have sufficient motivation.

It was only as I was pulling my socks over my still-moist toes that I realised Caroline hadn't just delivered tea (and fear).

My cycling clothes were gone.

I headed back through the poolroom and into the kitchen. It was empty, but I could see the blue and white colours of my cycling jersey spinning round in the washing machine window. I was going to be here for as long as they were.

I placed my empty mug beside the sink and called out. 'Hello!'

'I'm in here ... Come on through ...'

I followed Caroline's voice, passing through a set of double doors and into the dining room. My shoeless feet sank into the deep-pile carpet. There were bookcases on two walls, a stereo mounted on a third but nothing could take the attention away from the dramatic dining table. It was at least twelve feet long and instead of legs, the dark wood tabletop was supported by a granite plinth. It must have easily weighed a ton or more. Caroline was sitting at the near end of the table.

'I put your things in the wash,' she said. 'Now ... shall we play?'

On the table in front of her was a Monopoly board. I have fond memories of Monopoly. And bad memories, too. I don't think any of my brothers and I ever managed a game by ourselves without it ending in a fight; many's the time the board was tipped over in rage. It was always the same: we'd ask

Mum if it was okay for us to play Monopoly, she'd reply, 'All right, but only if you promise you won't fight this time,' and then a couple of hours later one of us would be purple-faced and screaming the house down. There's a reason it doesn't have a picture of two angelic kids happily playing it on the front of the box: it would be in breach of the Trade Descriptions Act if it did.

As a game it really is quite badly flawed. There's normally a point in a game of Monopoly where the outcome is a foregone conclusion. If that point came five minutes before the end it would be fine. But it doesn't. There's usually a good hour of play left to go, an hour in which the loser is expected to obediently go through the motions – rolling the dice, moving their piece, paying the rent – despite the fact that for them, there is no pleasure left to squeeze out of the experience. Meanwhile, the winner is effectively forced to bully his downtrodden friends because unless they are annihilated, the game hasn't been played to a proper conclusion. It's a tinderbox that can blow at any moment. In my experience, the trigger was normally the winning player daring to show that they were enjoying it.

As much as I find the new breed of board games – Settlers of Catan, Agricola and the like – difficult to grasp they have, I think, done away with this particular problem. They've been designed to give every player a stake in the game right to the end. Even Snakes and Ladders has a big snake just before the finishing line giving it a 'not-over-til-it's-over' quality that Monopoly simply hasn't got.

There *was* one way of playing Monopoly without a tantrum when I was growing up. We just had to add one special ingredient: Dad. Those are the games that provide a store of fond memories for me. Those are the games that mean I can forgive Monopoly its many flaws.

For some reason, we never played Monopoly with Dad at home. It was a ritual we saved for when we were visiting our gran's. Things were different when we were visiting Gran. We had a cooked breakfast every day, we said Grace before dinner and we'd get to spend one evening staying up late – just Dad and his boys – playing Monopoly.

Being allowed to stay up past our bedtime normally involved sitting quietly on the sofa hoping that none of the grown-ups noticed we were still there. It was an illicit thrill. It made us feel naughty. And, in a way, that only served to remind us we were still children. But the Monopoly nights weren't like that. The Monopoly nights made us feel like grown-ups. We weren't just staying up; we were staying up later than our gran. And she knew! And Dad knew! This wasn't naughty at all. This was us being invited into the adult world. The fact that it was happening outside children's hours confirmed to us that this was a grown-up's game. This was 'us' being allowed to join in with 'them'. (Or just 'him', as it was in this case.)

I assume the board we played with at my gran's had been bought in the 40s, when my Dad was a nipper. It was a set made during the austerity of the war years. It didn't have the metal tokens – the top hat, the car, the boot, etc. – instead, each piece was represented by a cardboard picture slotted into a wooden base to keep it upright. The houses and hotels were wooden, too. I always preferred this version of the game. The one we had at home – with the metal tokens and the injection-moulded plastic houses and hotels with their tiny chimney pot details – felt like the children's version of the game. But the old one? Well, that was for grown-ups.

The version sitting on Caroline's dining table had wooden houses and hotels too, but there was no wartime austerity about it. (I don't think there was much austerity in Caroline's life.) Her Monopoly set was of the modern era, but it was some kind of premium edition. The board was set into a rose-wood frame with polished brass inlay. The traditional trinkets were there, but instead of being pewter they were gold. Or at least gold plated. I didn't see the box, but I imagine it was the Monopoly Steampunk Bling edition.

'What piece do you want to be?' asked Caroline.

'I'll be the boot, please,' I said. I've always been the boot.

We rolled the dice to see who would have the privilege of opening the game, and the honour fell to me. I started with what I think is the quickest available circuit of the board. I rolled a seven, which took me to the first CHANCE space. When I turned the top card over it told me to advance to 'Go', so I did, taking my shiny golden boot back to the start of the board and picking up £200 for my troubles.

'Crikey,' I said. 'If only London was really like that.'

'If only,' agreed Caroline. She picked up the dice, blew on them for luck, and rolled.

'So, do you play a lot of Monopoly?' I asked.

'Actually, not that often.' Caroline's golden sports car had arrived at one of the light blue set. 'I'll buy that.' The money went in the bank and the first Title Deed of the game was added to someone's portfolio. 'We play with some friends at least once a year ... Apart from that? Not really. Your go.'

I rolled the dice but Caroline kept on talking.

'Keith's into his rugby,' she said. I counted my piece round. 'Every year when the Six Nations is on we go to one of the matches at Twickenham with friends. Giles and Ann, Bill and Ben ...'

'Bill and Ben?' I put some money in the bank and picked up my first property. 'The Flowerpot Men?'

'Ben is a nickname. Her real name is Caterina. She's Bill's third wife. Bill's wives are always nicknamed Ben.'

'How lovely for them,' said I. Caroline rolled the dice. A one and a five. 'So,' I prompted, 'the six of you watch a rugby game ...?'

'And then we all go back to someone's house for a bit of a party.' She moved her piece and bought whatever piece of real estate it was she had landed on. 'Which always involves Monopoly.'

'I never really thought of it as a party game,' I said as I rolled the dice.

'We spice it up a little.' Caroline paused for effect. 'We play with real money.'

'*What?*'

'I knew you'd like that! … We can do it now if you like?'

'I think,' I said squeakily, 'that's a bit rich for my blood! Bloody hell! Sorry. Excuse my language.'

'We don't have a whole bank of real cash!' Caroline protested – as if that was where the line between madness and sanity lay. 'It's just each player's starting cash that's real.'

I looked at the pretend notes in front of me. Having only recently counted out our starting wedge: two pink £500s, four orange £100s, one white £50, one green £20, two grey £10s, one blue £5 and five yellow £1s, I knew only too well how much 'money' a player started out with. But the point *is* that it is 'money' and not, um … *money*.

'You're talking about £1,500!' I said, managing to be even squeakier still.

'Exactly! We all put £1,500 in, in cash … and the winner takes all.'

'Hang on … you're saying someone takes home nine grand? For playing Monopoly?'

'Yes.' Caroline was clearly enjoying my astonishment. 'But we're all couples, so really it's just a six-grand profit.'

'Well, yes,' I said. 'But then really it's also a three-grand risk! That's a lot of money!'

'It's worse than that.' Caroline leaned forwards as if this next bit of information could only be divulged at close quarters. 'We play a six-player game but the first couple to go out has to buy the match tickets for next year … and the second couple to go out has to host the party.'

'So you could lose three grand *and* then have to spend hundreds on tickets?'

'Yeah.'

'But if you win, you get all the cash *and* everything laid on for you the year after.'

'Yeah. It makes it much more enjoyable.'

'That's one way of looking at it,' I said. 'If I play poker for more than twenty quid I get a bit edgy.'

'If I make another tea,' asked Caroline, 'can I trust you not to steal from the bank?'

'Of course you can.'

'Do you want one?'

'Yes, please.' I paused. 'Um … do you mind if I ask you what Keith does for a living?'

Caroline gestured to the board. 'This.'

What? This? Monopoly? I knew there wasn't a high-end Professional Monopoly League but I didn't have the wit to see what else she could mean. My head was still reeling from the idea of playing £1,500-a-pop games of Monopoly. It's when straightforward facts like that become hard to process that your brain's focus narrows and its nuance sensors get shut down.

'Sorry?' I asked. 'What?'

'He buys and sells bits of London,' came the reply. That made more sense. 'It's milk and no sugar, isn't it?'

As I cycled back to East London that afternoon – with perfectly clean Lycra clinging to my thighs – I wished I'd taken Caroline up on the offer of a cash game. I'd have been £1,500 better off if I had. Not that I was complaining. It had been a good-natured game, after all. Caroline had played out that last hour of slow defeat without any sign of temper. But then, why wouldn't she? By her standards it was a very cheap loss. When she finally fell into financial oblivion – thanks to a £1,400 stay at my Bond Street hotel – she was no doubt celebrating the fact that it was only Monopoly money after all.

CHAPTER 17

Devo's version of 'Working In A Coalmine' was playing in my pocket. I didn't have to look at the phone to know who was calling.

I'd programmed my phone to give a select band of friends and colleagues their own ringtones. My agent was on the line.

'Hi, Rob.'

'Dave? Rob.'

He rarely says more than is strictly necessary.

'Yes. Hi. What can I do for you, Rob?'

'You on a train?'

'Yeah,' I said, 'I'm on my way back from Cheltenham.'

'Cheltenham?'

He sounded confused. I could hear him rustling through some paperwork in the background.

'Yeah. Cheltenham. Don't worry, you don't need to check my diary. I wasn't working.'

'Oh.' The rustling stopped. 'Why Cheltenham?'

'I went to play a game,' I explained. 'Sevens.'

'Rugby?'

'No. Cards. It was fun.'

'Okay. Now, tomorrow?'

'What about it?'

'What're you doing?'

'Um … nothing. I think. Why?'

'I've got someone I want you to meet.'

'Okay …' I paused, waiting for more information to flow. Who was it? What was it about? There was nothing. 'Any clues, Rob?'

'How about eleven?'

'Yeah, okay ... but who is it?'

'Actually, make it eleven-thirty. Is that okay?'

'Yeah but ...'

'See you then. Bye.'

'Bye,' I said, but the line was already dead.

Rob was looking unusually businesslike. He's normally to be found wearing a jeans and polo shirt combination but on this occasion he was wearing a sharp, three-button suit.

If he was wearing it to try and appear more businesslike it wasn't working. Any seriousness was undercut by his decision to eschew the conventional office chair in favour of a huge, grey, shiny rubber ball. He wasn't bouncing very much. There was no more than a quarter-inch rise in height with each bob ... but he was in a constant state of motion: an on-going, non-stop, micro-bounce.

Luckily the rest of the office furniture was of the non-inflatable variety. There were two standard chairs on the other side of Rob's desk. A young man in a tracksuit top was sitting in one of them. I was in the other.

'So,' said Rob, 'this is Guy. Guy works for an independent production company ... Guy, this is Dave ... So, Guy ... why don't you take it from here?'

'Okay,' said Guy, swishing his fingers through his hair. 'I'll get straight to the point, Dave. We'd like to help with your new project ...'

I was a tad confused. What new project was he talking about? I looked to Rob for a clue. He bobbed, slowly. His eyes gave nothing away.

'Um ... I don't want to sound dim,' I said, cautiously. 'But I don't know what my new project *is* ... um ... I'm just doing the radio show at the minute and, um ... that's pretty much it.'

Guy smirked.

'I follow you on Twitter, Dave,' he said, as if that explained everything.

I looked at Rob.

'Twitter,' he said. 'He's,' *bob*, 'following you,' *bob*, 'on,' *bob-bob-bob*, 'Twitter.'

'Uh huh,' I said. 'I *am* using Twitter but I still don't know what this mysterious "new project" is ... er ... What are we talking about?'

'Your games thing,' said Guy. He seemed a bit miffed at having to spell it out.

'My games thing?'

'You've been playing games,' added Guy.

'Yes. I know. But ...'

'He was in Cheltenham yesterday,' said bobbing Rob. 'Weren't you, Dave?'

'Um. Yes.'

'Playing Sevens.'

'What? Rugby?' asked Guy.

'No,' said Rob. 'Cards.'

'Well, there you go,' said Guy. '*This* is your new project: games.'

'If you say so,' I said.

'Well, I want to be a part of it,' said Guy.

'Um ...' I paused. He seemed to be talking in riddles. 'I don't understand,' I said. 'Do you want to play a game? Because you could have just sent me an email or a tweet or ...'

'Ha! No. I don't really play games.'

'Then you're going to have to help me out here,' I said. 'I feel like I'm being rude but I genuinely don't understand what this is about.'

'Look,' said Guy, 'you're working on a show about games ...'

'No,' I said. 'That's where I'm getting lost ... what show am I doing about games?'

I looked at Guy. Guy looked at Rob. Rob shrugged at Guy. At least I think he did. It was hard to tell, what with the bobbing. Guy looked at me.

'Well, *that's* the thing,' he said, brushing his doubts aside. I got the impression that brushing his doubts aside was a tactic that had taken Guy quite far in life. 'We want to make *that* show. We want to put *that* show on TV.'

'What show?' I was sounding tetchy now.

'Your games show.'

'A game show?'

'No. The show you're doing. About games.'

'I'm not *doing* a show about games!' I squeaked.

'Yeah ... but games is your new' – he used air-quotes – '"thing", isn't it?'

'"Thing"?'

Guy sighed. 'Look, you've been meeting people to play games, right?'

'Ye-ess ...'

'So ...?' Guy let the word hang in the air. He raised his eyebrows cryptically as if inviting me to fill in the blanks.

I was blank.

'So ...?' I replied.

'So ... we've seen you do this before. You do a "thing" ...' – the air-quotes were back – '... and then you write it up and up pops a stage show!'

'Well, it's not quite like that ...'

'I think we can get a broadcaster interested in this, Dave.'

'In me playing games?' I was incredulous. 'That's not why I'm ... look ... I don't think it's really very telly friendly,' I explained. 'We're talking about card games and board games and, um, games?' I finished lamely.

'Well, yeah ... obviously we'd want to take a view about which games we let you play. We're not going to get much out of the card games, unless ... are you playing strip poker at all?'

'No.'

'But rugby would work. You played rugby, right?'

'No. I didn't ...'

'We brainstormed all this in the office last week. Sumo would be great ...'

'Sumo!' I scoffed. 'There's no way I'm *sumo*-ing!'

'Think about it, Dave,' Guy waved his hands in the air as if painting the scene. 'You'd get flattened!'

'Exactly! Why would I want to do that?'

'You squashed to the floor with some lardy Japanese fella smothering you!'

'You can stop picturing it because it's not happening!'

'Look, Dave ... I don't know if we can sell this ... but if you let us come with you to some of your *wacky* games ... we'll shoot some test footage, we'll cut it together, you just have to sprinkle a bit of *je ne sais quoi* over it in voice-over and then leave it with us ... I reckon we can get something off the ground if we speak to the right people.'

'I don't think you're talking to the right person,' I said. 'I appreciate you thinking of me, but I don't think I'm doing what you think I'm doing. I'm just ... playing games. Because they're fun to play. And I don't want to ...'

'But we could ...'

'Nah. Honestly. I'm enjoying having some time off. Even if I thought you could sell it – which I don't – I don't *want* to turn *this* into work. I don't want to change it ... I don't really want someone taking a view about which games I'm "allowed to play"' – I was doing air-quotes now – 'I'm sorry if Twitter's given you the wrong impression but just because you can see it, it doesn't mean it's a show. They're just ...

games! I'm enjoying them *because* they're just games! In fact
... d'y'know what?'

'What?'

'You should try playing some. You'll like it. They're fun
... And I'm not being rude,' I leaned in closer, 'but you seem
a bit stressed out right now.'

CHAPTER 18

If you're meeting a stranger in a train station I'm pretty sure you're meant to carry a copy of *The Times* or wear a red carnation or stand underneath a big clock. Or possibly all three.

I was doing none of the above. Instead, I was just standing in the ticket hall of Sheffield station giving every male stranger a meaningful look in case they turned out to be Ross.

The trouble with that was that a train station is just the kind of place that strangers agree to meet in, so meaningful looks abound. And the vast majority of them turn out to be meaningless. It's not always easy to tell the difference between a look that means, 'I wonder if you're my taxi driver?' and another that means, 'Are you the stranger I agreed to play cribbage with?'

It turns out they're also quite similar to a look that means, 'I'm about to show you my penis.' They must be. Because I made eye contact with a fiftyish-year-old man whose hands were in the pockets of his leather jacket and I could have sworn we both did the, 'I wonder if it's you? Ah, you're clearly wondering if it's me ... That significantly increases the chances that it *is* you and the longer this eye contact is maintained the more confident I'm going to be that it is you ... aaaaand, yup, what the hell, I'm going to go for it!' thing, only instead of coming up and saying hello, he just pulled his right hand away from his body, which moved his leather jacket aside and revealed his engorged member. Eye contact of a different kind. Charming.

It took me half a second to work out that this obviously wasn't the person – or indeed the penis – I'd arranged to meet. But by the time I had, it was too late: I'd already started speaking.

'Ross?' I asked. It's hard to imagine any word being more steeped in confusion.

His expression changed from, 'Ah, it is you!' to 'Shit, it's definitely *not* you and I've just flashed my cock!' He squawked a breathy apology – which was nice of him – and then legged it outside and into the night air, running awkwardly, the way men who have to keep their hands in their pockets are wont to do.

It was odd. And a bit unpleasant. Still, it could have been worse. What if he'd been called Ross? And now you'll have to forgive me for what I am about to type. I've got a sentence in my head and I don't think I can prevent it from reaching my fingertips. It's not a classy sentence. I'm not proud of it. But the facts have aligned so neatly that to ignore them would be almost rude. So here goes: when the real Ross turned up a few minutes later he, too, announced his presence by flashing six inches of wood in my direction.

There. We can pretend it didn't happen if you like.

I could, of course, add something about how it had dozens of small holes drilled into it ... but I'm assuming you've already worked out it was a cribbage board, so there's no point, really.

Let's move on.

The only thing I knew about Ross in advance was that he played cribbage. From that one, rather flimsy fact I had decided for myself that he was probably going to be in his fifties. Or maybe older. It turned out that my cribbage-profiling was way off. He turned out to be in his mid twenties. He had a neat goatee beard, dark-framed glasses and a chipped tooth that gave him a *Bash Street Kids* sense of cheekiness whenever he smiled.

'Bloody hell, this has changed since I was last here,' I said as we stepped out of the station. 'I like that.'

The 'that' in question was a huge sculpture-cum-water-feature made – with inevita-Sheffield-ability – out of stainless steel. It was a long, curved, mirrored snake, its contours changing over the course of its 100-yard length. At one end it's tubular and about three feet in diameter while at the other it looks like the tailfin from a 1950s Cadillac – albeit one that's fifteen feet tall.

'Nice, isn't it?' said Ross.

Nodding, I turned and looked back, past the sculpture, past the station to the housing estate on the hill beyond.

'Bloody hell … *that's* changed, too!'

Park Hill it's called. I'd first seen it twenty years ago when I was a callow youth making one of my first journeys away from home for a paid gig. It had scared me back then. It was concrete and it was enormous. Ten or more storeys high and a quarter of a mile or so long, it was a grey and forbidding sight. It looked as if a sliver of Communist-era Albania had been transplanted to modern Britain.

It had made the landscape feel yet more alien, intensifying the feeling that the nineteen-year-old me was out of his depth; that what I was doing was something a nice middle-class boy like me shouldn't really have been getting into. But now it was being renovated. Sections of it were hiding behind scaffolding while a huge swathe of it was looking fresh-out-of-the-box new. The concrete frame was still there but where it had once seemed to be a wall of grey, now there were alternating swatches of glass and brightly coloured glossy panels in red, orange and yellow. The locals used to call it San Quentin. Now it's being yuppified for Saras and Quentins. Actually, it looked like it was going to be bloody marvellous. (Of course, an unadorned hill might well have looked nicer, but seeing as it was already there it might as well be the best it can be.)

'It's been a controversial development.' Ross filled me in. 'D'you remember Channel Four doing a show called *Demolition*?'

'Vaguely.'

'The public voted for the buildings they most wanted to have torn down.'

'And that was one of them?'

'Number five.'

'I'm glad they're not knocking it down.'

'They couldn't even if they wanted to,' said Ross, turning on his heel and restarting our journey. 'It's Grade II listed.'

Our walk took us into the vibrant part of the city officially known as the 'Cultural Industries Quarter'. I think they might have to rethink that name as, these days, the balance seems to be swinging towards other, less cultural, pursuits. The Showroom fulfils the brief: built in the 1930s as a car showroom, nowadays this beautiful Art Deco building is an art-house cinema. Tick. But across the road from it is what used to be the National Centre for Popular Music. It's a pretty avant-garde building that consists of four large stainless steel drums designed to look like curling stones. It opened in 1999 but failed to attract enough visitors and closed less than a year later. In 2003, it was bought by Sheffield Hallam University and it's now their Students' Union. I'm pretty sure the main job of a Students' Union is to peddle cheap lager and alcopops, and to my mind this disqualifies it as a 'cultural building', no matter how many gigs it hosts. Even if you do count it, it's surely less cultural a building than it was originally intended to be. But it's its next-door neighbour that seals the deal. It's a Spearmint Rhino strip club. Is *that* considered a cultural industry nowadays? A sign told me that Tuesday night was student night. Times have certainly changed since I was a student.

I'm not really a strip-club kinda guy but with hindsight maybe I should have popped in for five minutes. I'd been exposed to a penis that evening so maybe the world owed me half a tit. Hmm. No. That's not really how it works, is it?

Just a little further up the road and we got to the Rutland Arms, the pub where Ross and I were to play cribbage. It was a traditional old boozer sitting in the crook of the road's U-bend. There weren't many right angles to it.

The walls were decorated with black and white photos of other Sheffield pubs, while a high shelf that circumnavigated the place displayed a large collection of bottles that had once contained a host of peculiar and exotic ales. There was an incongruously sparkly jukebox and a quiz machine, but I'm pleased to say everyone was studiously ignoring them both.

Ross settled into the red plush bench seat while I got the drinks in. When I returned, the cribbage board was on the table and he was shuffling a deck of cards.

'Have you played cribbage before?' he asked.

'No. I've seen people playing it … moving their pegs up and down the board and that, but I've no idea what they're doing.'

'The board is just a way of keeping score.'

'Really?'

'Yeah.'

'So you could play with a deck of cards and a notepad?' I asked. 'You don't need to carry a lump of wood around?'

'Well … yeah, I suppose not.'

'But you wouldn't?'

'No. Probably not.'

Ross set about explaining the rules of the game. It sounded complicated, in large part due to the fact the game has developed a language and etiquette all of its own, and that just makes a beginner feel more excluded. For example, instead of referring to the dealer and the non-dealer, it's the dealer and the pone.[39] But strip the jargon and the formalities away and what's left is a very simple and very playable card game.

By the time Ross and I had played out two or three dummy hands I pretty much had a handle on it and I was enjoying it immensely – that said, I would need to play it a few hundred times before I could start to really appreciate the tactical decisions involved – but the fact that I could make a decent fist of it having only just picked it up says something about the game's DNA.

For a card game to work, it has to get the blend of luck and skill just right. I think cribbage has a pretty good recipe. It's possible for a weaker player to win because of the cards they're dealt but, over time, a stronger player will definitely win far more often than they lose. That means each player is rewarded for his or her efforts. You know when you've played well – or badly – which means the game (and the world) feels fair, but you also know that sometimes there's just nothing you can do.

RULES

Cribbage

The deal:

Each player is dealt six cards. They then discard two cards face down. This means they each have four cards in their hands and four cards have been discarded in total. These four discarded cards form a third hand – the crib. You won't need the crib for a little while, though. I'll tell you when.

The turn up:

The top card of the remaining deck is turned over. If it's a jack the dealer scores two points. Why? I've no idea. It is referred to as 'Two for his heels'.

---

39. Presumably this is an abbreviation of 'opponent'. I might be wrong. But I'm going to use it as such anyway. Just you see if I don't.

Why? I've no idea. Look, this game is 400 years old. The rules have evolved over time. They work. They no longer need reasons. When someone sneezes I say, 'Bless you.' I don't do it because I believe their soul might have been violently ejected from their body and that invoking God's blessing will protect it from being grabbed by the ever-present Satan. That might well be where the custom started, but I do it simply because it's the custom. So, if the top card is a jack, the dealer scores two for his heels.

The play:

This is the start of the game proper. The pone goes first. He lays down a card and declares its value. (An ace counts as one. A picture card counts as ten.) The dealer then lays down a card and declares the cumulative total. So, for example, if the first two cards played were **7♦** and **K♣**, the pone would declare 'seven' as they played their card, after which the dealer would then say 'seventeen' as they played theirs. Play continues in this fashion with the total increasing. So if the third card laid down is **4♠** the pone would then declare 'twenty-one'. And so on.

As you lay down cards you are trying to score points. You score points in several ways.

- If the total reaches **exactly** 15, you score two points.

- If the total reaches **exactly** 31, you score two points.

- If your card pairs the card before it, say: **6♦ 6♣**, you score two points.

- If you follow a pair with a third card of the same value: **6♠**, for example, you score six points. This isn't called 'a triple' or 'trips' or 'threes' or anything sensible like that. Rather ridiculously it's a 'pair royal'. (We've already talked about this sort of thing. Please don't ask me to explain.) By the way, in the unlikely event that the **6♥** followed next, the player laying it down would score twelve points. And 'double pair royal' since you ask. (I know.)

- If the last three cards played form a sequence you score three points. If the last four cards form a sequence, you score four points and so on. The cards don't have to be in order and they don't have to be suited. For example, if the sequence went: **6♥ 8♣ 9♦ 7♠**, the player laying down the **7♠** would score four points because it completes a sequence.

- The total cannot rise above 31. If you can't play a card without taking the total beyond 31 you say 'Go' and your opponent scores one point.

- If the total reaches 31, or someone says 'Go', the play continues, starting from zero.

Spelled out like that it all looks rather complicated, but in reality it's just four things to remember: pairs, runs, 15 and 31. By the way, when you lay your cards down, don't put them in one central pile so that they all get mixed together. Keep the dealer's and the pone's cards separate. You're going to need them during the next phase of play: the show.

The show:

This is the second phase of the game proper. This is basically a second round of point scoring. The pone goes first.

You use the four cards in your hand plus the turn-up (the card first turned over at the beginning) and score as follows:

- Flush: if the four cards in your hand are of the same suit, score four points. If the turn-up card is also of the same suit, score five instead.

- Pairs: score two points for a pair, six for a pair royal and twelve for a double pair royal. (See how quickly you pick these things up ...?)

- Fifteens: score two points for every combination of cards which totals 15. Cards can be used in more than one combination. For example, if you had **K♣ 5♦ 5♥** your king would count with both fives, giving you four points total.

- Runs: a sequence of three, four or five cards scores three, four or five points respectively.

- Finally, if you have the jack that matches the suit of the turn-up card, you score one point, not for his heels but for his knob.

('I've already given someone a point for his knob tonight,' I said when Ross explained this seemingly arbitrary rule to me.

'What?' he asked.

'Oh ... nothing.')

Again, it seems far more complicated written down than it does when put into action. When you have the actual cards in front of you and can move them around the table to visually represent each scoring combination it soon becomes a speedy process.

Once the pone has scored his hand, the dealer does the same for his hand **but** then the dealer scores **again** using the hand you both contributed to when you discarded two cards at the start of the game: the crib. You can see now that when it comes to discarding those cards the dealer and the pone have very different incentives.

Winning:

You continue to play games, alternating the deal and totting up the points as you go. The winner is the first person to score 121 points or higher.

The cribbage board:

As I've already noted, you could easily score the game with a pen and paper, but that would involve doing lots of complicated sums, and who wants to spend their evening adding 8 to 75? That's where a cribbage board comes in handy.

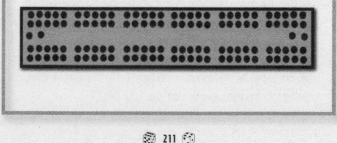

I really did feel a bit stupid for not already knowing what a cribbage board actually was. I'd always assumed it was a fundamental part of the game, that it was the field of play. I always thought people were moving their pegs around the board tactically, perhaps akin to the way people move their counters in backgammon. But as Ross explained it to me – and as I'm sure you already know – all it really is, is a scoreboard.

Each player uses their own half of the board, which consists of two rows of thirty holes. That's sixty holes in total. Start at one end. Move a peg up for every point you score. When you get to end of lane one, return in lane two. Complete one circuit and then go round again. Up one lane, down the other, up one lane and down the other. That takes you to 120 points. One more point and you win. Simple.

One of the reasons I think I'd always assumed it was more complicated is that each player actually has two pegs. But this turns out to be a stroke of genius. The pegs leapfrog each other because you always leave one peg where it was – to show where you were – and you then advance the other peg the right number of places beyond it. That way nobody can ever lose their place.

This two-peg system is such a brilliant idea I'm surprised it isn't commonplace in other games. You know that argument you had playing Monopoly as a kid because your older brother Richard rolled 11 and moved his piece really quickly to land on Free Parking, when you were pretty sure he was meant to land on Vine Street which you owned and had a hotel on? You remember? He insisted he was right but when you counted it back you knew you were right because you knew full well that he'd started on Euston Road but he just lied and told you he'd been on Pentonville Road, actually, and there was no way of proving it either way because the token had been moved and anyway he was bigger than you and would have punched you if you'd gone on about it even if it did mean the whole game was ruined now and it was never as good when your dad wasn't there to make sure everyone played fair? You remember? To think that he's a policeman now! I know! If they only knew what he used to do back then!

Anyway ... none of that would have happened if the cribbage board two-peg system had been employed. His first token would have stayed on Euston Road, his second token would have advanced eleven spaces beyond it – landing on Vine Street – and there would have been no doubt in anyone's mind as to where he was meant to be. You'd collect your grand in rent, nobody would end up getting punched, and thirty years later that sense of injustice you've been harbouring all these years wouldn't be spilling out in the pages of a book. Now, you're not seriously telling me that wouldn't be a better system? Come on, game manufacturers! Start using the two counters! Think of the children!

Cribbage turned out to be a brilliant pub game. It occupies enough of the brain to engage you, without using up so much brain space that it crowds out the conversation.

In Lewes, I'd given Ben my theory as to how the playing of games would lead me to a better quality of pub, and this was a perfect example. This was a pub where two men could play dominoes. This was a pub where a head-butt was unlikely. I liked the Rutland Arms.

'I thought you were going to be older,' I said. I hadn't felt able to say it when we first met. It wasn't meant rudely, but you never know how things will be taken.

'What made you think that?'

'I guess I associate cribbage with the older generation,' I confessed. 'But I hadn't really thought it through. I was forgetting the Sheffield factor.'

'How do you mean?'

'I've a theory about Sheffield,' I said. Pubs tend to bring the theories out of me. 'Sheffield is an old-man city. Everyone I've ever known from Sheffield has been an old man ... or an old man waiting to happen.'

'Huh?'

'I've got a few friends from Sheffield,' I said. 'Even when they were eighteen they had middle-aged sensibilities. Crosswords. Cardigans. Walking. Fresh air. They're all people who wouldn't look odd if they were smoking a pipe. Jarvis Cocker's from Sheffield. You put a pipe in Noel Gallagher's gob and he'd look like he was taking the piss. You give Damon Albarn a pipe and he looks like he's taking himself too seriously. You give Jarvis Cocker a pipe and he looks like he smokes a pipe. That's Sheffield for you.'

'Ah, but I'm not from Sheffield,' countered Ross.

'So that means you *chose* to move here,' I said. 'You were attracted here because you're an old man waiting to happen. Sheffield breeds them and it attracts them.' I drained my glass. 'Do you want another drink?'

'Yeah, go on.'

'What is it again?'

'Pale ale.'

'I rest my case.'

At the bar I surveyed the room. Two goths were drinking in romantic goth silence in one corner, and five or six men were having a gently heated conversation in the other corner. I tuned into it partway through.

' … Well, you say that,' said one, 'but there's a reason. That's not a public right of way, that bridge.'

'Well, actually,' declared another, 'it's not *technically* a bridge.'

'What d'y'mean?'

'Well …'

The speaker went on to back up his not-a-bridge declaration with a lengthy discourse. His friends protested.

'But it is a bridge,' they said. 'It's a road that goes up and over the railway line … of course it's a bloody bridge!'

He was having none it. He quoted by-laws A and B and historical precedents X and Y, and eventually the rest of the group conceded that the bridge wasn't – at least from the local council's legal perspective – a bridge.

'Okay,' said one of the group. 'I accept that the bridge isn't a bridge. But what makes you think it's not a public right of way?'

'Well …'

It started all over again.

It was a fantastically arcane conversation. I like hearing people *choose* their words and enjoy their language. It was an old-man conversation. But not one of them was over thirty-five.

Back at the table, I resumed our conversation: 'So, if you're not from Sheffield' – I plonked a pale ale on the table – 'where are you from? Your accent's South West-ish. Bristol way?'

'Devon, actually. Barnstaple.'

'And what brought you up here?'

'Work. I studied in Cardiff. When I graduated, I applied for jobs there as well as London, Birmingham and here. This is the one that came up.'

'What d'you do?'

'Cancer research.'

'The charity?'

'No. The research.'

For some reason I heard myself saying an incredulous, '*Really?*' I've no idea why. It didn't need any clarification. Why would he make up a job? It's not like he was on the pull. I imagine there were men inventing jobs for themselves at Spearmint Rhino but even they wouldn't opt for cancer research, would they? Airline pilot? Footballer? Record producer? Not cancer research. I felt foolish for sounding doubtful. He didn't seem to mind.

'Yeah,' he said.

'And how have you found Sheffield?' I asked.

'I love it. It might sound a bit sad,' he said, 'but there's a website, a Sheffield forum, and I got involved in that. There's some mad local politics and stuff that I ignore, but there's a walkers' group and ...'

'Y'see?' I said. 'Walking.'

' ... and I've got involved in community radio, too.'

'None of that sounds sad,' I said. 'Sounds like fun to me.'

'It is,' he nodded enthusiastically. 'You wouldn't do community radio if it wasn't fun.' He supped his ale. 'I used to do a science show. That started off as fun but then the guy I was working with just started taking over. He'd say, "Can you just record a link saying, 'Hmmm, that's very interesting,' and I'll edit it in later?" and I was like, "Well, no, I can't really, because I don't know what it is you're going to be saying." But he didn't seem too bothered about anything like that. So a mate and I looked at it and just thought we'd do a breakfast show instead. We picked Fridays because you can tell people what's coming up on the weekend and that. It's great fun.' He sipped his pint. 'So ... what about you?' he asked. 'What brings you to Sheffield?'

'What? Tonight?'

'Yeah. You can't have come just to play cribbage.'

'I sort of have,' I said. 'But it's more that I wanted to go *somewhere* and do *something*. And being here and playing cribbage seems as good a suggestion as any.' Ross didn't seem convinced so I added, 'I'm thinking of it as a holiday.'

'I don't think many people come to Sheffield for a holiday.'

'They should,' I said. 'It's nice. One of the reasons I chose to come here and play cribbage with you instead of, say, Twister in Leeds, is that I found a really good place to stay here.'

'Go on ...?'

'I'm staying on a narrow boat.'

'Really? In Sheffield?'

'Yeah. I've always wanted to do a boating holiday. I'd love to spend a couple of weeks pootling up the canal. Lovely.'

'That,' said Ross, 'is because *you* are an old man, too.'

The truth was out. 'I know. That's why I like coming to Sheffield. I'm going to sit on my boat tomorrow morning, have my breakfast, feed the ducks and do my crossword. Heavenly. It might not be two weeks. There won't be any pootling. But it'll do for now. It's a bite-sized holiday.'

'Where's the next bite?'

'I'm spending tomorrow in Nottingham.'

'Playing?'

'Cluedo and "sock golf".'

'What the hell is sock golf?'

'Your guess is as good as mine,' I said. 'Ask me tomorrow night and I might be able to tell you.'

Ross and I walked back the way we'd come and parted company where we'd met, at the station. Passing through the station and out the other side to where a tramline zipped past, I traced round the foot of Park Hill and began my walk to the Houseboat Hotel.

A footpath runs alongside the tramline that runs above and beside the railway, which runs parallel to the road that in turn travels over the River Sheaf, which flows largely unseen, sheathed in concrete, beneath the city that took its name. That's five channels running in concert with one another. There's no standing still here: the world wants you to move and it's already decided what direction you should be heading. North if you like. South if you must. Nothing else will do.

I was heading north. I'd printed off the directions but they were so simple I didn't bother getting the piece of paper out of my backpack. I just followed the path of the tram to the point where the line split and then ignored it, holding my own course, taking a footbridge (it definitely *was* a footbridge) over the main road and into Victoria Quay.

Sitting at the end of the Sheffield and Tinsley canal, the quay opened in the early part of the nineteenth century, when most freight travelled by canal. Victoria Quay meant narrow boats could reach the heart of the city for the very first time: it is close to the city centre, yet so calm, peaceful and serene. It was almost impossible to imagine it as the noisy, industrial hub it must once have been. There's an old block and tackle still in place, and an old crane that must have seen it all; but they're not giving up their secrets. Typical Victorians. Stiff upper lip and all that. There's also an old grain warehouse at the city end of the quay and another, the straddle warehouse – doing what its name suggests – partway along.

In the still water, their reflections were sharp: it was only because I knew where my feet were that I could tell what was real and what was illusion. There were cobbles underfoot and a small flotilla of narrow boats on my right. The only sound was the oh-so-gentle lapping of water against craft. Or at least it would have been the only sound if a couple's conversation hadn't carried quite so clearly through the still of the night. They both had broad Yorkshire accents. They weren't shouting. In fact, they spoke in urgent whispers, but the hollow quay amplified it all.

'I'm just saying it might be a bit of fun, that's all,' said he, with a petulant tremor.

'Oh … just piss off, Stan,' said she, witheringly.

Across the water I could see two little orange lights glowing as they inhaled on their cigarettes. As my eyes tuned into the darkness, their silhouettes became clear. They were sitting side by side, arses on the cold stone ground, staring out at the water.

'You don't have to take it so serious,' he continued. 'She's up for it and I thought you would be, too. For a laugh!'

'For the last time,' she said – although I very much doubted it would be the last time – 'I am not having a bloody threesome!'

Ouch.

'All right, all right, I get it,' he hissed. 'I just thought …'

'*Listen*, will yer? I'm *not* having a threesome!'

(I told you.)

I wanted to let them know that their conversation was being broadcast but it seemed a little late now. The conversation – like their love life – had no room for a third participant. (Maybe he'd have had more luck if he'd asked her to take part in a pair royal. It sounds much less grubby than a threesome.)

I found my boat: *Mallard*. A forty-three-foot-long narrow boat with a glossy red paint job. I hoped the brusque sound of me unzipping the tarpaulin porch – an impersonal, metallic, *zhush* – would carry as clearly to their ears as their words were carrying to mine.

There was no check-in desk at the Houseboat Hotel. No one to see; no key to collect. I already had the combination for the lock. That was all I needed. Once inside, *Mallard* would be mine, all mine.

I pulled the wooden doors apart and found a light switch. And there she was. As snug as you like. A small kitchen that opened onto an even smaller lounge and, beyond that, a door to the bedroom. Actually, the word 'bedroom' is a bit of a misnomer. It was really just a bed. I shut the doors behind me, sealing me in my wooden cocoon, and shutting out the *ménage-à-troisgument*.

I filled the kettle and lit the gas hob. I waited for the whistle to sound. I nosed around, pointlessly enjoying the dolls' house furniture, playing with every cleverly hinged bit I could find. If it was possible for a piece of furniture to fold out of sight when not in use then it did so. More often than not, it

looked like something Wallace and Gromit had come up with.
I bloody loved my floating caravan. I loved it even more when
I had a cup of tea in my hand. I really did feel like I was on
holiday. It was the perfect hotel room: my ideal crib.

CHAPTER 19

I slept well. It was the kind of deep sleep that holds on to you even after you wake. It took me a few moments to work out where I was. And why the world was moving. Only gently. But moving. Slowly the grogginess ebbed away and I realised I was afloat in Sheffield. All the excitement I'd had on arriving at the boat the night before returned.

While waiting for the kettle to boil again, I unlatched a set of doors positioned halfway along the side of the boat. There were hinges on the corresponding bit of roof too, so once I'd swung the doors open I lifted the lid and let the early morning sun warm my face.

In the dark of the night before, I hadn't appreciated how low in the water the boat was sitting, but as I stood in the open doorway, looking out over the quay, it felt as though I was below the water line from the waist down. I'd probably slept below water.

I lit the grill and put a couple of slices of bread in the pan. With fresh tea, fresh toast and a day-old crossword – I'd saved it specially – my idyll was almost complete. All it needed was some ducks. Sadly, there were none to be seen. Spoilsports. There was just one big *Mallard* and I was in it.

So I fed the carp instead, which I thought was even better because from a distance, it would have looked like I was feeding invisible ducks. The water was murky, and it was only when I was standing directly over them that I could see the fish. A gang of five or so carp – a couple of them getting on for three feet long – competing with each other to grab the bits of bread

I tossed their way, swooping aggressively with a *plip* and a *plap* and an occasional *pliplop*!

It was an idyllic moment in the heart of an industrial city, and it beat any hotel breakfast I'd had in a good long while. I took a photo of the view from my fish-feeding hatch and posted it on Twitter with an accompanying message:[40] 'Stayed in a houseboat last night. Really cosy. View from the window this morning.' (Oh, yeah – *that's* the kind of sizzling informa-tion I share on Twitter.)

I showered (alarmingly compact, surprisingly hot, oh look, there's the toilet!) and then went on my way, retracing my steps to the station to catch the train to Nottingham. A care-free, car-free, ten-minute walk.

Every time I've been to Nottingham – and I've been going off and on for twenty years – someone tells me the following fact: Nottingham has more women than men. As facts go, it's lacking just one thing: truth. What's more, it's normally accompanied by some figures to make it sound more *facty*. Some people will tell you it's a 60–40 split while others claim it's a truly ludicrous three-women-to-every-man scenario. It obviously isn't true: you'd soon notice if there really were three times as many women as men. It's one of those things that seems to have become accepted as 'fact' simply by being repeated often enough. Y'know, like carrots help you see in the dark (they don't), goldfish have a three-second memory span (they don't), and there's nothing quite like a McDon-alds (there is). If anything, this spurious gender-fact has always led me to expect the exact opposite: I've heard it repeated so often and with such conviction that I expect instead to find huge hordes of men wandering forlornly around Nottingham's streets, all wondering where on earth

---

40. http://yfrog.com/j9kh1qj

the women have got to. Of course, in reality, the balance appears to be roughly 50–50. (Mind you, it's been some time since I experienced Nottingham on a Friday night.)

As the train trundled to Nottingham, I killed some time by looking through the incoming Twitter messages on my phone. A couple of handfuls of people had commented on my photo of the quay … and every one of them seemed to be taking a guess as to where it might have been taken. I hadn't meant it to be a 'Where am I?' quiz question.

'Are you in Birmingham? They have more canals than Venice,' read one. 'I recognise that. Are you in Manchester?' asked another.

Of course there were right answers, too: 'Victoria Quay, Sheffield – do I win a prize?' Answer: yes and then no.

And there were also a couple of tweets from people who remembered my would-you-like-a-game? tweet from a few weeks earlier: 'Looks like you're in Sheffield. Do you fancy that game of dominoes?' tweeted Ian. 'We work just up the road from there. Darts?' tweeted Martin.

Hmm. It would be nice to stay another day in Sheffield and get the full old-man trifecta of cribbage, dominoes and darts! Perfect. Just thinking about it made me feel like I was wearing corduroy. (I like getting older. I like wallowing in such easy pleasures.) I decided to do something about their suggestions.

The line of taxis – black cabs, although not black, green – stretched for as far as the eye could see on Station Street. On the other side of the road, a community art project was breathing life into some of the old Victorian buildings. What was once a railway hotel had become studio space, what was once a hardware store was now a gallery and tea bar. They were decorated with street art, and the station – a big baroque, terracotta structure – seemed to tut disapprovingly at it all like a disappointed parent saying, '*You know you don't need all that make-up, darling; you've got such a lovely face!'* while the beat-nik buildings scowled back as if to say, *'Look, at least I'm doing something with my life! Why don't you have a go at my brother? Yeah, he calls himself a "hotel" but look at him ... he's just a tacky pub that's gone to seed!'* The tacky pub that's gone to seed remains silent, its soul crushed long ago.

A fifteen-minute bus ride took me to the right part of town, St Ann's, which quickly felt like the wrong part of town when a bunch of kids hanging around outside the local shop greeted me with loud hollers of, 'Oi! Twat wiv a bag!'

I'm pretty sure it was aimed at me. I was still fifty yards away from them but there was no one else on the street that it could have been directed at, and I *did* have a bag on my shoulder. (I am also a bit of a twat, but there's no way they could have known that.)

It's always tricky working out how to handle confronta-tional kids. They were occupying as much of the pavement as they could, so I knew that in thirty seconds' time I'd be nego-tiating my way around them. Should I acknowledge the greet-ing? Whichever course of action I chose I already had a pretty good idea as to how the script would play out:

Option 1:
```
YOUTH: Oi! Twat wiv a bag!
ME:    What?
YOUTH: Ha ha ha ha … he answered! He knows
       he's a twat! Ha ha ha!
```

Or:

Option 2:
```
YOUTH: Oi! Twat wiv a bag!
ME:    (SILENCE)
YOUTH: You ignorin' me? You gotta problem?
```

Whatever you put the behaviour down to – maybe they're testing boundaries, exploring how far they can push things; maybe they're just showing off – what it amounts to is creating a confrontation they know they'll win. And of course they'll win – you can't lose if you're the only ones competing.

I decided to plump for option 2 on the simple grounds that it delayed my involvement by a few seconds.

My guess wasn't far off the mark.

'Oi! I was talking to you!' one of the lads said accusingly as I drew nearer.

His friends: one leaning with his back to the shop wall, one draped across the handlebars of a BMX bike and two others posturing behind his shoulders, had arranged themselves to be as obstructive as possible.

'I'm sorry,' I said, 'I didn't realise. Do you mind if I come through …'

I walked on. They rotated their shoulders and let me pass. Two paces on I heard him say, 'Oi, mate. There's somethin' fallin' out o' ya bag!'

I looked, pulling it round in front of me to check. Nothing was falling out. But that didn't matter. That was the moment they declared victory.

'Ha ha ha ha ha!' they screeched. 'He fuckin' looked. What a twat! *What a twat!*'

Yep, they had got me all right! I had indeed looked at my bag. I'm not sure I'll ever live it down. Tricked again! I'm *so* gullible. Honestly, once, someone rang my doorbell and when I opened the door there was *nobody* there! What a klutz! A winner wouldn't have done that. A winner would have stayed on the couch and left the door unanswered, wouldn't he …? Grrr! Why do I always fall for these things? I'll never learn, me.

I strode on up the road confident in the knowledge that

unlike them I wasn't wasting my life. Oh no. I was on my way to play Cluedo.

Oh.

'Nice place you've got here,' I said with an appreciative nod.

It's one of those things you say to fill an awkward silence, isn't it? Don't get me wrong, it's not that it *wasn't* a nice place – it was – but it wasn't so nice that it had to be pointed out. And it wasn't that things were especially awkward, either. It was just that run-of-the-mill, level-3 awkwardness you'd expect under the circumstances.

Level-1 awkwardness, as I'm sure you're aware, is what occurs when two Englishmen meet for the first time in a public place. Level-2 awkwardness is what happens if the meeting occurs in one of their homes. It ramps things up a little bit because the visitor knows their behaviour doesn't just have to conform to society's norms; they have to divine the particular house rules, too. Are they shoes-off or shoes-on people? Are there coasters and is their use strictly adhered to? You know the sort of thing. Level-3 awkwardness is what happens if the meeting takes place in the home of one of their parents. It doesn't matter how long the visitor has been an adult; they automatically snap into parent-friendly, not-just-a-guest-but-a-guest-of-a-guest mode.

Graham, my Cluedo pone,[41] lived in Worcester, but his initial tweet and subsequent emails had only ever suggested we play in Nottingham at his mother's house, so Level-3 on the awkwardometer it was. Which was nothing to worry about, obviously. You have to get to Level-14 (which involves unilateral nudity) before it's truly worrisome. With Level-3 you just have to sprinkle in a few platitudes to tide you over.

---

41. I told you I would.

A 'How was your journey?' here, and a 'Nice place you've got here!' there.

'It's a nice place,' shrugged Graham, 'in a rough area.'

'Really?' I tried to sound surprised. I pretended my own welcome to the area hadn't been tinged with youthful intimidation.

'St Ann's,' said Graham wryly, 'is the gun-crime capital of Nottingham.'

'Well, I suppose Cluedo's quite appropriate then.'

As soon as I'd said it, I winced at my own glibness. It had sounded fine in my head but out loud it sounded a bit insensitive. In truth, I think it's the phrase 'gun-crime capital' I'm insensitive to. It's a phrase that was often applied to Manchester during the time I lived there and it always felt more like tabloid scare-mongering than any kind of perceptible truth. But Graham wasn't a journalist trying to scare me off St Ann's … he was a young man whose mum lived there.[42]

Luckily he didn't seem offended. He just smiled and said, 'Yeah … I suppose it is. Although I had a bit of trouble getting it.'

'What do you mean?'

'Cluedo. I thought my old version of it was still here,' he said. 'But we couldn't find it …' – he raised his voice – '… could we, Mum?'

'No, we couldn't,' came the voice of his mother, Margaret. She was in the kitchen preparing lunch. 'It'll probably be here somewhere.'

'So I bought a new one,' Graham continued. 'But the thing is,' his face dropped, 'they've changed it.'

'They've changed it?'

---

42. Two weeks after I was there, a gun was fired outside the shop where the kids had taunted me for a) having a bag and b) looking at it. A few days later, a man was arrested on a charge of attempted murder.

'Yeah.'

'How d'you mean?'

'I mean, it's different.' Disappointment dripped from every syllable. 'It's ...' he paused, as if anxiously searching for the exact word, ' ... *worse*.'

'Worse?'

He curled his lip. 'It's all *modern*.'

'*No!*'

My shock was genuine. I have a soft spot for Cluedo. When I did my first one-man show at the Edinburgh Fringe, I performed in a venue called the Attic. (It seated forty thin people or thirty fat ones.) The show had no theme but convention dictated that it needed a title so I called it, '*Dave Gorman: In The Attic With The Microphone*' in homage to Cluedo's familiar 'Colonel-Mustard-in-the-library-with-the-candlestick'-style grammar. The poster even parodied the classic Cluedo card. The cards of old used to be black with two white, round-edged stripes at either end. They had a picture of one of the playing pieces – brightly coloured, long-necked plastic pedestals – only instead of the small plastic bobble on top there was a face painted in the style of a 1940s movie poster. My 1995 stand-up poster looked exactly like that, only the face – rosy cheeked and youthful – was my own.

The game was invented in the 1940s by a prat. Sorry. No. The game was invented in the 1940s by A. Pratt. Yep. That's better. Anthony E. Pratt to be precise. Anthony Ernest Pratt to be even preciser. Pratt, a Brummie, was inspired by his friend and neighbour, Geoffrey Bull, who had already devised a successful game by the name of Buccaneer. Buccaneer – a game of adventure on the high seas – was manufactured from 1938 right through to the mid 80s and was recently given a new lease of life when a *Pirates of the Caribbean* version was released to tie in with the Disney blockbuster.

I love the idea that two such enduring games were invented by next-door neighbours from Kings Heath, Birmingham. Given the numbers that have been sold, I'll bet somewhere in the world there is a cupboard where the two games are stacked one on top of the other, maintaining the neighbourly bond.

'Here, have a look at this,' said Graham, placing his modern Cluedo board on the table.

The old board depicts a very basic floor plan for the Tudor mansion in which the mystery is set. It's an architect's drawing, no more and no less. In the new version, however, the board tries to create the impression that you're looking in on a real house. The remains of dinner can be seen on the stylish dining-room table, and there's a flat-screen TV on the living-room wall. It's no longer a Tudor mansion in Edwardian England … it's some ghastly, *nouveau riche* home that wouldn't look remotely out of place on MTV's rich-people-showing-off extravaganza, *Cribs*. There's no longer a stuffy billiard room – it's become a modern, whiz-bang, twenty-seat movie theatre. Where there was once a conservatory there's now a spa with a hot tub and a massage table, and what was once a ballroom is now a patio with dark-stained wood decking, sun loungers and potted ferns. (I'm not sure, however, that the designers have seen the bling-tastic revamp through, properly, in every room. The kitchen is a particular let-down: there's no dishwasher and the basic two-slice toaster would never do given the number of houseguests.)

There are more weapons in the new version, too. Candle-stick, dagger, revolver, rope, lead pipe and spanner: that's the classic list. The first four of them have survived in the new format, but there's also an axe, a baseball bat, a dumbbell, some poison and a trophy. This last fully confirms that the game is now set in the glamorous world of celebrity. It's not an old-fashioned cup. It's a shiny, shooting star. It doesn't look like the kind of trophy the Dog and Duck Sunday League football team might win. It looks like the kind of trophy they hand out at slightly tacky showbiz dos, the ones that celebrate those niche parts of the industry that have traditionally been looked down upon. My guess is that it's the award for 'Best Actress In A Daytime Soap As Voted For By The Readers Of *Bella*' or similar.

You might be wondering what Colonel Mustard and Professor Plum are doing in this swanky pad. Hip showbiz types don't invite old duffers like that round for dinner, do they? No, they don't. 'Jack' Mustard is an ex-footballer turned TV pundit and 'Victor' Plum is a self-made, computer-game-designer billionaire.

But that's got to be a mistake, hasn't it? If you're modernising a board game to make it more appealing to kids, surely the last thing you want to do is mention computer games. Aren't computer games the opposition? Having one of your characters remind kids that they could also be playing a computer game is like having a character in *EastEnders* tell you that *Coronation Street* is on the other side.

'This is ... ghastly!' I said, slack-jawed at the sight of it. 'What have they done?'

'I know,' said Graham, nodding his agreement. 'When I got it out of the box for the first time I knew immediately it was all wrong. I thought I'd let you down ...'

'Well, you didn't need to buy one on my account, anyway!'

'I've bought two.'

'What?'

'I found an old one in a charity shop.'

'Fantastic. Well done.'

'Only it's incomplete.'

'Ah.'

'Some of the cards are missing. But I think we can make a hybrid version. We'll have to use the new board because we haven't got a full set of cards for the rooms otherwise. But we can use the old playing pieces, and um … well, just those, really.'

'Sounds like a plan.'

'You'll have to clear the table first,' said Margaret, suddenly entering with two plates in her hands. 'These are hot … make some room.'

Salmon, boiled potatoes, carrots and peas. Lovely.

It wasn't hard to work out where Margaret's passion lay. Crochet. Half of one wall was taken up by a bookcase that was stuffed to the gills with books, each and every one of them devoted to needlework in general or, more often, crochet in particular. The rest of the wall was given over to a large cabinet with clear plastic square drawers full to overflowing with balls of wool. Wherever I looked there were hooks and needles, threads and yarns.

'You like your crochet, then,' I said.

'Oh, yes,' said Margaret between mouthfuls of lunch. 'I teach. If you're interested.'

'Not really my style,' I smiled. 'So how come you're in Nottingham?' I asked. Their accents were distinctly London. 'Did crochet bring you?'

'No … I moved for work,' said Margaret.

'She moved to work in a homeless shelter,' added Graham. 'It was a live-in job. But then they got rid of the job, ironically making another person homeless.' His tone was sarcastic. If the modern Cluedo axe had been within reach I'm pretty sure he'd have been grinding it.

'Except it didn't,' said Margaret. 'I'd already bought this place.'

'What about you, Graham,' I asked. 'Why Worcester?'

'He drives trains, don't you, Graham?'

'Yeah. I'm a train driver. Well … technically what I drive isn't *actually* a train. A train is an engine and ten carriages. I drive a single unit.'

'If you drive it up to Sheffield one day, you can drive your
not-technically-a-train under a not-technically-a-bridge,' I said.

'Huh?'

'Oh … it doesn't matter. Just something I overheard last
night.'

It was a good hearty lunch. For pudding we solved the
murder of Dr Black. Three cards – one suspect, one weapon
and one room – were put, sight unseen, in the black envelope
that was then placed in the centre of the board. In the old
game it would have been the cellar; on the new board this
space was the pool. It looked nice enough. (But I'd seen a
nicer one in Windsor recently.)

We divvied the other cards up between us, took our pieces
– I was Reverend Green, Margaret was Mrs White, and Graham
a surprisingly chunky Miss Scarlet – and began playing.

If you've not played the game before, the idea is to move
around the mansion by rolling a couple of dice. When you get
to a room you're then able to suggest a suspect and weapon
combo to go with that room. So, on moving my piece into
the hall, say, I might suggest that the murder was committed
there by Mrs Peacock using the revolver. My opponents would
then get the opportunity to prove my suggestion wrong. For
example, one of them might show me (and *only* me) that they
hold the Mrs Peacock card. I now know that the Mrs Peacock
card can't be in the envelope and so I can eliminate her from
my enquiries. Slowly, you whittle down the options – with six
suspects, six weapons and nine rooms, there are 324 unique
combinations – until you are able to make an accusation. You
name the murderer, the room and the weapon, have a look in
the envelope and if you've got them all right, you're the
winner. If you've got one or more wrong you put them back
in the envelope and the game continues – only with you no
longer allowed to make any more suggestions or accusations.

It's a simple game in which you try to give away only as much information as you really have to, while acquiring as much as you can. For some reason, it always used to say on the box that it was a game for two to six players. It's not. It's utterly ridiculous with only two players as you just end up sharing the same pool of information and both working it out at exactly the same time.

I got lucky, discovering that I, Reverend Green, was the killer with my first suggestion. So much for the sixth commandment, Reverend! Forty minutes later and I knew it was the axe but I couldn't be sure of the room. It was either the patio or the observatory. My guess was that Graham was holding on to the patio card himself. To test that theory I'd have to reach the patio ... but that would take me four or five goes and I was sure one of the others would be making their guess soon. So I went for it. I backed my hunch.

'I'm going to make an accusation,' I said. 'It was Reverend Green, in the observatory with the axe.'

'Ack,' said Graham, under his breath. 'I was going to do that next go.'

'I know you were.'

I reached for the envelope and pulled out the three cards. Right, right and right. Handshakes all round.

'That was fun,' I said.

'Yeah,' my pones concurred.

The truth – I think we all knew it – was that it's not really that good a game. Not for adults. It's not as childish as Guess Who? ... but this Guess Whodunnit comes close. Graham hadn't suggested it because he plays the game. He'd suggested it because he remembered it fondly. And so do I. But I think it belongs in the childhood memories file and not the present day.

'So, what else have you got planned?' asked Margaret.

'Well, I'm playing sock golf this evening,' I said. 'And before you ask, I have no idea what that means.'

'I guess it's a bit like golf,' said Graham.

'Only played with socks,' added Margaret.

They'd been playing Cluedo. Their deductive powers were finely honed.

CHAPTER 20

The sign was encouraging: 'Sir Charles Napier. Pub Games.'
The picture showed a draughts board, some dominoes, bowls,
a pool cue and a dartboard.

I was forty minutes early for my sock golf appointment and
the Sir Charles Napier seemed like the perfect place to while
away the necessary time. One drink, a few darts, and I'd be set.
I wandered inside. It was quiet. There was nobody behind the
bar. A middle-aged woman sat at a table near the window with
a glass of orange juice. She was doing a crossword. The kind
of crossword that takes up a whole page of a woman's magazine and has a photo of a celebrity in the middle of it.

Nicholas Lyndhurst, since you ask.

To my right was a little room where they were exhibiting
some not-very-exciting modern art. A series of square
canvasses hung on the walls. Most of them just big bold stripes
of two colours. Purple and blue. Red and orange. Above the
fireplace it was white and cream. Hmm. The games area must
be round the other side of the bar … I walked round and there
was a pool table but no, no sign of a dartboard.

Maybe the sign outside was out of date? I turned to leave.
I was halfway out of the door when I heard a voice.

'Can I help you?'

It was the crosswording woman. Either that or a magical
Nicholas Lyndhurst. My left leg was still in the pub. I leaned
back so that my head was, too.

'Sorry, I was just looking for a dartboard but you don't …'

'Why didn't you say?'

She put the magazine down, stood slowly and walked through to the room where the modern art was hanging. Without saying a word she approached the cream and white painting above the fireplace, reached up and picked the canvas off the wall to reveal a dartboard underneath.

Wow. A real water-into-wine magic trick. I felt like giving her a round of applause. I didn't though. I just ordered a rum and coke. And then made a phone call: 'Hi Kathryn ... it's Dave ... I stayed on one of your houseboats yesterday. *Mallard*. Yep ... well, I was ... no ... no ... I haven't forgotten anything. No, I was just wondering if you had a vacancy for tomorrow? Uh huh. Yeah. Ack ... you don't? Oh. No, it does-n't have to be *Mallard*. If one of the others is free then ... you do? Fantastic! Excellent! That's great! Thanks. Bye.'

And then I tweeted a man about some dominoes. And another about some darts. I was a man of leisure. Why not turn my two-day jaunt into a three-dayer? Why not go back to old-man Sheff for another day? Isn't doing what you want the point of being on holiday? There was still Simon and sock golf tonight ... but there'd be old-man Sheff tomorrow.

Simon lived in a three-storey townhouse. Which is another way of saying he lived in a two-storey house that's been built on top of the garage.

I was approaching his front door but on hearing the murmur of voices and the clink of bottles I jinked round the side of the house instead. The up-and-over garage door was up and over. There was no car at home. Instead, the garage was the hub of a small, seven- or eight-person party.

'You made it! Well done,' said someone. He wore a stripy T-shirt and combat shorts. 'I'm Simon. D'you want a beer?'

A bottle was thrust into my hand before I had the chance to say yes or no. So I said, 'Yes.'

I was introduced to everyone but it was a blizzard of names and it was impossible to hold on to them all. As the evening progressed, I tried to tune in to the conversations unfolding around me hoping I could pick the names up as I went along.

'Right,' Simon said eventually, clapping his hands together and getting our attention. 'Let's get down to the real business. Sock golf. Follow me.'

I traipsed upstairs, following the crowd, turning at the top of the stairs onto the landing and then into the living room. The cream walls were bare. The wooden floor home to piles of magazines. There was a big TV and several games consoles. It was a bachelor pad.

'This is the first tee,' explained our host. He pointed to a small piece of paper on the window ledge. It had '1st tee' written on it in felt-tip pen. There could be no doubt as to what it was.

'The first hole,' he continued, 'is the sun visor over there.'

He pointed towards the window at the far end of the room where a stocky guy with a stubbly beard – Gerard – was adopting a magician's assistant stance to indicate the precise whereabouts of the sun visor. There was a heavy cardboard box on the window ledge. The visor was wedged under it peak first, so that the headband was suspended in mid-air like an improvised hoop for basketball practice.

'Now, we've got a load of socks here,' said Simon and indeed, a whole pile of rolled-up socks were on the couch to his right. 'I'll just demonstrate the correct technique. You do not – I repeat – do not *throw* the sock. That wouldn't be golf at all. You bat it … like so …'

He picked up a pair of rolled-up socks and held them loosely in his left hand. He then swung his right arm so that his palm made contact with the sock, batting it across the room. It landed on the floor at Gerard's feet. Maybe they were homing socks.

'There're pens and paper down here,' he explained, 'so you can all keep your own score as you go round. Everyone got it?'

We had. But we didn't announce it loudly enough for Simon's liking.

'I said has everyone got it?' he asked again, the cajoling Redcoat determined that we should have fun.

'Yeah!' I roared, doing my bit to play along. I wasn't the only one.

'Right … seeing as I'm already on the tee I'll go first.'

He batted another pair of socks across the room. They landed in almost exactly the same place as before.

'Right,' he said, standing aside. 'Choose your weapons.'

We dived in, picking up the various socks, weighing them up, getting used to the feel of them in our hands, rejecting some and selecting others. I opted for a weighty pair of rolled-up football socks. They felt firm yet spongy and had a little bit of heft to them. I thought I'd have more control with them than the weightless, thin, grey cotton pair I'd first assessed.

Yes. I was taking it that seriously.

Almost everyone managed the first hole in two strokes although one player – a man wearing a retro T-shirt to match his retro moustache – came remarkably close to a hole in one. His sock hit the edge of the sun visor and pinged upwards. The room gasped and held its breath while we watched the sockball spinning, waiting to see which side of the hoop it would fall. It didn't pass through the hole but we were all suitably impressed nonetheless.

'Aaggh! Unlucky, John!' said one of the crowd and I made a mental note of another name.

John's little display of virtuosity seemed to change the mood slightly. It focused the mind and made a stupid game feel more respectable. We might only have been batting old socks round a house, but now we knew the game was capable of producing moments of beauty and that meant we knew it was worth putting the effort in.

Hmm. How many beers had I had?

Simon had certainly taken the game seriously when he laid out the course. A full eighteen holes ranged around the house, each one starting from where the last one had concluded. Hole two ended in the fireplace – you had to get your socks inside the grate – while hole three was an awkward dog leg that turned the corner as you left the living room, travelled down the landing and into the bathroom, holing out by landing the socks in the basin. I don't think there was a room in the house we didn't visit.

The front nine ended upstairs in the back bedroom, where we paused to take stock of the score. Tom, a lanky lad with fair hair, was in front with an impressive four below par. I was three below and playing a steady game.

Hole ten started with a long drive through the open bedroom window, landing outside behind the garage. You needed a lucky bounce here. I was quietly smug about my choice of sock. A fruit bowl, nestling just inside the garage door, was our hole. I left myself a longer putt than I would have liked ... but chalked up another par.

Tom didn't fare so well. His first shot failed to make it outdoors, clattering into the window frame and landing on the floor beside the bedside table. He dropped two shots. I'd got my nose in front.

From there we matched each other shot for shot and by the time we approached the final hole, my slender one-shot advantage was still there. Hole eighteen was short but blind. The tee was at the foot of the stairs and the hole – an empty shoebox – was sitting at the top. It was set back beyond the brow of the top stair so as to be unseen from the tee position.

I turned to Tom. 'Shall we walk the course?' I asked.

'Let's.'

We stood at the top of the stairs and stared meaningfully at the shoebox. We considered the angles, the breeze, the humidity and the socks. We stroked our chins. It looked tricky. We returned to the tee.

I went first. I landed four inches from the hole. A tap in. Tom's turn. If he got a hole in one it would be a tie. If he didn't, victory was mine.

A couple of the girls wanted to come upstairs, so Tom was forced to wait – you can't play when there are people on the fairway. He froze, holding his socks – fluffy white ones – aloft, not wanting to move, not wanting to break his concentration. When the path was clear, he paused some more.

'Fore!'

It was a good contact. The socks arced through the air. I knew where they were heading. I knew before they'd landed that he'd done it. It was a hole in one. It was beautiful.

'Did it go in?' he yelled from down below.

'Oh, yeah.' I said. 'Good shot. You bugger.'

He bounded upstairs to see the evidence for himself.

'Well played,' he said, shaking my hand. 'Good game.'

'A fair result. Well played.'

'Beer?'

'Why not.'

We congregated in the living room, chatting in small groups. As I looked round it suddenly occurred to me that I really didn't know any of the people I'd spent my evening with. I knew some names but no details. It hadn't seemed necessary. The sock golf had occupied the space where conversation would normally sit. We hadn't played in silence. It's just we'd largely talked about, um, sock golf. If that sounds like a negative note, well, it's not supposed to be. I'm not a confident party guest. I don't know many people who love the idea of going to a party where they know no one. Don't we all get that 'new kid at school' feeling? The evening hadn't been about me meeting Simon to play a game. It was a party ... in a sock-golf disguise. In that kind of situation, 'getting to know people' isn't necessarily as important as people make it out to be. Getting *on* with people: that's the important thing. I'd got to the end of a party without noticing that I was a stranger in the mix. That's a good thing.

'Hang on!' The voice was Simon's. It was loud enough to break through the background chatter. He had an announcement: 'I've just thought – we should be having a play-off. We shouldn't have a draw. Dave? Tom? You up for it?'

We both shrugged our agreement.

'Yeah,' I said. 'Fine by me.'

'Okay ... this is what we'll do,' said Simon. 'You replay hole one. For the win. If it's still a tie you move to hole two. And so on. Who wants to go first?'

Tom took his place at the window ledge. He played a confident approach shot, landing right by the sun visor hole. He couldn't miss from there. He didn't miss from there.

My turn. A hole in one would win it. But that was nigh-on impossible. Wasn't it? At this distance? I had to go for it. I lined up the shot. I swung my right arm. And I completely ballsed up the contact, slicing the socks off to the right, landing only halfway down the living room. Three yards from my target. Arse. I wasn't even on the green. I was going to have to chip it into the hole from distance to stay in the hunt. I tensed. All eyes on me. I didn't come close. I'd lost my sock-golf mojo.

'Well played, Tom,' I said. 'Deserved.'

'You too,' he said, and then, 'I meant the "well played" bit, not the "deserved" bit, you know; I didn't mean you deserved to lose, although I did win, so ...'

'I know,' I chuckled. 'Well played.'

'Do you want another drink?' asked Simon, clapping his hand on my shoulder.

'Thanks but no thanks,' I said with a glance at my watch. I wasn't really concerned with the time. The games were over. The party was now just that: a party. And I was a stranger. It felt strange. It was time to go.

CHAPTER 21

The tannoy crackled into life to tell us we would be calling at, 'Mansfield, Chesterfield, Dronfield and then Sheffield.' I looked out of the train window. It was all fields.

A young man sat down across the table from me. He wore moss-green corduroy trousers held up by a pair of leather braces. If it had been winter I'm sure he'd have been wearing a tweed jacket with leather elbow patches. But it was too hot for that. Not that he was going to go without his leather elbow patches: they were sewn onto his shirt instead. He had a short back and sides that was so short and so high it looked like his ears might have been lowered. He was seventeen going on fifty. Was he a Nottinghamian visiting Sheffield or a Sheffielder returning home? I knew where my money lay.

Nottingham was Cluedo and sock golf: childish games played by grown-ups who should know better. Sheffield was cribbage. Sheffield would soon be dominoes and *proper* darts. My impression of Sheffield as a city – that it's a place for old men and old-men-in-waiting – was being reinforced at every turn. The young fogey opposite me had to be a Sheffielder. I bet that if he'd taken his shirt off there'd have been leather patches on his actual elbows.

Station pubs are rarely the best. They don't have to compete for custom: weary travellers waiting for the 8:15 from Manchester will sup their ales, no matter what. So I was surprised to find that the Sheffield Tap – which sits on platform one – was a genuine, genial, old-fashioned pub. It's an old Edwardian refreshment room that's been tastefully refurbished, and the barman chatted proudly about the work that had gone on.

'It was turned into a waiting room in the 60s,' he said. 'They took the fireplace out, moved the counter and basically left it to the vandals.'

'What happened then?'

'They vandalised it.'

'That makes sense ... and then what?'

'It was locked up in the 70s and left to rot. The ceiling collapsed.'

'Leaky roof?'

'Aye.'

I looked up. The green plaster panelling – the colour of a teenage-pensioner's corduroy trousers – was beautifully ornate.

'It's a replica. Handmade. Using moulds of the original. And this,' the barman stroked the bar tenderly, 'is mahogany, salvaged from the original ... Polished up nice.'

'I've not heard of Thornbridge,' I said, pointing at one of the pumps. 'Local brewery?' Asking a barman about a local brewery is like asking a girl about her hair. They're flattered that you're interested. So you learn to ask, whether you're interested or not.

'They're Bakewell way,' he said.

'Home of the tarts?'

'That's the one. Derbyshire. Just up th'road, really. We always have Thornbridge on. But there're plenty of others. Guest beers and that.'

'I'd recommend Harveys,' I said.

'What?' He was aghast. 'The *sherry*?'

'No ... it's a brewery. They're based in Lewes. They brew a good ale.'

They brew a good ale?! What on earth was I was talking about? I'd never even tasted the stuff and wouldn't know a good ale if it slapped me. Here I was again, just trying to fit in.

'I'll make a note of it,' said he, not making a note of it. 'Can I get you a pint of something?'

'I'll just have a coffee,' I said.

I didn't want to fit in that much. I could still feel the effects of last night's boozy endeavours.

I found a table and took a seat. I waited with my refreshment in the refreshment-room-turned-waiting-room-turned-pub. I'm always one step behind the curve, me.

I feel naked if I'm not wearing a watch and yet, when I want to know the time, I sometimes find myself checking my phone first. It doesn't matter that my phone is normally in a pocket or a bag *and* inside a protective case; I still go through the more complicated manoeuvre of getting it out, instead of just glancing at my wrist.

When I looked at my phone in the Sheffield Tap it was time to ... plug my phone in. The battery was dead. I had plugged my phone in the night before in Nottingham, but I had realised too late that the hotel had a crafty energy-saving feature that meant that unless my room key was in a slot by the door there was no electricity being delivered to the socket.

Oh, well. I guess *that's* why I wear a watch. I slid my phone back into its case and then back into my jacket pocket ... and then I glanced at my wrist. Ian should be here any minute now.

'Dave?' A hand appeared in my peripheral vision.

The smiling gent proffering it was suited and booted: a shiny cufflink glinted in the sunlight that poured in through the large windows behind me. I shook it.

'Ian?'

'D'you want a drink?'

'I could go another coffee,' I said. I knew he was on his lunch break so I figured we'd both be staying teetotal.

I was wrong. He returned with a coffee for me and a pint of Czech lager for himself. Oh well.

There's a certain kind of suit that certain kinds of men wear. It's a suit that says, 'I-have-to-wear-a-suit-for-work-and-this-meets-the-minimum-requirements-in-that-it-is-a-suit-now-please-don't-look-at-my-shoes-as-you'll-only-be-disappoi-nted.' That wasn't the kind of suit Ian was wearing. Ian wasn't that kind of man. His was more of the 'I'm-expected-to-wear-a-good-suit-and-I-quite-like-it' variety. I glanced down at his shoes. Nice. He was wedding-or-funeral smart.

'You're turned out nicely,' I said admiringly.

'This?' he finessed his lapel. 'It's all right. I'm an accountant ...'

'That explains it.'

' ... in a law firm.'

'And that explains it twice.'

'So ... dominoes?'

'Yeah.'

'I wasn't sure which set to bring. I've got a normal set and a *Charlie and Lola* set for my lad.'[43]

'So which did you bring?'

---

43. *Charlie and Lola* is an animated TV show for young children about a boy – Charlie – and his younger sister, Lola. I was once in a bar when a stranger asked me if I wanted any 'Lola'. I had no idea what he was on about (or what he was on).

'What?' I had asked.

'You know ... *Lola* ... coca-cola?' said he with a wink.

'Coca cola?' I was confused. 'Are you asking me if I want coca cola?'

'Coke,' he said. The word came from the side of his mouth.

'Coca cola?' I asked again, still not up to speed. (Or coke.)

He raised his eyes to the heavens. 'Do. You. Want. Some. Cocaine?' he asked.

'Oooh,' said I, finally on the same page. 'No thanks.'

I wonder if the slang existed before the series – in which case there's a chil-dren's TV show where the two main characters are named after slang terms for cocaine. Or maybe the slang has come about *because* of the series. Odd, either way.

'The normal set.'

Of course he had. This wasn't Nottingham. This was Sheffield.

He produced a box, and emptied the white tiles, *clinkily-clankily*, onto the wooden table.

'So, do you play often?' I asked.

'Only with George, and he's five.'

'It's odd, isn't it?' I said. 'You see kids playing with them. And you see old men playing with them. But you don't see many people in between.'

'You're right. I used to like those displays where they knock them all over … y'know, when they fan out and fill a whole room …'

'Oh, I *love* them. They go mad for that in Holland, y'know?'

'Really?'

'They have a Domino Day every year where they try and get the world record for most dominoes toppled. It's a big TV event over there. It's worth YouTubing.'

'I'll have a look for that.'[44]

'Now,' I said, 'you'll have to give me a refresher on the rules …'

'Well, I only know the way I play with George.' Ian started turning all the dominoes over so that they were face down. 'We both pick six dominoes' – we started to do just that – 'and then we take it in turns to play. If you can't play one, you have to pick up. The winner's the first to play out.'

'Simple enough. Who goes first?'

'Have you got the double six?'

'No. You?'

'No. Double five?'

'Got it.'

---

44. http://bit.ly/DominoDay if you're interested.

'Then you do.'

I placed the double five in the centre of the table.

He added another tile. I followed suit. Him again. Me again. Hmm. I couldn't go. It was a two-headed snake with a three at either end.

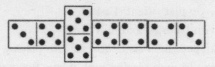

I didn't have a three. I knocked – a little rap of my knuckles on the table – and picked up a new tile.

I hadn't thought this through. I was the one who'd played the [image] knowing full well that I didn't have any more threes in my rack. I hadn't been forced into it. There were other fours I could have played. It was a bad move. I wouldn't do that again.

And I didn't. I lost that first game but then went on to win the next seven on the trot, before Ian finally pulled one back. Still, 7–2. I was the domino dominator. The Dominotor.

'How am I going to tell George that his dad lost?' said Ian, loosening his tie.

'Just lie to him.' I shrugged. 'Tell him you won. You can't be worried about lying to kids. You must do it all the time.'

'Yeah, I s'pose. But I do try to tell him moral lies.'

'Like what?'

'Well, for example, with our cat … someone shot him with an air rifle and he's had to have one of his legs off.'

'Ouch.'

'Yeah. So I told George that the cat had lost his leg because he was naughty and was playing in the road.'

'Good work!'

'Ah!' Ian looked at his watch. 'You've just reminded me. Work! Sorry. I'm going to have to run. Been nice meeting you.'

'You, too. And do lie. Tell George you beat me.'

'Nah. He'll be all right. He won't be too disappointed. Bye.'

I crossed over the train tracks and started the walk towards Victoria Quay again, only pausing to take a photo or two of the Park Hill estate. The red, orange and yellow panels were looking even more vibrant against the clear blue sky.

'It's revolting, isn't it?' said a voice to my left.

The speaker was wearing a red-and-white-striped football shirt. Sheffield United. A small dog padded impatiently about his feet.

'To be honest,' I said, snapping one more photo, 'I quite like it.'

'No,' he said, 'it's not right. Not for Sheffield. That's like something out of *Leeds*, that is.'

If you're a fan of techno music, in particular the sub-genre known as IDM (intelligent dance music), you've probably heard of a band called The Black Dog.

They're techno legends. They are pioneers in their field. They play to crowds of thousands at European festivals devoted to electronica. They're avant-garde superstars.

I'm not a fan of techno music and was blissfully unaware that the sub-genre intelligent dance music existed. I had not heard of The Black Dog. At least, I hadn't heard of them until I was about ten minutes into my time playing darts with two-thirds of them. Even then, they weren't especially forthcoming.

We met in the Harlequin, a tatty-round-the-edges but charming pub, next door to a beautiful big old flour mill. With the River Don on one side and Sheffield's first railway the other, the mill had been built in the perfect location for its job. Grain was brought up from the fields of Lincolnshire and flour was sent out to the world. It doesn't mill flour any more.

These days, it's serviced offices – a business centre. But the red brick chimney is still standing tall, square and proud, and the amateur photographer in me was still finding that blue sky appealing.

In trying to capture the full height of the stack I almost lost my balance and toppled backwards into the road. For a split second I was caught up in that strange, giddy, weightless sensation that comes when you're no longer supporting yourself and yet not falling, either. My toes were off the ground, wriggling inside my shoes like Wile E. Coyote trying to gain purchase on thin air, yet somehow they won the day. I looked around. Nobody had seen my strange off-balance dance. I felt a bit light headed. I enjoyed that. So I did it again. Leaning backwards, trying to find my balance point, my moment of equilibrium. But it's not as much fun when you do it on purpose. Oh well. I headed into the pub.

They do pubs well in Sheff. Like the Rutland Arms and the Sheffield Tap, the Harlequin was a real-ale pub. I might not be a real-ale drinker but I like people who are and I like the pubs that serve it. They're nicer places to drink rum in. It was a big, old place but there were only two customers that day. They were on the dartboard. Martin and Rich.

Martin had a real physical presence: tall and broad shouldered, his square jaw was covered with a thick, stubbly, greying beard. If he had wanted to adopt a look of brooding menace he had all the equipment. Luckily he didn't want to. Rich, however, would be hard-pressed to look brooding and menacing no matter what. He was small and wiry and had a natural bounce to his stride. Either that or he spent the whole time needing to use the loo.

We spent a while warming up, just taking turns to throw some arrows as and when we felt like it. The three of us chatted aimlessly – almost as aimlessly as Rich was throwing – and it was then that I discovered they were part of a band.

When I asked them what they did, 'Music ... we're in a band,' definitely wasn't the answer I was expecting. For a start they'd already told me they were based in the business centre next door, and somehow a serviced office just doesn't seem like a very rock and roll base. But on top of that, their demeanour was as un-rock and roll as it was possible to be. They were so unassuming, so avowedly unshowy, so easy-going and down to earth, that I was expecting them to be involved in something far more gritty and hands-on: 'We install fruit machines,' or 'We rip out old fireplaces,' or even 'Oh, you know, a bit of this, a bit of that.' Those were the kind of answers I'd been expecting. But no, it was, 'Music ... we're in a band.'

'Really?' I said. 'What kind of stuff?'

'Oh, y'know, electronic 'n' that,' said Martin, casually.

'Techno,' added Rich, in an equivocal, some-people-call-it-that way.

'Ah,' I said, 'not really my scene, that.'

They didn't mount a defence of their art form and they didn't sound stung by the idea that it wasn't really on my cultural radar. They just shrugged.

'It's not for everyone,' said Martin.

I wouldn't discover quite how successful they were until a few days later when I thought to Google them. And they had nothing to prove. They were successful. They knew it. There was nothing to gain by telling anyone else.

Besides, what Martin really wanted to talk about was darts. 'Let's have a look at yours,' he said, picking up my arrows. 'Bloody hell, these are hefty! How heavy are they?'

'Twenty-six grams,' I said. 'Let's have a look at yours.' Martin passed them my way. 'Oo ... these are nice,' I said, admiringly. 'But there's not a lot to them.'

'Eighteen grams,' said Martin. 'They're John "Boy" Walton's old darts,' he added.

Now *this* was something he was happy to impress me with. Rich just looked confused. Unsurprising, really. From his point of view, Martin had just claimed that his darts used to belong to a fictional character from a TV show. I thought about stirring in even more confusion by telling him that my darts used to belong to The Fonz. But before I could, Martin had already started to explain: 'John Walton's a darts player,' he said.

I handed the darts back to Martin. 'He's from Sheffield, isn't he?'

'Yeah.' He held the darts in his hand like an archaeologist holding some recently unearthed rare treasure. 'He won the World Championships in 2001. These were his darts.'[45]

'You mean these are replicas, right?' I asked. Most of the big players have something similar available.

'No, I mean these were his *actual* darts.' Martin glowed at the memory. 'I was at the Lakeside when he won it. They auctioned them off for charity. Cost me an arm and a leg. Bloody lovely darts, though.'

'Well,' I couldn't hide the fact that I was impressed. These

---

45. The World Championship in question is the one run by the BDO. Darts has two ruling bodies – the BDO (British Darts Organisation) and the PDC (Professional Darts Corporation) – and consequently it also has two World Championships. The schism happened in the early 90s but even now, many of the people involved seem to be the bitterest of enemies. Opinions on the two associations vary. Some people think the PDC is a mercenary organisation that's only interested in making money and that the BDO is the friendly face of the sport: a cuddly, community-minded bunch devoted to the grass roots. But then there are others who think the PDC is slick, professional and ploughing much-needed money into modernising the sport and that the BDO is out of touch, out of date and mired in the kind of petty bureaucracy you'd expect to find in a 1970s working men's club entertainment committee. The players are caught in the middle. They have to align themselves with one or the other organisation and are only allowed to compete in their tournaments. There are good players on both sides of the fence, although at a push I'd say the higher prize money on offer in PDC events means there's greater strength in depth there.

darts had won a World Championship! 'Do you want to play a proper game with them?'

'Sure. Do you want to play 301 down?'

'Sounds good.'

'You're playing as well, aren't you, Rich?'

'Yeah,' he said. And then, 'What?' And then, 'I don't really know what's going on.'

This is one square centimetre:

This is three square centimetres: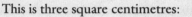

The treble 20 (and indeed every other treble on the board) is *smaller* than three square centimetres. It's small. And you're looking at it from a distance of seven foot nine and a quarter inches. Throwing a dart over that distance to hit a target that small is an utterly ridiculous task. And this is why I love the sport.

As a spectator you watch professionals hitting that tiny target with ridiculous frequency. It starts to look easy. So much so that when a stray dart lands a few millimetres high and to the right and only scores one point you tut and roll your eyes at the lack of ability on display. For some reason we don't hold every sportsman to the same standards. When a footballer takes a free kick and the ball loops over a wall and grazes the cross bar on its way out of play, we 'Oof' and we 'Aagh' and we 'So close!' But when a darts player misses his smaller target by an even smaller margin we think, 'Well, that just isn't good enough.' It's a hard world.

And then you try and do it yourself. And it is *almost* impossible. Almost. It's that word '*almost*' that's key here. It's the '*almost*' that makes the game so compelling to me, and so addictive. Because it *is* possible. You *can* do it. You *can* touch greatness. And every time you do – *every single time* – it is thrilling. It is thrilling because for a moment you are as good as it is possible to be. If I throw two out of three darts into the treble 20, I am in raptures. If I throw all three into the treble 20 the excitement is so raw, the rush of adrenaline so tangible, that my brain is thrown off balance. A part of me wants to never throw another dart again, to be frozen in that moment of darting glory, to always know that the last time I threw darts they were perfect ... But that could never happen because a greater part of me wants to repeat the feat immediately, to taste that joy all over again.

But despite having thrown a small number of 180s,[46] I know that I am rubbish and that I will always be rubbish. I can only ever visit that place briefly; I can never live there. When I miss I don't miss by millimetres. I miss by inches. I am crap. My average score is, well, incredibly average. But that is a part of why those tiny moments of joy are quite so joyful.

In Martin I recognised a man with the same addiction. The same affliction. While in Rich's eyes I saw a look familiar to me because I was used to seeing it in Beth's. A look that is one-part pity and three parts bemused amusement.

In the 80s and early 90s, the darts-themed game show, *Bullseye*, was a huge TV institution. Contestants competed in pairs – with one of them answering quiz questions and the other throwing darts. At the end of the game the winning couple would be presented with a gamble. They were invited to risk what they'd won so far in order to win the star prize.[47]

---

46. I know this is pathetic but I am sad enough to have filmed myself playing in order to capture a couple of them. For example: http://bit.ly/gorm180
47. There was a brief moment in time when it seemed as many as one in four stand-up comedians had a routine mocking *Bullseye*'s lavish prizes. It was almost impossible to go to a comedy club and not hear someone point out that the contestants probably didn't have anywhere to keep a speedboat. I suppose that's just more evidence of how big a part the show played in the cultural firmament of the time.

To do this they had to score 101 or more with six darts. The non-darts player would throw three darts first of all and then the darts player would try to finish the job. The tactic here was almost always the same. The non-darts player (for some reason, it was always taken as read that they were *actually* a non-darts player and not just the one who-hadn't-played-darts-yet-in-the-game-show) would be urged to aim for the left-hand side of the board.

If you're not a good player you will most likely achieve higher scores by aiming to the left, in particular around the 14 because, while the 20 is book-ended by the dangerously low-scoring 5 and 1, the 14's neighbours are, relatively speaking, friendlier.

Even if every one of your three darts misses the 14, if they've gone in roughly the right direction they should end up scoring more than thirty. With a bit of luck you might get over forty – and that was really all the non-darts player was hoping to achieve. After all, their team mate was normally a pretty decent pub player: someone you'd back to score sixty-plus points.

I'm not a decent pub player. I wouldn't back myself to score sixty-plus. If I was taking part in the *Bullseye* Star Prize Gamble I'd hedge my bets and aim for the left-hand side of the board. With a star prize at stake, I'd have to be pragmatic. I'm not good enough not to be.

But in the pub, playing with Martin and Rich, pragmatism didn't come into it. It never does. Because it's not as simple as outscoring your opponents. The point of playing the game is to try and reach perfection, to treasure those moments when you get an incredibly difficult task right.

During our games, Martin and I focused on the 20s while Rich just scattergunned his arrows all over the board. But Martin and I missed more often than we hit, so our scores fluctuated wildly and by the time it got to the business end of a game, the three of us were always pretty much level.

The first game started with Rich taking an early, unexpected lead. I hit two 5s and a 1 – scoring eleven, Martin hit a 5, a treble 5 and a 12 – scoring thirty-two, and Rich hit a treble 17, a 16 and a 4 – scoring a remarkable seventy-one. Or, as Martin grumpily called it, 'An un-fucking-*believable* seventy-fucking-one!'

Of course, while the scattergun approach might keep you in touch with two misfiring players, it won't win you any games. To win a game you have to get your score down to zero – and your last dart needs to hit a double. Or the bullseye … which technically is a double: it scores fifty – double the twenty-five points for the ring that surrounds it.

So let's say you're down to a score of eighteen. The scattergun approach is no longer of any use. You don't *need* to score highly. You need to score precisely. To win the game you need to hit a double 9. It isn't a big target.

This is how big the bullseye is:

While a double is smaller than this five-square-centimetre rectangle:

Martin was the first to experience the ecstasy of hitting his double – it made up for the agony of his third turn, in which he scored only two. No mean feat that, with three darts. The first two had landed firmly in the 1. His third had hit the wire and bounced out scoring nought. But the wire it hit was the wire bounding the treble 20.

'Did you see that?' he asked. 'Unbelievable. That was the treble. Did you see that?'

We had both seen it. We both told him we'd seen it. But that didn't stop him asking over and over whether or not we'd definitely seen it. He only stopped asking when a few goes later, he stepped up needing a score of ninety.

'What's the best way from here?' he asked.

'Treble 18, double 18,' said I. 'I think that's the route the pros take.'

'How about bull, double top?'

'Nah ... if you miss the bull you could hit anything,' I said. 'You'll have to stop and work it out, break your rhythm ... you want 18s ...'

'Hmm. Let's see. Let's try bull double top.'

His first dart landed dead centre. I froze. I wanted to congratulate him but manners dictate that you wait 'til the whole turn has been completed. He was in the zone. His second dart was a quarter of an inch too high. His third dart was perfect. Double top. Beautiful. Martin pumped his fist.

'Get in!' It was a roar but also a whisper.

'Amazing shot!' I said. It was, as well.

His points path from 301 to 0 had gone as follows: thirty-two, twenty-three, two, forty-three, twenty-seven, eighty-four and then ninety. His eighty-four was decent. His ninety was brilliant. He could stop asking us if we'd seen him hit the wire now. He'd experienced perfection.

The next game went my way with my scores following a similarly haphazard path: fifty-two, twenty-six, twenty-four, ninety-eight, twenty-two and then seventy-nine. I checked out with a 19, a 20 and then a double top. I'd never won a game with such a high check-out before. I was cock-a-hoop.

It seemed pretty clear by then that Rich was there for the beers and the conversation and that when it came to the darts, he was just making up the numbers. He was scoring random thirties and forties and hadn't yet aimed at anything except the board as a generality. He was like a control experiment, showing us where we could be if we just threw at random, instead of wasting our time on *aiming* and stuff. But then he surprised everyone by nailing a double 11 to win the third game.

'How the hell did you do that?' asked Martin. 'Your first dart missed the bloody board!'

Rich smirked. 'I've no idea.'

Martin shook his head in disbelief. 'I need a drink.'

We stopped playing for a while. Or rather we stopped keeping score for a while. We never actually stopped throwing darts. Every time the oche was unoccupied for even a minute one us would get drawn in and start practising and then the others would join them and after ten minutes or so of that someone would say, 'Shall we have another game, then?' and so the scoring would resume.

I told them about the dog-walking man who'd dismissed the new-look Park Hill flats as being like something out of Leeds. They chuckled.

'That's what Sheffield's like,' said Martin. 'We don't like to shout about ourselves.'

'Sheffield doesn't do much to promote itself,' added Rich. 'It's hard to get things going here.'

It sounded like a mild grumble, a quiet dig at their home town. But secretly I think they liked it that way. Thousands of people download The Black Dog's latest tracks and follow their every move. They storm the festival stages of Europe. But in Sheffield, they keep themselves quietly to themselves (which is also why I haven't mentioned that Martin also threw a rather spectacular 140 at one point. He wouldn't want you to know about that. He wouldn't want that kind of thing mentioned in a book. He wouldn't want to make a fuss).

I pushed the wooden doors back and stooped as I stepped into my waterborne home. I filled the kettle, struck a match and – *whoomf* – lit the gas hob. I kicked my shoes off, flicked on the telly and flopped back onto the couch. I wished Beth was there. Which reminded me. I'd left my phone plugged in for the afternoon.

I stretched my arm out as far as it would go and then shuffled my bum up the couch the few inches necessary to put me within reach of my phone. I unplugged the cord and turned it on. It seemed to take an age for it to go through the various home screens so I took the opportunity to update my notepad.

Rest of the World: **42**
Me: **37**

The first few pips and squeaks started to emerge from the kettle's whistle. It was comfy on the couch. Comfy enough that I probably wouldn't have roused myself to get up and make a tea if it had been an electric kettle. But a whistling, stove-top kettle can't be ignored so I found the strength in my arms to push myself up and turn off the gas.

It was as I was pouring the water that my phone finally completed the complicated process of connecting itself to the outside world. A series of beeps trilled. I had more messages than normal. That was odd.

With tea in hand I slumped back down on the couch and looked to see what all the fuss was about. My heart stopped. There were eight voicemails and a dozen or more texts. Most of them were from Beth. I didn't need to listen to them. I didn't need to read them. I already knew what they said: I wasn't meant to have spent the day in Sheffield. I wasn't meant to have spent the day playing dominoes and darts. I was meant to have been in London. We were supposed to have met our caterer to 'discuss menus'.

I've never had a burning desire to discuss menus with anyone, but that wasn't really the point. Beth had taken a day off work specially. I was meant to be there. And I wasn't.

Arse.

I called. It went to voicemail. I tried to pretend that the tone of voice in her 'Please-leave-a-message' message was an accurate representation of her current mood. I knew it wasn't.

'Hey, Beth. I'm sooo sorry. I just forgot. I was in Sheffield and it was lovely and then I went to Nottingham but a couple of blokes from Sheffield got in touch,' I gabbled, 'and it just seemed like the right thing to do to go back the next day but obviously it wasn't the right thing to do at all but I just forgot and I'm sorry and ... and ... I love you. Call me. Love you. Bye.'

Arse.

I flicked through the texts. The first ones were worried that I was late. The next couple were angry that I'd missed it. Then there was angry-and-concerned. Then just angry. Then just concerned.

For a moment I wished I'd been hit by a car. It would be so much easier. If the concern was justified, her anger would evaporate. But it wasn't. The anger was justified. So it was the concern that would burn away. Fuelling more anger.

We'd never had a row before. I didn't want to start now. But it was a bit late for that. I was an arse. I'd hurt the person I least wanted to hurt. For the sake of dominoes and darts.

Arse.

CHAPTER 22

'I'll stop if you like,' I said. The apology dinner appeared to be going quite well. Beth was smiling but I wasn't out of the woods yet; this still needed to be said. 'I cancelled tonight's game and I can cancel the rest if you like.'

'No,' she said. 'You don't need to do that.'

'I know. But I will if you want me to. I should be around more. We've got a lot to organise.'

Beth sighed. 'I was just embarrassed,' she said. 'I'm sure they thought I was some kind of fantasist who isn't really getting married at all!'

'I'm sure they didn't.' I tried to sound reassuring.

'You didn't see them! "Oh, is your fiancé not coming then?"' She laughed at the memory. 'I looked like a right idiot!'

'I can't apologise enough ...'

'Well, at least you got that bit right ...'

'I'm so sorry.'

'S'okay. Honestly. It is. I mean ... it wasn't. But it is.' She sipped her wine. 'And I don't want you to cancel any more games. I like it when you come back from these trips. You're happy.'

'Am I?'

'Yeah.' She smiled. Her eyes smiled too. They were green with a hint of grey that night. They were whatever she wanted them to be. 'You don't like doing nothing. You're not you when you're doing nothing. You need to go and do something like this. Just don't ever stand me up for a game of dominoes again!'

'It wasn't just dominoes,' I explained. 'There was darts and a night in a narrow boat too, and when you think about it, that means there were ...'

'This isn't helping.'

'No.' I reached across the table and held her hand in mine. 'Sorry.'

'You know it's not just the games you like, don't you?'

'Isn't it?'

'No. The games are just an excuse. It's the places. And the people. For what it's worth ... I like that you like people. It's sweet.'

I felt like my heart was going to burst.

CHAPTER 23

I felt like my lungs were going to burst. My calf muscles were on fire. There was the faint taste of blood in my mouth. 'Ultimate Frisbe' is insane. Gloriously, fiercely insane. I was loving it. But I definitely wasn't fine.

Things had started quite gently. It was a beautiful evening. The sun was only just beginning to think about setting and a couple of coxless pairs were sculling on the River Exe.

Flowerpot Playing Fields, a long thin stretch of grass that runs beside the river, is divided into football and rugby pitches that are all laid out end to end as if an efficient chef has tried to get as many pie lids as possible out of one wonkily rolled-out slab of pastry. As well as the sports fields, it's home to the Flowerpot Chill Zone. That's the council's 'down-with-the-kids' name for their skate park. I wish they wouldn't try to be down with the kids. Do kids want to be down-withed? I doubt it. Why didn't they just call it something prosaic and helpful? Like the Flowerpot Skate Park? That would have told people what it is – a skate park – and where it is – the Flowerpot Playing Fields. That would have been informative. Then if the skateboarders that used it had wanted to call it something else they'd have done so. And it would be *their* name. And it would give them a sense of ownership. The skateboarders of Exeter don't call it the *Chill Zone*. Why would they? That's what the council granddads called it. So they've had to come up with something of their own. They call it the Flowerpot Skate Park.

I'd been to Flowerpot Playing Fields once before. Not to use the fields or the half-pipe, but to ride the cycle path that winds its way under the railway and through the fields, beside the river and out of the city. I'd cycled that way on the start of my ride from Exeter to Taunton: a painful day four.

The first member of the Second Wind Ultimate[48] team to arrive was James, the man who'd invited me. James looked like the boy at school who'd forgotten his P.E. kit and been made to wear stuff out of the lost property box instead. Thin grey office socks were sticking out of the top of his trainers. He wore a black and red T-shirt and Hawaiian shorts.

Nobody wears Hawaiian shorts for sport. Not even for surfing. Not really.

Next to arrive was Phil. 'Call me Scraggy,' he said as he shook my hand. 'Everyone calls me Scraggy.'

I don't know why everyone called him that, because Scraggy definitely wasn't scraggy. He was lean, for sure, but not scraggy. He was taut and muscular. That rare kind of person who makes sportswear make sense. You see someone like Scraggy in his sports kit and you think, 'Ooohhh, so that's what it's supposed to look like!' He wasn't just physically fit … he had a commanding presence. Scraggy looked powerful. Mind you, he *was* standing with the sun at his back and as it shone through his mop of auburn hair it *did* create the illusion of a halo. I guess a hint of divinity would make most people look kind of powerful.

Scraggy is a professional sports coach. He runs a company that offers coaching sessions and courses as well as staging tournaments.

---

48. The word 'Frisbee' is a registered trademark of the Wham-O toy company. While most people would use the word to describe *any* flying disc toy, legally, only discs made by Wham-O are actually Frisbees. This is also the reason why the sport that started out being called Ultimate Frisbee is now called simply 'Ultimate'.

'Scraggy,' said James, 'coaches the Ultimate British Under-17s, don't you, Scrag?'

'Yep.'

'How're they doing?' I asked.

'Good ... we got gold at the European Championships in Vienna last year. Beat Germany in the final.'

'Wow!'

My wow was two-fold. Scraggy's credentials were impressive and wow-worthy for sure. But he'd just told me as much about the sport as he had about himself. It has European Championships. Proper ones. Ones that are evolved enough to have different age brackets. That's a whole lot more infrastructure than I was expecting. That was wow-worthy, too.

While we waited for the rest of the team to arrive, Scraggy and James gave me a quick lesson in frisbee throwing.

I admit that when the word 'lesson' was first used I bristled slightly. I didn't think I needed to be taught how to throw a frisbee. How wrong I was. In the space of just ten minutes I acquired two brand-new skills, which made it the perfect lesson for my brand of impatient curiosity.

Learning to do something new is always exciting to me. It doesn't matter what it is especially, it's always good to bring another tiny slice of the world under your own control. So long as I can pick it up in a hurry, anyway. If I could sit at a potter's wheel and be throwing a serviceable bowl in less than ten minutes I'd be on it at the first opportunity. If I could pick up a trombone and bang out a recognisable tune within half an hour of wetting my lips, I'd bloody love it. It's the knowledge that these things take days, weeks, months or years that puts me off.

But, oh no ... Here, we're talking two skills in ten minutes!

Imagine you're holding a tennis racket in your hand. Imagine playing a backhand, a forehand and then a smash.

Now swap the imaginary racket for a frisbee and go through the three strokes again.

I'll wager that your normal frisbee throw (if you have one) is most likely the backhand. That's how most people instinctively throw a disc. I know I do. The forehand is something I've seen a few show-offs doing in the park but it's always eluded me. I could sort of do it ... in that I could make the disc travel a few yards in the right direction ... but it would never *really* fly. Not in that floaty-drifty way that frisbees are meant to fly. And if a flying disc isn't flying ... well, then it's just a disc.

But with Scraggy's tutelage I was, for the first time in my life, throwing forehand frisbees. I wasn't consistent. It was nowhere near as strong or accurate as my regular backhand. But I could do it.

Now, I didn't ask you to imagine an overhead smash for no reason. I'd never seen it before, but something of that ilk exists in the frisbee world, too. It's called *the hammer*. The disc seems to wheel through the air vertically for a split second before suddenly remembering that it's a frisbee, at which point it flips onto the horizontal axis – as if it's hoping nobody noticed – and flies as a frisbee should. Sort of. The disc must confuse itself in that moment of transition, as it ends up *flying upside down*, with its 'lid' facing the ground. Silly frisbee. Silly, magical, over-arm-smash frisbee!

The first time I pulled off a successful hammer it felt like I'd performed a magic trick. When you throw a frisbee with a conventional backhand, you can see how the flight of the frisbee is a continuation of the momentum you gave to the disc. It flies in a way that is predictable given the movement of your arm. But the hammer seems completely counter-intuitive to me. There's nothing about the initial movement of the thrower that leads me to suspect that outcome. But it happens. And it's ace. Frankly, if nobody else had turned up that day it would have been worth travelling to Exeter just to learn to do the hammer. But of course they did turn up. And so there was a game.

When you ask someone to describe Ultimate to you, the first thing they say is normally, 'It's a bit like American Football … only with a frisbee.' And they're right, in that the idea is to pass the frisbee into the end zone and there is a player operating a bit like a quarterback – but that's really as far as the similarities go.

Unlike gridiron, it's a non-contact sport and teams are often mixed in gender. There are seven players on each side. You're not allowed to run with the disc so you can only advance it towards the end zone by throwing it. Once you catch the frisbee, you have to stop travelling and look to make a pass … and you have only ten seconds to do so. Luckily, you don't have to count the ten seconds for yourself. One of the opposition team will be marking you and, as well as waving their arms all over the place and generally making a nuisance of themselves, they'll help you out by counting to ten. If you haven't thrown the disc by the time they reach the 't' sound in 'ten' then possession of the disc passes to the other side. And that's pretty much it as far as the rules are concerned.

The only thing I've missed out is the *Spirit of the Game*.

This, in my opinion, is the single best part of Ultimate. Here's the thing: there are no referees in Ultimate. Ever. At any level. Messing around in the park? No ref. Playing a rival club? No ref. World Championship final? No ref. Players call their own fouls and have to settle their own disputes. If you're going to play Ultimate, you just have to accept that playing the game fairly is more important than winning.

When Scraggy first explained the Spirit of the Game to me I confess I thought it sounded a tad overbearingly, cloyingly hippyish, but it only takes a moment's thought to realise that actually we have all played games without officials many times and it works just fine, thank you very much.

Along with a group of friends I used to play in a regular Tuesday night five-a-side football game. It fizzled out when our numbers dwindled, but we were there in strength most Tuesdays for a year or more and in all that time there was not one argument.

I'm sure hundreds of thousands of games are played up and down the land each week with exactly the same attitude: you compete in those circumstances but you don't dive, foul or hand-ball because, well, what would be the point? Of course it was easy for us to be honest – the only things at stake in our kickabouts were friendships. Maybe if someone had invested millions of pounds in our games and paid us all ninety grand a week to take part it would have been different.

Luckily – or unluckily – Ultimate doesn't have to deal with the kind of financial high stakes that wield so much influence on the game of football, but even if it did, I still think the Spirit of the Game would survive. Besides, a ref-free game can often get better results than a refereed one: in November 2009, a football game took place between Ireland and France. The stakes were high. The winning team would qualify for the 2010 South Africa World Cup. Financially, qualification was worth millions and to the players involved, a win would give them an opportunity to compete at the highest level: to perform on the biggest stage available to their profession. It was huge.

France won the game in famously controversial circumstances. The winning goal – scored by William Gallas – came about as a direct result of a double handball from Monsieur Va Va Voom himself: Thierry Henry. Pictures of the handball were beamed around the world. It was pretty blatant. It was pretty embarrassing. Everyone agreed it was wrong. Including Henry. Of course the football authorities, in their usual, intransigent way, did nothing. It was too late. The referee hadn't seen it and that was that.

Did Henry handle the ball because of the money it would earn the French Football Federation? Did he handle it because of the potential glory of another World Cup? I don't think so. To my eyes it all looked instinctive – which, I suppose, is damning enough in its own way. But to me, the far greater offence takes place immediately afterwards. The real offence is in the way Henry celebrates the goal. The real offence is in his willingness to get away with it. That's no longer instinctive. That's calculated. You can see the cogs turning behind his eyes. He looks haunted. He knows that he has cheated. He knows that his reputation – a magnificent one at that – will be tarnished. But he also knows that it is his *job* to get away with it. Because he can. Because in football it's not the players' responsibility to play fairly … it's the refs' responsibility to make them.

'Yes, it was a handball,' said Henry later, ' … but when it comes down to it, I'm not the referee.' Well, there you go. That's football's malaise in a nutshell: '… *when it comes down to it I'm not the referee.*'

Well, in Ultimate, *you* are the referee. All of you. Collectively.

Imagine the France–Ireland game being played in a parallel universe where football has no referee and no linesmen. In a world where the players know they have to resolve any dispute themselves, Henry simply couldn't – and wouldn't – have tried to get away with it. It wouldn't have mattered that World Cup qualification was at stake: there simply isn't a way in which he could have maintained the lie. With a referee in place, he knows he has to con just one man. With no referee he has to con the whole world, and that isn't possible.

Of course this could never happen in football for all sorts of reasons. Some refereeing decisions are really judgement calls and you'll always need a ref for those … but it goes deeper than that. Football has lost its innocence. It's allowed dishonesty to become a part of the game's culture and that's an irreversible process. You can't put the genie back in the bottle. In Ultimate there is no genie … there's just the Spirit of the Game, and there's never been a bottle to put it in.

This lack of referee also means that the game tends to move very quickly. There's simply no respite. One team launches the disc from their end zone towards the other. A member of the receiving team picks it up and from that point on, it seems nobody is allowed to stop running. Depending on whether your team is in possession of the disc or not, you're either trying to lose your marker or you're marking someone and trying not to be lost. Either way, it comes down to a never-ending series of zigzagging runs and sudden surprise jinks, and it is completely and utterly exhausting.

It's a far more explosive form of exercise than the steady plod of cycling that I'm more accustomed to. When I'm cycling, I'm never going at full tilt. I just get going and keep going. Sprinting hurts me. I don't understand how anyone maintains a sprint for any serious amount of time. Doesn't sprinting involve working at your capacity? In which case, how can you not be spent the moment you start doing it? Within five minutes, I was gasping for air. Within ten minutes I was wondering if it would double my oxygen intake if I breathed through my arse as well.

I'd like to say that my struggle to keep up with the pace of the game was down to my age. At nearly forty, I was older than almost all the players there by a good fifteen years. But I can't use that excuse because while I was older than most, I wasn't the oldest of all. I was only the second oldest player in the game: the penultimate Ultimater. The oldest was in his early fifties.

For most of the game we were marking each other. For most of the game he was running me ragged.

I ended up playing on the same side as Scraggy and against James. In our first pre-game huddle, Scraggy issued some quick-fire instructions and then asked if we all knew who we were marking. There were nods and positive murmurs all round. 'I'll take Jamie,' said one voice, 'And I'm on James,' said another.

'I haven't got a clue who anyone is,' I whispered. I don't know why I was whispering: the opposition must have been sixty or seventy yards away. 'Who's left? Who am I marking?'

Scraggy popped his head out of the huddle for a moment and then dropped back down into our circular fold. 'You go for Shaun Sheep,' he said.

'Shaun the Sheep?'

'No. Shaun Sheep.'

It was my turn to pop my head up and out of the huddle. The opposition team were lined up in their end zone. I wanted to know which one of them was Shaun Sheep. I took a short shufti. Surely Shaun Sheep should shtand out? Surely Shaun Sheep was going to be a nickname for someone who either looked like a sheep in general or like Shaun the Sheep (the animated character from the *Wallace and Gromit* stable) in particular. Nobody matched that description. I dipped back into the huddle.

'Which one's Shaun the Sheep?'

'Not Shaun *the* Sheep ... just Shaun Sheep,' said Phil. 'It's his name.'

'Really? His *real* name?' I was incredulous. 'Shaun Sheep?'

I popped my head out of the huddle, took another look in the other team's direction and then dropped back into the circle. If it had been possible to view our donut of shoulders from above, we would have looked like a very slow and predictable bit of Busby Berkeley choreography.

'So which one is he?'

'Most of us call him Santa,' said a female voice. 'The older guy with the beard.'

Up periscope. Down periscope.

'Great,' I said. I was quietly confident. 'I'm on Santa.'

Just as Scraggy didn't look scraggy, Santa didn't look like Santa. Yes he was an older gent and yes he had a beard, but it wasn't a white, cuddly Santa beard. It was more rusty brown in colour. And it was more ZZ Top in style. Later, as he was leading me on a merry dance around the field of play, I'd see that as well as the beard, his face was augmented by several ear piercings, too: he had five or six studs, pins and rings in each ear. You could slide a pencil through the hole in one of his lobes. (Not that I did. It's a non-contact sport and I wasn't marking him *that* closely.)

One thing was for sure, Santa didn't give me any presents. Whenever we were both on the pitch he made my life difficult – just as he was supposed to.

'Bloody hell, Santa,' I would later wheeze. 'Can you stop being fitter than me, please?'

'I'm not really,' he said. 'I just know the game.'

When we started we were just fourteen players but more people started turning up and it wasn't long before we had a bunch of subs hoping to get a game too. But substitutions were only allowed when a point had been scored. It didn't matter how purple I was or how much my lungs wanted out … until there was a score it was just run, run, run, run, run. At one point, Santa did a little feint to the right and then legged it into the end zone where he skilfully plucked a disc out of the air above his hairy head, and I'm ashamed to say that I was, ever so briefly, glad that I hadn't been able to prevent the score. Any score was welcome by that stage. It was a chance to take a much-needed breather.

When I rejoined the game we were 5–2 down.

'Okay, Dave? How are you feeling?' asked Scraggy before the restart.

'Okay,' I said. 'But I don't know how long for.'

'Right … here's the plan.' He patted the solid shoulder of the man to his right. 'Either J.B. or I will collect the disc. We line up as normal. But Dave and Heather … you go long.'

The opposition launched the frisbee. It travelled about three-quarters of the field where it was promptly scooped up by J.B. The rest of us were hurtling into our positions in what is called 'the stack' – a column of players, running up the field. I didn't stop though. I was heading for the end zone. Heather too.

I could hear J.B.'s defender counting the seconds. 'Two … Three …' I planted my right foot and turned as if to collect a disc. 'Four … Five …' But instead of stopping, I used my right foot as a pivot and changed the angle of my run, now propelling myself towards the far left corner. 'Six … Seven … Eigh–' The count stopped and I heard the disc take flight. And I heard my heart pounding. I checked over my shoulder to see the flight of the disc, changing my course slightly as a result. I sped up … but the disc slowed down so I did the same and it drifted … down … down … over my right shoulder and … I thrust my hand out. It clipped my index finger and tried to get away but my thumb had snapped shut like a mousetrap and … yes! I held on. Touchdown! (Except they probably don't call them touchdowns in Ultimate.) It was a score, though! It was a point. It was my biggest – and quite possibly my only – contribution to the game. And it was bloody satisfying.

In the pub afterwards, Scraggy and James were offering plenty of encouragement.

'You picked it up really quickly,' said Scraggy.

'Yeah,' said James. 'Really quickly. You even did a point block against me … that's a *very* tough defensive move.'

'Did I? What's a point block?'

'When you swat the frisbee out of the air just as it's released,' said James. 'It's tough.'

'I don't remember that,' I said. I was lying. Now I knew what it was I remembered it well. It had been a reflex defensive move. There you go. I knew I'd contributed *something* else. 'I must have got lucky,' I said.

'Are you interested in playing some more?' asked Scraggy.

'I am,' I said. 'Realistically, I'm not going to be able to keep coming down to Exeter but ...'

'I didn't mean that ... though you'd be welcome, obviously.' He sipped his drink. 'But I can help put you in touch with some people if you like. There are a few teams in London.'

'I'd like that,' I said. 'I *really* enjoyed it.'

'Yeah ... we were unlucky not to win at the end. 6–7. I thought we were going to nick it. Mind you, you were on the field every time we scored a point.'

'Yeah ... I don't think I touched the disc for four of them though ...'

'No,' said Scraggy taking another sip, 'but *you were on the field*.'

'And how many of their points was I on the field for?'

'Don't think about that.'

How much liquid do you think can be contained by a standard-issue frisbee? If you turn it on its back, place it on a completely flat surface and then pour very carefully, you can get three full pints of lager into it. It's really quite astonishing. It certainly doesn't look like it will fit all that. At two and a half pints it really looks like it's about to spill, but it finds a way – if you pour gently, the meniscus will bulge out above the frisbee's edge and the surface tension will hold out for the full three pints. But please just take my word for it. Don't actually do it. Nothing good can come from filling a frisbee full of lager.

Especially when there are straws in the vicinity.

From: Steve
To: Dave Gorman
Subject: Just checking in

Hi Dave,

You said you'd get back to me 'nearer the time' but I still haven't heard from you. Or maybe you have sent an email and I haven't seen it for some reason? Are you still planning on coming to Portsmouth?

Steve

From: Dave Gorman
To: Steve
Subject: Re: Just checking in

Hi Steve,

Really sorry I haven't been in touch yet. I've been away from home for a few days and then busy with wedding plans. (I'm not a wedding planner on the side — I'm getting married in a few weeks!)

I'm pretty booked up for the next couple of weeks. The wedding's early October and when we get back from honeymoon I'm going to be working more regular hours which will make travel tricky … So how about mid-to-late September?

Dave

From: Steve
To: Dave Gorman
Subject: Re: Re: Just checking in

Dave,

You're getting married! Great news! Congratulations. It's definitely a busy time. Have you
had your pre-wedding interview yet? Is your
vicar nice?

Late September is good for me. Looking
forward to teaching you IDVE.

Will you be wanting to stay over? I've got a
spare room.

Steve

From: Dave Gorman
To: Steve
Subject: Re: Re: Re: Just checking in

Steve,

We're not having a church wedding so there's
no vicar to meet (nice or otherwise!)

I really do appreciate the offer of a place
to stay but I'll get a cheap hotel in town if
that's okay.

Need to check wedding plans and train times
before I commit ... is it okay if I get back to
you in a bit?

Dave

From: Steve
To: Dave Gorman
Subject: Re: Re: Re: Re: Just checking in

Yes.

CHAPTER 24

There is only one place in the whole of the British Isles to have an exclamation mark as part of its official name. I refer, of course, to the village of Westward Ho! in Devon which was named, punctuation included, after the novel by Charles Kingsley.[49]

Adding an exclamation mark to a place-name is like giving it Botox: it doesn't matter what sentence you write 'Westward Ho!' in, the words always look surprised to be there. But if exclamation marks *are* allowed, I think a few other places should consider adding them to their names, too.

First on my list would be the Cardiff suburb, Splott. If ever a word demanded an exclamation mark it is that one. Splott! You see? It just looks right, doesn't it?

The last time I'd played a game in Cardiff it had been a very profitable game of poker. However, there was no money at stake today. It was a good job, too. I didn't fancy my chances. Today's game was a game of skill. It was a game I'd played before, but not for more than twenty years, and even then I was rubbish. Today's game was Subbuteo.

---

49. Neither the book nor the village should be confused with 'Westwood Ho' which is what preposterous Radio 1 DJ and hip-hop guru Tim Westwood calls a special kind of lady. Probably.

Attentive readers might remember that in Chapter 13 I asked if there were any Tims in the world who were not mild mannered and softly spoken. You might be thinking that Tim Westwood proves that there are. I beg to differ. I simply refuse to believe he *really* talks like that. As many other people have pointed out before me, he is an upper-middle-class white man from Lowestoft whose father was the Bishop of Peterborough. The real Tim Westwood is surely mild mannered and softly spoken.)

My opponent, Ron, had given me very strict instructions not to arrive before 1.30 p.m. so I killed a bit of time wandering around the streets of densely packed terraced houses, marvelling at the amount of stone cladding on display.

A house with stone cladding is normally the aberration but not in Splott. In Splott it was very much the norm. I saw as many as ten houses in a row standing behind fake stone shells … it was as if the residents had thought, 'Well, maybe if we *all* do it, people might think it's real.' But an unclad brick house will always pop up eventually to give the lie away. (I'm surprised there aren't midnight raids to clad the deniers against their wishes and bring whole streets into line: 'Good morning, you've been splotted!') Some people had even painted the stones in gaudy colours, often with an equally gaudy but contrasting colour for the posts, lintels and quoins. It didn't disguise the stone cladding at all, instead it highlighted it and showed it for what it was.

Maybe that's the point. Maybe it's a brash confession, a new owner saying, 'Look, the house might be stuck with this stone cladding but at least I'm not trying to pretend it's real, okay?'

Ron's house was also stone clad – I'd have been almost disappointed if it hadn't been – but unpainted. 'Ah-ha! Dave Gorman!' he said as he opened the door. 'Very good timing! I've just put the kettle on. You'll be 'aving tea, will you?' He didn't hang around to hear my answer; just turned and headed back towards the kitchen, his voice trailing behind him as he went. 'Come in, come in … milk and sugar, is it?' He was spry for a man in his late fifties: he was in the kitchen before I'd so much as crossed the threshold. 'Did you want sugar?' he asked.

I found my way into the kitchen. He was standing with a heaped teaspoonful of the sweet stuff poised and ready to go, his eyebrows raised, awaiting my answer.

'Um, no thanks,' I said. 'Just milk, ta.'

'Fair dos.'

He handed me my mug and then sweetened his own tea by adding first one, then two, then three spoons of sugar. He stirred it vigorously, sipped it and then added a fourth for luck.

'So,' he said. 'Subbuteo?'

'Yes,' I said. 'Subbuteo.'

In his Welsh accent, the word took on a very distinct sound, a sort of clipped 'Sir-booty-ho'.[50] Instinctively I found myself wanting to copy his pronunciation – otherwise it sounded like we were talking about two different things – but I resisted the urge and so 'Sir-booty-ho' and 'Suh-beauty-oh' it was.

'Do you play?' he asked, pushing his wire-frame specs back up to the bridge of his nose.

'No,' I said. 'Not really. I did. As a kid.'

I took a sip of tea. My life, it was sweet. Either he'd stirred a spoonful of sugar in before I'd made it into the kitchen or this was an unwashed mug from an earlier four-spoon cuppa. Or maybe every mug in the house had been exposed to so much sugar over the years that they themselves were now sweet.

'I'm sure you'll pick it up again,' he said. 'Follow me.'

Ron was wearing a pair of navy-blue tracksuit trousers and a T-shirt in the same colour. Across his ample chest, four big, bold, white letters spelled out 'CWRW'. As it happens it's one of the few Welsh words I know. It's pronounced 'kuru' (sort of) and it means beer.

Despite knowing the word, my brain still went off for a little dance with it. At first glance my English eyes had – reasonably enough, I think – seen it as a set of initials and so a small part of my brain had instantly started trying to guess what they might stand for. In almost the same moment, another part of my brain had realised that it recognised the

---

50. If Sir Booty Ho isn't one of Tim Westwood's friends, then he obviously should be.

string of letters as a Welsh word but it was too late by then: the synapses were firing.

The playful side of my brain – the bit that does crosswords – was already running through the options and the sensible part of my brain – the part that knew what was going on – seemed powerless to stop it. As I followed Ron upstairs it felt like my brain was bickering with itself: 'Is it Cardiff Women's Rugby World?' 'No. It's beer.' 'Okay ... how about the College of Western Rural Wales?' 'No ... I just told you, it's beer.' 'Hmmm ... I know, Conan Wrestles Real Wrestlers?' 'Stop it! You're being silly now.' 'Can Whistle: Roger Whittaker?' 'Look, no, it's–' 'Clean With Running Water?' '*No!* It's *beer*!'

At the top of the stairs Ron thrust his mug of tea in my direction and said, 'Hold this for a minute, will you?'

The warmth of the mug in my left hand brought me out of my reverie and back to the here and now, but with the woozy uncertainty of someone emerging from a hypnotist's trance.

'It's beer, isn't it?' I said, my words sounding disconnected.

'No.' Ron furrowed his brow. 'It's tea.'

'Oh. Yes. I didn't mean *this*,' I said, nodding mug-wards. 'I meant on your shirt ... the word on your shirt ... that's "beer", isn't it?'

He glanced down at his chest to check. 'Yes, it is, Dave,' he said. 'Would you like a glass of *cwrw* while we play? It's still too early for me but you're very welcome if you'd like some ...'

'No, no, I'm very happy with my tea, thanks.'

'Right, oh,' he said and then, pointing skywards, he added, 'Up there is where we're playing.'

I looked up. The hatch to the attic looked back at me. I looked down. Ron had a pole hook in his hand. I looked up again and watched as he skilfully slipped the hook into a loop and gave a gentle tug. The door swung open. Ron then jabbed the end of the long pole into the black hole above our heads a few times as if fighting off the attic-elves, but eventually he found the contact he was fishing for and with a jerky one-two he gave a tug. A set of aluminium steps unfolded their way down to the landing with an impressive *kersshhhhuck*. Blimey. To get into my loft at home I have to use a rickety old stepladder that lives in the spare room. Standing on the top step puts my head and shoulders into the attic space and I can heave myself up from there. This was no ladder. This was a sturdy staircase. It was geekily beautiful.

'Good, isn't it?' said Ron with pride. 'Come on up' – and up he went – 'into the mothership!'

I followed, taking the gentle gradient with no hands. Well, I *was* carrying two mugs of tea.

'I've got staircase envy, Ron,' I said. 'I want some of these.'

'They're very swish,' he said. 'I'll give you that.' He enjoyed saying the word 'swish' and I enjoyed hearing it, too. And he was right. They were swish. They were swishing excellent.

Safely up the ladder, I looked round the attic. A proper floor had been laid and there was carpet down, but apart from that it looked pretty much as I would expect any other attic to look. There were cardboard boxes stacked up one on top of the other, and a pair of old curtains had tumbled out of a burst bin bag. There were a couple of battered suitcases, and a bent and twisted plastic Christmas tree.

'This is the good bit,' said Ron with a twinkle in his eye. 'Come here.'

What I couldn't see from my place by the hatch, but could easily see the moment I'd taken just two steps in Ron's direction, was that the attic was much longer than it first appeared. Which was obvious the moment I thought about it because, like most attics, its footprint was the size of the house on which it sat.

Ron had stacked his boxes carefully. They acted as a partition wall, dividing the space in two. On the one side it looked like, well, an attic, but on the other, secret, side – it was a winter wonderland, a mystical landscape stretching as far as the eye could see, a whole world full of magical creatures and ... (No, tell a lie ... I'm thinking of the wardrobe. Wrong book.)

On the other side of the boxes, there were two pieces of furniture. At the far end of the attic, against the wall, there was an old 1950s chest of drawers that had seen better days, and in the middle of the space there was a very old kitchen table that had been cannibalised and turned into a permanent base for a Subbuteo pitch.

'Nice work, Ron!' I said. 'Nice work, indeed!'

'It's my pride and joy,' he said. 'My pride and joy.' He paused. 'I love it. Only thing is,' he added, 'Mary – that's my wife – she doesn't like me playing it. So this is my secret.'

'Really?' It seemed hard to believe.

'I only play it when she's out,' he said. 'She's got bad hips, has Mary. She never comes in the attic. Mind you, she never did. The attic is a man's place, isn't it? Like a shed. Do you 'ave a shed, Dave? Or an attic?'

'Just an attic.'

'And does your wife go in the attic?'

'Um ... no,' I said. 'I mean ... she's not my wife. Yet. But she's going to be. And no. I don't think she's ever been in the attic. But if we had a *swish* staircase like yours, I bet she would.'

Ron peered sceptically over the top of his spectacles at me. 'Really?'

'Yeah. I mean I came up those stairs no hands ...'

'I doubt it, Dave, I really do. I think you'll find the attic is all yours. That's why I had to ask you not to come 'til after one-thirty. Mary leaves for work at one, see?'

'I see,' I said. But I didn't really see. I stared at the Subbuteo shrine in awe. It was wonderful. Why would anyone want to keep it a secret?

Ron must have sensed that the question was on my mind because he answered it of his own accord.

'She'd hate it, Dave. She'd *absolutely* hate it. She's a serious sort, is Mary. I love her to bits but she doesn't go in for fun, bless her.' He reached out his hand and I passed him his mug. 'Now, come on' – he slurped noisily at his tea – 'let's have ourselves a game.'

> **RULES**
>
> For those unfamiliar with Subbuteo, the game is a miniature version of football. The players are small figurines, mounted on hemispherical bases about the diameter of a penny. The smooth surface on the underside of the bases means they can be flicked around the green baize pitch, as you try to manoeuvre the ball (which is almost as big as a player) into the back of the net.
>
> In The Undertones' song, 'My Perfect Cousin', Feargal Sharkey sings, 'He always beat me at Subbuteo / 'Cause he flicked to kick, and I didn't know.'

I didn't really know what to believe. Was he really keeping this a secret from his wife? Did he *really* have to? It seemed a bit far-fetched. I suspected he was gilding the lily: trying to make the game seem more adventurous. True or not, it didn't really matter. I shrugged and joined him pitchside. Two teams were already on the pitch. One blue, one gold.

'I'll be Cardiff City,' said Ron. 'I thought you might like to be Brazil.'

'Thank you,' I said. 'But I don't think it'll help me much. We used to have a Brazil side when I was a kid and I was never very good with it.'

'Did you have all the gubbins?' he asked as we started to arrange our men, ready for kick-off. 'Did you have spectators? The floodlights? Anything like that?'

'Oh Lord, no,' I said. 'Our set-up was pretty much like this … just the pitch and the players, really. We had a scoreboard but that was it.'

'Man after my own heart.'

'To be honest, I don't think it was a style choice. I think we wanted all that … we just couldn't afford it. We used to save up our pocket money and buy new teams but we didn't use them … We already had the ones we wanted.'

'Which were?'

'Liverpool, England and Brazil,' I said. 'I can still see the boxes. I can tell you from memory that Liverpool was Team 41 in the catalogue. It was Liverpool to us, but the all-red kit meant it was also Brechin City, Canada, Dubai and Scunthorpe.'

'Very impressive!'

'I saw Scunthorpe on TV a couple of years ago, though, and they weren't wearing red. I was shocked. Either Subbuteo had got it wrong or they've changed their kit.'

'I imagine they've changed their kit.'

'I imagine you're right.'

I tapped the tabletop. The pitch was glued to a chipboard base. 'This is nice,' I said. 'We had to unfold ours and lay it out on the bedroom floor. It had a huge crease on the halfway line that would throw the ball off at odd angles. Plus as you moved around to take your next flick you'd pull the pile of the carpet around so the pitch would move a bit, too. This is definitely the way to do it.'

'If a job's worth doing …'

But I wasn't done yet. 'Just having it at this height changes it,' I enthused. 'I must have played table football hundreds of times but I think this is the first time I've seen it actually *on a table*. It's just so much better!'

'Especially with my knees …'

'Are they still making it?' I asked.

'What? My knees?'

'No. The game?'

'Oh. Ha,' Ron smiled. 'You know what, I don't really know. I think there's some Italian company doing a version of it. Very accurate-looking things they are. Got the sponsors' logos on the shirts and all that.'

'Of course!' I said. 'I hadn't thought about all that. So now Brechin City is Brechin City and Canada is Canada, and never the twain shall meet?'

'Exactly.'

'Oh, well,' I said. 'I suppose that's what people want. I guess football's changed.'

'But Subbuteo doesn't have to,' said Ron ruefully, as he flicked some imagined dust off the pitch. 'I don't know. I'm not a part of the table-football community, so to speak. I can't talk for them. There are people out there who take it all very serious ... very competitive they are. Play in leagues an' all sorts. I'm not bothered with any of that. I've got my old set up here and that's all I need.'

'Well, you need someone to play *with* ...'

'I got Karl for that,' he said. 'Comes round once a week. Most weeks, any road.'

'While Mary's out?'

'Oh, yes, of course, yes ... Now, are you happy with the way you've set your team out?'

I nodded my agreement. 'Yes,' I said. I'd gone for an unconventional 3-5-2 formation. 'I'm trying to crowd out the midfield.'

Ron smirked. He'd gone for a more traditional 4-4-2.

'Okay. How 'bout we play fifteen minutes each half,' he said, 'and take a three-minute break for half time. Good with you?'

'Yep. Good with me.'

'Then heads or tails?'

'Tails.'

He tossed a shiny ten-pence piece. It turned somersaults as it rose towards the bare light bulb and back down to the back of Ron's hand. He opened his mouth to speak but the voice that emerged wasn't his. Nor was it in the attic.

'*Coo-ee!*' The word hit the same notes as their ding-dong door chime. 'It's only me!'

I smiled. But then I looked at Ron. Ron wasn't smiling. There was a mild sense of panic in his eyes. I froze.

'... It's Mary,' whispered Ron urgently. 'Stay here. Don't make a sound.' He walked back around the wall of boxes and to the hatch. 'I'm in the attic, my love,' he called down. 'Just sorting through some old bits and pieces.' He paused. Then added a less than convincing, 'Oh, it's a right old mess up here, it really is.'

She replied but the words were indistinct.

'Right you are, my dear,' I heard Ron holler, 'right you are!' Footsteps. And then his head appeared around the edge of the boxes. 'She's got her shifts wrong.' He was back to his whispering ways. 'She's not needed at the shop for another thirty minutes. I'm going to pop down and keep her company – have a cup of tea and see her off, okay?'

'But I ...'

'Shh! Don't move. Don't make a noise. I won't be long.'

'But what if ...'

'I'm going to have to turn the light off,' hissed Ron from the hatch. 'Sorry.'

The room was plunged into semi-darkness. I listened as the ladder slid up again and nested at the top of the hatch with a *shucckk-kersssshhhh-dunk*. And then the hatch closed and the darkness was total. I was trapped. Alone. In an attic. In the dark.

Okay. Maybe it really *was* a secret.

I stepped to my right and the floor creaked. I felt guilty. Why? Thankfully, my phone was in my back pocket so I took it out and used its light to guide me to the edge of the room.

I lowered myself to the ground carefully, quietly, cocooned by the wooden eaves above.

I stared at the phone. If it rang now, it might be heard downstairs and then I'd be found and his secret would be blown. Would that be so bad? There are far worse things that a man could hide in his attic. If it happened, it wouldn't be my fault. It would just be one of those things.

One of those things that happens when you trap a stranger in your attic.

I stared at the screen, willing it to ring and then ... then some strange sense of loyalty got to me. I felt guilty. I switched it to silent.

I watched the clock. Was time moving slowly because I was watching it or because I was trapped – alert yet constrained with nothing to stimulate my brain? One minute felt like five.

I sent a text message.

```
To: Beth
I am being held hostage in an attic in Splott!
D x
```

Two minutes felt like ten. The screen flickered silently.

```
To: Dave
Ha ha. I take it you're playing another one of
those fantasy games then? B x
```

```
To: Beth
I wish. No. Splott is a real place. As is the
attic. And I am trapped. Sort of. I mean, I'm
not ... but I am. This is weird. D x
```

Four minutes. Four minutes! It felt like a day.

To: Dave
Sounds like you're having fun! I have to turn my
phone off now — we're filming. Love you. B x

Beautiful. What to do? Did my phone contain any games? I
wouldn't know where to begin if it did: I wouldn't know
where to find them or what to do with them. Instead, I
just stared at the screen. I thought if I counted the seconds
down in my head I might bring reality to my senses: it might
force each minute to *feel* like an actual minute. One Mississippi, two Mississippi, three Mississippi, four Mississippi, five
Mississippi ...

I won't keep going now. *You're* not trapped in an attic,
after all. Besides, it was nigh on impossible to count past
twenty Mississippis before the boredom drove me to distraction ... at which point I'd stop ... only to realise that there
was nothing else to distract me and that actually, as boring as
the counting was, it was the *only* thing available to me. So I'd
start again. Weirdly, it seemed to prove that time really was
going slowly in there ... I repeated that cycle – from nought
to twenty – three times over and still a new minute didn't tick
by. I became obsessed with seeing the time change. I wanted
to see a new minute arrive so that I could begin counting at a
proper moment, but it was as if my phone was playing a game
of cat and mouse. If I stared at the screen it would do nothing.
You know what they say: a watched clock never boils. (Hang
on. They don't say that, do they? They should, though. It's
definitely true.)

Well, if the minute was only going to change when I
looked away I thought I'd try and double bluff it and see if I
could speed up time by looking away more frequently. Unfortunately, time was wise to my ruse and simply refused to play
along. You can't kid a kidder. Arse.

Thirty minutes passed.

Eventually.

First a triangular shaft of light. Then a *kersshhhhuck*. Then Ron's voice: 'Helloo! Are you still there, Dave?'

Was I still there? Of course I was still there! There was only one way out and it'd been closed! Where did he think I could have gone? The light overhead blinked and flickered to life.

'Yes,' I said. 'I'm over here.'

'I'm sorry about that,' he said, emerging around the side of the boxes. He looked baffled for a moment, expecting to find me at head height. 'Oh, there you are,' he said, as his eyes alighted on my prostrate frame. 'I made you another tea by way of an apology. You do 'ave sugar, don't you?'

'Not always,' I said, pulling myself upright. I felt a little light-headed. 'But I'll take it.' I tasted it. My gums tried to run away. I tasted some more. Crikey. 'Thanks, Ron. This is lovely.' I was surprising myself with my manners: is it possible to suffer from Stockholm syndrome after just thirty minutes in an attic?

'Are you sure this is a secret worth keeping, Ron?' I asked.

'Oh, yes.'

'But she probably thinks you're having an affair!' I said. 'She probably thinks you've got a stash of porn and a torture chamber up here ...'

'Now, where were we?' said Ron, ignoring my reasoning. 'Ah yes, you'd just called heads or tails, hadn't you?'

'Um, yes.'

'And you said ...?'

'Tails.'

'That's right. And it was heads, as I recall.'

'Was it?'

'Oh, yes. I think so. Anyway, I'll kick off. Fifteen minutes each way ... here we go.'

I'd forgotten the speed at which Subbuteo can unfold. After each of Ron's attacking flicks I was entitled to make a defensive flick, but he was under no obligation to wait for me and he quickly got into a rat-a-tat pace that I struggled to keep up with.

His two centre forwards skilfully swapped possession, carrying the ball into the final third of the pitch and into shooting range. His shot was ridiculously powerful.

The goalie is unlike the other players. You don't flick to kick. Instead, he sits on the end of a plastic paddle that extends under the back of the goal. I'd like to pretend that I skilfully jerked my keeper to the right and pulled off a spectacular save but the truth is the ball clattered into the crossbar and bounced out of play behind me.

'Ooooof,' said Ron with a wince. 'Goal kick.'

'You're a bit good at this, Ron,' I said admiringly.

'Do you want me to slow down for you?' he asked.

'No,' I said. 'There's no point in that, is there? You've got to play a game to the best of your ability.'

I took my goal kick. The ball travelled twelve inches or so, landing only three or four inches from one of my five midfielders. Ron made his blocking move, sending one of his midfielders forward to close me down. I lined up my next shot and missed the ball spectacularly. So possession passed to Ron ... and he didn't miss the opportunity. Using the midfielder he'd advanced moments before, he expertly flicked the ball back into the shooting zone. The striker who'd hit the bar evaded my blocking move by nudging the ball towards the penalty spot, where his strike partner clinically swiped it into the bottom left-hand corner of the net.

'One nil to Cardiff!' growled Ron. 'Come on the Bluebirds!'

It was obvious I was in for a drubbing.

'Well played,' I said, picking the ball out of the goal and putting it on the centre circle.

'Can I give you some advice, Dave?'

'Of course,' I said. 'Anything to improve my game.'

'The thing is,' said Ron, adopting the philosophical 'been-there-done-that' tone of a man in the know, 'you've got to have secrets in a marriage.'

'Really, Ron?'

'Oh, yes,' he said. 'You take my word for it. You'll see. You'll see.'

CHAPTER 25

I'd booked my accommodation in advance – you have to if you're going to spend Bank Holiday Monday in Cornwall – but even then, finding anywhere close to my game was tricky. I hadn't been invited to play this time: I'd invited myself.

I was going to play in the 'Smite' World Championships. Tiny St Neot – the village that was hosting the event – was full. As was sizeable Liskeard, too. I scoured the internet looking up the villages that lay between the two – Doublebois, Dobwalls, St Cleer – but there were no beds to be found in any of those either, so I was forced to look further afield, east to Merrymeet, Quethiock and then Menheniot, where I finally found a B&B with a vacancy. Phew.[51]

I suppose most people taking advantage of the bank holiday do their travelling on the Friday evening after work or, failing that, the Saturday morning. I was a Sunday afternoon traveller – having spent the morning wittering on the wireless – and so found myself one of only three passengers leaving the train at Liskeard.

'Excellent,' I thought, ' … shouldn't be much competition for a taxi.'

I was right about that. The only problem being there were no taxis either. I looked at my phone. No reception. Hmm? Oh well. I started to walk into town.

---

51. Incidentally, if we're going to add punctuation marks to place names and make Splott into Splott! surely Quethiock can get the question mark it deserves and become Quethiock? too.

I wouldn't describe Liskeard as a pretty place. It's more prosaic than that. If you think of all the little villages around and about as gorgeous old vintage sports cars – high maintenance, impractical, but lovely for looking at – then Liskeard is the rusty-but-trusty family saloon. And while those vintage automobiles are all very well, when you want to do the shopping you know which car keys you pick up. (If you want to stick with this motoring analogy, it follows that Plymouth is, um … a transit van.)

In the centre of Liskeard, a trio of thirty year olds had gathered outside the local shop to drink tins of cider and scowl at passers-by. That's not a typo. They *were* thirty. Thirty-year-old men. They definitely weren't thirteen. Maybe they'd started doing it when they *were* thirteen but, unlike the rest of us, had discovered they actually liked it …?

I looked at my phone but there were still no bars. I didn't know the way to Menheniot and even if I did I wasn't really in the mood for a four- or five-mile yomp so I popped into a phone box where – under the watchful gaze of Liskeard's own Larry, Curly and Asbo – I called a cab.

'I've got a driver just pickin' up in Pensilva,' said the female voice on the end of the line. 'She's dropping off in Liskeard so I can do you in about forty minutes. Is that okay for you?'

'Yep, that's fine,' I said, putting my London-living, want-it-now impatience aside. It was time to embrace the Cornish pace of life: this was supposed to be a holiday after all. And besides, I'd tried four other cab companies already and this was the only one that had picked up the phone.

'Whereabouts are you?' she asked.

'I'm in the town centre.' I peered out through the phone box's glass panes. 'Oo … I tell you what,' I said, spying a pub across the way, 'I'll be in the White Horse. Is that okay?'

'No probs. See y'in abou' forty, all right?'

I crossed the road with the self-conscious gait of a watched man. I was trying to appear unconcerned by the cider boys' attention – I wanted them to think I hadn't even noticed they were there – but instead, I ended up walking so deliberately I must have looked like I was trying to balance an invisible pint pot on the top of my head. No, it was actually more awkward than that. Make it an invisible pint pot filled with invisible heroin that I was trying to smuggle through an invisible 'Nothing to declare' channel at an invisible airport. That's more like it.

There were six or seven regulars hanging around at the near end of the pub – either propping up the bar or lounging on a tatty, out-of-place sofa – and they all gave me the once-over as I stepped inside. And there was me hoping to leave my self-consciousness outside in the street! Nope. It must have sneaked in just as the door was closing. Well, if my self-consciousness was going to follow me in, I thought I might as well get him a drink, so I bought us both a rum. One for me, and one for my self-consciousness.

I walked – with the same awkward, over-studied gait – to the back of the room and took a seat. I had the very definite sense that I was still being assessed. Was I being paranoid? Or *was* I being judged? In fairness to them, they were probably thinking, 'I wonder what's up with Mr Paranoid here? He's so on edge he can't even walk properly.'

The music selection wasn't making the place feel any less judgemental, either. Merle Haggard's country classic, 'Okie from Muskogee', was on the jukebox. According to the song, the list of things they don't do in Muskogee, Oklahoma, includes smoking marijuana, growing long hair and 'making a party out of loving' ... while the list of things they *do* do includes holding hands, wearing leather boots and respecting the college dean. To some it's an anti-hippy rallying cry but I think of it more as an affectionate character study: a warm but wry look at blue-collar life, a paean to the simple, homely values of conservative, middle-of-the-road, middle America. Country music does little for me but in the right mood I quite like 'Okie' … But I wasn't in the right mood, and the we're-from-a-small-town-and-we-don't-want-any-of-your-beads-and-sandals-nonsense message made me feel more self-conscious still as I flicked through the pages of my Sunday paper.

On a visit to the Gents I found a stronger hint that at least one person in these parts was wont to cast unsavoury judgements on others: scratched into the paint on the wall above the urinal – with some unsavoury text to back it up – was a swastika. Nice. I wondered how long it had been there. Too long, surely.

'I need to get to St Neot tomorrow morning,' I said as I paid for my cab. 'I don't suppose you're free then, are you?'

'Oh, no,' the driver said. 'I'm fully booked.'

'What about if I call the main number?' I asked. 'Do you think I'll be able to get one of the other drivers?'

'No.'

'Ach, are you sure?'

'There aren't any other drivers, dafty!' she said. (*Dafty!*) 'It's jus' me.'

Once at the B&B, I was pleased to see I had mobile phone reception in my room. Well, technically the reception started fifteen centimetres outside the window, but at least I could make calls with my legs in the room, and that was good enough for me.

With a list of taxi numbers kindly supplied by my landlady, I set about trying to arrange a ride to St Neot in the morning. I'd managed the first 250 miles of the journey, how hard could the last ten be?

Impossible. That's how hard.

I really was more than happy to put my London-living, want-it-now impatience to one side ... I just wanted some relaxed, Cornish, you-can-have-it-eventually-ness to replace it. But no. Even a company called Anytime Taxis had an answering-machine message that started, 'We're not working on Bank Holiday Monday, but if you'd like to make a booking for another time then ...' There was nothing. My landlady had no more suggestions. I asked if St Neot was walkable and she scoffed. Hmm.

In desperation I called the Smite Master, Roger. Roger was the man responsible for organising the Smite World Championships. Roger is Mister Smite. I had his number scribbled down in amongst the details for the tournament.

'Hello there!'

For a moment I thought I'd called the wrong number: he sounded just like Ron, my Cardiff Subbuteologist.

'Hello,' I said, 'is that Roger?'

'Uh huh.'

'Look, I'm sorry to trouble you as you must have your hands full the day before the tournament and things ...'

'Well, we *are* busy but go on ...'

'Well, this is going to sound ridiculous ... I've come down from London for the World Championships tomorrow and I've got as far as Menheniot ... But I can't find a cab for love nor money that will get me to St Neot in the morning. I was wondering if you knew of any companies at your end or ...'

'Oh, don't you worry about that,' he said. 'We'll pick you up. Can't have you stranded now, can we?'

'Well, that would be amazing but ...'

'It's no trouble. We'll send one of the tournament courtesy cars for you.'

'Wow! Really?'

'How does 10 a.m. sound?'

Hmm. The Smite World Championships? Tournament

courtesy cars? I'd assumed their use of the word 'world' was tongue-in-cheek, a silly claim to global status from an event that was knowingly – pleasingly – parochial. You know, like Lewes does with Toad In The Hole and America does with baseball. I certainly wasn't expecting the tournament to have a fleet of courtesy cars! Maybe it was more serious than I'd imagined?

Or maybe Roger was just using grand phrases like 'tournament courtesy cars' to mean, 'I'm sure we'll find someone willing to pick you up … I'll ask Dan in the village if he'll pop over.'

Yeah. That was it.

The sun had bleached Dan's hair and tanned his face. He wore baggy jeans and sandals that would have met with disapproval in Muskogee.

He was curious to know how I'd found out about the tournament. You might be, too. Smite isn't on everyone's radar.

It was a year to the day since I'd set out on a bicycle to zigzag my way between Britain's cardinal points. Eleven months since I'd arrived at the northernmost point and gone down on one knee to Beth. Five weeks before I would tie the knot.

When I set out to cycle across Britain, a friend asked me why I'd chosen to start the journey at the southernmost point and work up the country, instead of going the other way round.

'Wouldn't it be easier,' he asked, 'to go from north to south?'

'Huh?' I was confused. 'Why easier?'

'Well, you'd be going south, wouldn't you?' he said, as if it was the most obvious thing in the world. 'So you'd be going downhill.'

'Ha ha … nice one.'

'What? What's funny?'

'I'm sorry … do you *actually* mean it?'

'Well, it's obvious, isn't it? North is up. Isn't it? People live up north … and … down south …'

He wasn't joking. He genuinely believed that the north was uphill, and there was nothing I could do to persuade him otherwise. According to him, the only reason a football dropped in Aberdeen doesn't roll all the way down the hill to Brighton is that '… there are buildings and trees and stuff …' in the way. Remarkable.

Having said all that, there was a moment – three or four days into the ride – when I started to think that maybe he was right, that maybe *I* was the idiot and that maybe 'north' really was 'up'. Because for those first few days it definitely did feel like it was uphill all the way. For those first few days I was knackered. For those first few days I was in pain. I was spending all day in the saddle and following it with two hours on stage each evening. It was taking its toll. By the end of each night I was completely spent and no matter how much sleep I got, I'd wake up feeling tired in my bones and heavy in my legs. I worried that it wasn't going to be possible to maintain this routine for thirty-two consecutive days. I thought I'd bitten off more than I could chew.

As it happens, my fear didn't last long. After only six or seven days my body started to attune. It was as if a switch had been flipped and my muscles had suddenly said, 'Oh, *every* day – you should have said! Right then … we're up for it if you are …' From then on, I found that instead of waking up with less energy than the day before, I started waking up with more.

During that first week, a sixty-mile bike ride had been achievable – just painfully, thigh-burningly so. But in the three weeks that followed it became, dare I say it, comfortable. The first 400 miles of cycling might have hurt … but it turned out to be the perfect training regime for the 1,200 miles that followed. Who knew? I didn't. Certainly not on day two anyway.

On day two I was still very much mired in fear. On day two I cycled from Grampound, a village near Truro (and another of Thomas Paine's former homes), to the venue for that evening: an open-air theatre, which sat high on the moor a couple of miles beyond Liskeard.

A couple of weeks earlier, a friendly Cornishman called Dave had emailed, suggesting that I break up that day's journey and spend the afternoon in St Neot. As his email explained: '… it would only involve a small detour of six or seven miles.' He wasn't suggesting it simply because he thought the village was beautiful – although it is – but because it was hosting an event that day that he thought I might like.

Smite, he explained, was a skittles-like game of Cornish origins. More importantly, there would be a barbecue, booze and sunshine.

He'd judged me well. It did indeed sound like the kind of day out I'd enjoy. But it was day two of my ride. There was dread in my belly and lactic acid in my legs. I wasn't taking a seven-mile detour for anything. There wasn't time in the day for an afternoon of skittles-like fun … and there was definitely no lunchtime boozing to be done. So I didn't stop at St Neot that day, but I did make a mental note of it and filed the Smite World Championships away for another time. And now was that other time. A year later: a year to the day since I'd started my ride, eleven months since bended knee, five weeks before 'I do'.

Dan walked me down through the grounds of St Neot's striking fifteenth-century granite church, across the road and along a winding footpath to Doorstep Green: a subtly landscaped public garden that contains a series of footpaths even more winding than the one that brings you to it. Whichever path you take, the chances are it'll lead down to the lawn – about the size of a tennis court – bound at one end by a semicircular arch of stone steps. The steps act as a public gallery and turn the place into a tiny amphitheatre. With hardly a cloud in the sky, the whole place looked rather idyllic.

'Blimey, this is nice!' I said.

'We were Village of the Year in 2004,' said Dan, not with untrammelled pride but with a restrained, self-aware grin.

'I had no idea such a competition existed.'

'It's run by Calor,' he said. 'You know … the gas people? We were Village of the Decade in 2006, too.'

'Who on earth has an of-the-decade competition in a year that ends in six?'

'Calor.'

'I see. They like it here, then.'

'We probably use a lot of gas.'

'Fair enough.'

'Ah … there's Roger. I'll introduce you.'

Dan didn't need to introduce me to Roger. Nobody needs to be introduced to Roger. Roger will always introduce himself first.

'Ah, you must be Dave!' he said, his fruity Welsh voice carrying across the garden. 'We're just setting up for the day … what d'y'think?'

He stood, hands on hips, a king surveying his domain.

There was a small green, canvas gazebo set up on the lawn which had been divided up into seven or eight Smite pitches – or smitches – all roughly seven or eight yards long. Each smitch was labelled with a small numbered flag, and had a wooden box a bit bigger than a shoebox that looked like a washed-up-on-the-shore treasure chest nearby.

'It's looking good,' I said. 'Looking good.'

'Have you played before?'

'No. This'll be my first time.'

'Well, let's get you practising then, eh?' He pursed his lips as if trying to work out which of the identical empty smitches would be best to use. 'How about we put you on smitch five for now, Dave? Dan, you'll give Dave a practice game, won't you? Do you want a beer, Dave? You're very welcome.'

'No ... I'll be fine for now,' I said. It was still only half past ten.

But Roger had already dived into a nearby cooler. 'Here,' he pressed a tin of cold lager into my hand, 'have one anyway, in case you change your mind. Now, I've got a bit of organising to do still, so I'll leave you in Dan's more than capable hands, okay? Great! That's looking great. I warn you though, Dan's good ... he's a two-time world champion aren't you, Dan? Super. Actually ... he's never been beaten in competition! Have you, Dan? Very good record, very strong ... carry on.' And with that he marched off, moving from smitch to smitch like a wasp buzzing between jam sandwiches. Roger's whirling-dervish-like energy was impressive. No wonder he was so annoyingly slim.

'I had no idea the man giving me a lift was the World Champion!' I said. 'You play your cards close to your chest!'

'A *former* world champion,' said Dan. 'I moved away for a while so I've missed some tournaments. I'm still unbeaten, though. I'm putting my reputation on the line today!'

'What brought you back?'

It was a stupid question in such an uncommonly beautiful place.

'I think I agree with Calor,' said Dan with a casual shrug. 'So ... do you know the rules?'

'Not really.'

It took him one minute to explain:

Smite:

At the start of the game, the ten numbered pins are arranged in a triangle with the ⑩ at the back and the ①②③ and ④ pins facing the throwing line, which is about four yards away.

Players take turns to throw the smiting stick (a wooden log about the size of a bottle of wine), using an underarm throw.

Throwing Line

If you knock over just one pin you score that pin's number. If you knock over more than one, your score is the number of felled pins.

So, if you only knock over the ⑥, say, you score six points but if you knock over the ①, ⑥ and ⑩, you score just three.

Of course at the start of the game – when the pins are tightly packed – it would be impossible to knock over just one pin. But the feature that makes Smite so playable is that after each go, the pins are stood back up wherever they fell.

It's not long before they're spread out. Individual pins get separated from the pack and some of them will doubtless end up several yards from where they started.

The winner is the first player to get to fifty points. But it has to be **exactly** fifty points. If you go over, your score is reduced to twenty-five.

Oh, and if you fail to score for three consecutive goes, you forfeit the game.

I took first smite and used it to give the pack a hefty thwack at the front of the triangle … All ten fell over. Ten points.

'Ah, the perfect start,' said Roger, who'd already buzzed back our way. 'Now, it won't have escaped your attention, Dave' – it had – 'that it's possible to win a game in just five goes.'

'Of course!' I said.

'Five tens,' he continued, 'and you're home. It's the maximum break: the one-four-seven of Smite! The nine-dart finish, if you prefer. Magnificent! We're offering a bottle of champagne to anyone who does it today. In competition only, of course! Fancy your chances?'

'Ha! I very much doubt it,' I said ... but Roger wasn't there to hear the answer. He was already off, welcoming another couple of early arrivals and passing on a few instructions to his fellow organisers, otherwise known as his wife, Sue and daughter, Jess.

I had stormed into an early lead over Dan. I definitely fancied my chances of picking up a win. It was hard to believe that Dan was really a former world champion. Unbeaten in competition? Really? Had he burned out? Or was he just keeping his powder dry and saving his A-game for the tournament proper?

The answer was neither of the above. He easily beat me. Scoring heavily early on is relatively simple. The tricky part is closing the game out. I ended up on forty-seven points and with no obvious way of scoring the three I needed to win. There was no way of knocking over the 3-pin without also taking out several others and there was no obvious group of three that could be knocked over in one go. Almost inevitably, I ended up going over fifty ... and busting myself down to twenty-five points. Two shots later and Dan had cleaned up.

'Well played,' he said. 'Pretty good for a beginner. And it was only a practice game. It's when the competition starts that they really count.'

Practice games were breaking out on smitches left, right and centre. People had arrived in dribs and drabs, gathered in cliques and claques, and I hadn't really taken in how large a group we smiters had become. It was only when I heard Roger's voice addressing the crowd via a PA system that I looked around me and saw what must have been nearly 400 people. Pretty much the whole village. Most had come to play but some were there purely as spectators.

I wasn't the only interloper. I wasn't even the furthest travelled. One family had come down from Liverpool specially, and Roger's daughter, Jess, had come all the way from Japan where she was working as a teacher. I don't think she made the journey back just for the World Championships ... but given the family's evident devotion to all things Smite, I might be wrong.

When it was totted up, some 300 people had registered to play. The children's tournament (on the back field) and the adults' tournament (on the lawn) would happen concurrently, then there'd be a break for some entertainment and then play would resume with the doubles.

I couldn't imagine how it was all going to fit into one day. It was a house of cards. It only needed one 'Sorry-I-didn't-realise-I-was-meant-to-be-playing-I-just-went-to-get-a-burger!' and the whole thing would be out of whack. It was going to require military-style scheduling and, looking around at the giggly, chatty crowd, the tins of lager and the sunshine, I found it hard to imagine them being that easily corralled.

But Roger's enthusiasm was infectious. If you boiled his opening speech down to its bare bones it was a, 'Look, I know you all want to have some fun *but* ...' speech, but it was perfectly pitched, so that wasn't how it came across. Whenever the necessary information was in danger of becoming overwhelming, he'd spoon in a load of more 'unnecessary' information to lighten the mood. So, as well as learning that we were being divided into groups of five or six and that this group was playing on that smitch and that group was playing on this one, we also found out who were the favourites, how they'd fared in previous years, who their big rivalries were with and so on. Visitors from other parts of Cornwall were playfully teased as if they were unwelcome intruders, while those of us from further afield were heralded as evidence of Cornwall's superior appeal: '… so I ask you, ladies and gentlemen, how many people have travelled from Cornwall to Liverpool for the bank holiday?' asked Roger with a music-hall wink. We all played along. It was a summer-time panto.

'It's good, isn't it?' said the woman to my right.

'Absolutely,' I said. 'It's like being at Butlins. Roger's a great Redcoat.'

She wrinkled her nose at me for a moment, confused as to whether or not my words were complimentary.

My tone of voice was positive so it must have been the word 'Butlins' that threw her. I understand the confusion. If someone tried to persuade me to go on a particular night out and said it was like Butlins, I'd probably wrinkle my nose, too. They're not words that would persuade me to go along. Which is ridiculous because I went to Butlins several times as a kid and I loved it.[52] Did I only enjoy Butlins because I was a kid? Did grown-ups always think it was a bit naff? Or have perceptions of the brand changed over the years? Either way, it's true that at some point between then and now I have grown snobbish about the whole world of 'organised fun'. I suspect I'm not alone. Holiday camps? Karaoke? Guided coach trips? 'Oh no … it's a bit vulgar … I might have to – ugh – *take part*!' I instinctively recoil from such things but I don't know why, because all empirical evidence suggests I'll enjoy them. Surely organised fun is something Britain is especially good at? I can't find any evidence of Butlins-style camps in other cultures and yet they thrived over here. I loved my child-hood holiday-camp holidays. I enjoy karaoke. Guided coach trips, too. I *think* I don't. But I do. And so do you.

---

52. Pwllheli, on the Lleyn Peninsula, North Wales as it happens. It's there that I first hear the word 'cwrw'.

There was something timeless and quintessentially British about the mood in St Neot that day. If you'd swapped Roger's microphone for a loud hailer, and given the various Justin Bieber-like boys a haircut, it could have been the 1950s. If someone had tried to organise a knobbly knees competition partway through, it would have gone down a storm. And *you* can stop wrinkling your nose at that, as well. Don't try to hide it; I know you were. I mean it as a compliment. When we throw our cynicism aside there's so much more to enjoy.

The singles competition started off with a group stage. Everyone was to play everyone else within their group, and the person with the most wins would go on. Most of them were groups of five but mine was a group of six, meaning I had to play Trish, Josie, Merryn, Adam and Graham ... and they all had to play each other, too. I knew from Roger's opening monologue that Graham was amongst the favourites: '... a formidable player who'll be keen to add to his doubles title of three years ago.'

When we arrived at our smitch there was no debate about who was going to take control of the clipboard and keep track of everyone's scores. Adam – the mayor of Saltash – was one of life's natural administrators. As the old saying goes: 'You can take the mayor out of Saltash, but you can't stop him picking up a clipboard and making sure his Smite group runs like clockwork.' (Or something like that.) When he was playing, the clipboard was instead entrusted to his wife, Merryn – herself a town councillor – and when they played each other, well, the clipboard was abandoned.

My first two games went exactly the same way as my practice game with Dan. I started strongly and built up a healthy lead but then made a complete hash of the endgame and found myself all too easily overhauled. I was determined to toughen up for my next encounter.

The formbook wasn't on my side, however. The mayor of

Saltash had played two, won two. I'd played two, lost two. I knew where the smart money was.

Having accrued thirty-eight points, I scanned the smitch looking for the best available shot. I was trying to learn from my defeats; I was trying to plan a shot or two in advance. The 10-pin was loose at the back of the pack. In my previous game I'd have gone for it and taken my score to forty-eight. But what use was that? Being on forty-eight just made going bust more likely. I knew what would happen next if I went that way: Adam would throw at the 2-pin and knock it into the heart of the pack, making my next move impossible.

Adam was skilled when it came to playing short shots in tight spaces, whereas I was turning out to be surprisingly good over long distances. So I made the tactically astute move – and there is something incredibly satisfying about the first time you do that in any game – and went for the 2-pin first. That put me on forty points: so much harder for Adam to deal with. I'd given the mayor a 'mare.

He went for a spoiler shot. He aimed at the 10-pin, hoping to send it even further away, hoping to send it out of my range … but really it was already out of his. He missed. I didn't … I was delighted. My arm hadn't got better. Nor had my eye. But my head had. I'd started to think like a smiter.

My first win had blown the group wide open. My second win, even more so. With one game left to play – me versus pre-tournament favourite, Graham – there were still three people who could win the group.

	P	W	L
ADAM:	5	3	2
DAVE:	4	2	2
GRAHAM:	4	3	1
JOSIE:	5	2	3
MERRYN:	5	2	3
TRISH:	5	2	3

If I won against Graham, I would draw level with him and Adam, as they both had three victories already. That would force us into a three-way play-off game.

But if Graham won it, the group was his, and both Adam and I would be eliminated. Adam was well aware of the game's importance and was there to cheer me on.

Graham carried himself with a certain nonchalance about the smitch. A cigarette was a permanent fixture between his lips and a drink was always in his hand. Even while he was throwing. (Mind you, I don't recall seeing the cigarette lit at any time so, really, it was just an obstacle to his drinking.) His *insouciant* demeanour was topped off by a Panama hat which had seen better days (by which I mean a Panama hat that had been made ragged by worse days).

I hadn't really studied any of Graham's earlier games but, my life, he was good. He played – cig in gob, can in hand, hat on head – and never looked like he was trying. If he was a footballer he'd be the cultured but lazy midfielder, the one that does no running but who always seems to have plenty of time on the ball, the one with his socks rolled down to his ankles.

I didn't get a look in. He romped home in some style. If someone had been running a book I'd have put my life's savings on Graham after that display. Especially when I heard that Dan – courtesy car driver and unbeaten Smitist – had been rushed to Derriford hospital.

Oh, I know Smite might sound like a gentle, country pursuit but it's not without its dangers. Dan had been stung on the inside of his mouth by a wasp that had hidden inside his can of beer.

There's no easy way to put this – and I know it's not where you thought a book like this was going – but, sadly, he died soon after. Nobody even knew his name. He was just 'Waspy'. On the bright side, I'm pleased to report that Dan made a full recovery. I suppose that'll teach Waspy not to steal someone else's beer. Still, at least he died doing something he loved. It's what he would have wanted. (A rumour went round that the wasp incident was actually a deliberate act of Smite sabotage by Graham: a man who wanted more than a three-year-old doubles title and was prepared to go to any lengths to get it. Of course, there was no truth in the rumour. I'd even go so far as to say that I regret starting it now. Oh well.)

As it happens, Graham did go on to win the singles in a closely fought final with Andy – himself a former champion. I was thrilled for him and childishly thrilled for myself. Yes, I'd been knocked out of the World Championships in the first round, but at least the man who'd knocked me out went on to win the thing. There's a smidgen of sporting dignity in that. *And* Dan could still claim to be undefeated, too. Entered thrice. Won twice. Retired through injury once. There's *more* than a smidgen of sporting dignity there.

'So, where did the game come from?'

I was lying down on a patch of grass listening to a young girl with a big voice belting out a few songs. I had a couple of cheese sandwiches in my belly and I'd topped it up with a couple of cans of lager – the drink I don't drink except when playing darts. Or sock golf. Or Smite.

It was the first time I'd seen Roger at rest all day, and I was interested to hear about the game's Cornish heritage. I wanted to hear about Smite being played by tin miners and pirates.

'Well,' he said. 'Sue and I are retired teachers.' He rolled all the Rs. 'We started looking around for something else we could do … because, well, you can't stand still, can you?'

'I'm not sure *you* can,' I said. 'But I think I can manage it.'

'We started looking into Scandinavian throwing games …'

'Huh? Scandinavian?'

'Yes. They have a lot of throwing games.'

'Have you heard of a game called Kubb?' I asked.

'It rings a bell. Thing is, we wanted to find something we could take into schools. We found one we liked – a Finnish game. It's a bit like this, only with twelve pins. We tried it but we thought, "Nah, this'll never work," so we started tinkering with it, refining it … and we came up with this …'

'So it's not ancient and Cornish?'

'No. It's a young Cornish child of Finnish parents.'

'People obviously love it,' I said. 'I love it.'

'Did I tell you we had a perfect game? Al Hoare did it in five shots. He's won the champagne.'

'Fantastic!'

'Yes and no.' Roger squinted into the sunlight. 'I fancied that bottle myself. So … are you staying for the doubles, Dave?'

'I'd love to, but I've got nobody to play with.'

'Oh, that's no problem … I'm sure we can sort that out.'

'But don't you want to play with Merryn?' I asked.

Adam shook his head. 'I think I've got a bit more appetite for the game than she has,' he said. 'She'll be very happy enjoying the sun this afternoon.'

'Then that's a deal.' We shook hands. I pulled Adam in a little closer and adopted a conspiratorial whisper. 'Okay … let's talk tactics,' I said. 'How do you want to play this?'

'I think the important thing,' said Adam, playing along, 'is to keep talking … make sure we discuss each shot …'

'Exactly. Keep each other's strengths in mind. If they push the game long, I can go there … if they want it all short and tight …'

' … then that's my zone.'

'Exactly.'

We were more than aware of how silly we sounded. Our boot-room-style tactical discussion was designed to make each other laugh. It was also designed to disguise our true feelings. 'Look how little we care,' we were saying to each other. 'We're so relaxed and uncompetitive, look at how we mock the over-competitive fools!' But we both knew it was a bluff.

The mayor of Saltash and I were desperate to win.

We turned out to be a bit of a dream team. Our respective strengths really did blend well. We blitzed our first three games. But we weren't the only team playing well in our group. Another team matched our three-win streak.

They were a good team: a useful blend of youth and experience. The youth came in the surf-dude shape of a young chap called Jack, while the experience came in the shape of – oh, dear – the newly crowned World Champion of Smite: Graham.

The game between them and us was to be the group's decisive rubber. Adam made a perfect ten-point break to get us off to a good start and we didn't let up. We couldn't afford to. It was nip and tuck all the way. Unfortunately, the game would turn on a refereeing decision that, even now, still rankles.

Our score was called as thirty-two. It was my go. Adam and I had our tactical conflab and came up with a strategy. It was high risk but it offered us the highest reward.

I don't mind saying that I played it pretty damn well. Before my throw we needed eighteen points and the 9-pin was in relatively crowded territory. After my go, we needed nine points and the 9-pin was out in the open. Perfect.

But our celebrations were cut short when we heard the ref say, 'Oh! I'm terribly sorry, I think I've miscounted … yep … yep … sorry … my mistake.'

'What do you mean?' The two of us spoke together; we spoke as a team.

'I said you needed eighteen, didn't I? But you actually needed seventeen. So sorry.'

'But I hit the 9-pin,' said I, a Gorman-aghast.

'Yes,' she said, 'so that leaves you needing eight …'

We turned to examine the smitch. The 8-pin was being hugged by three other pins; two in front of it and one behind. Scoring eight was impossible.

'But … but …' Adam didn't quite know what to say. 'But …'

'But,' I picked up the slack, 'I played the 9-pin deliberately so as to leave us needing nine more. If I'd have known we needed seventeen I'd have done something different …'

'Hmm. Yes,' she said. 'But you *did* hit the nine and you *did* need seventeen … so you *now* need eight.' The logic was faultless. If only the maths had been. 'Sorry!'

Adam and I looked at each other. Our we're-not-really-that-bothered bluff was being called.

'It's okay,' he said, with jaw-jutting stoicism. 'It's okay.'

But that was it. Our fate was sealed. There was no way back.

I was gutted. I knew Adam was gutted, too. But he sighed a heavy sigh and opted instead for the careworn, philosophical approach.

'I'm a Lib Dem,' he said. 'These things happen.'

From: Dave Gorman
To: Steve
Subject: IDVE

Steve,

Firstly … how are you set for Tuesday evening?

I haven't booked a train yet as I wanted to see if you were around. Also, I wasn't sure which train station I should be booking for … is Portsmouth Harbour or Portsmouth and Southsea best?

Dave

From: Steve
To: Dave Gorman
Subject: Re: IDVE

Dave,

Tuesday's great. The best train station would be Cosham. It's north side.

Let me know what time your train gets in and I'll pick you up at the station.

You are very welcome to stay over if you like.

Steve

From: Dave Gorman
To: Steve
Subject: Re: Re: IDVE

Steve,

My train gets in about 7.20 p.m. Is that ok?

I really appreciate the offer of a bed for the night but I've already booked a hotel in town. It's just easier and makes me feel less of an imposition.

Looking forward to IDVE!

Cheers,

Dave

From: Steve
To: Dave Gorman
Subject: Re: Re: Re: IDVE

I'll meet you at the station.

CHAPTER 26

Rest of the World: 53
Me: 49

'How was the train? All right was it? Have you eaten? I've got some pizza in for later. Is that all right for you? It's just cheese and tomato. Margherita, they call it. Oh dear, what am I thinking? Here, let me take your bag ...'

Steve was certainly more talkative than his emails had led me to expect.

'Pizza sounds great,' I said. 'And don't worry, there's hardly anything in the bag. I'm fine.'

'Go on ... let me take it ... I should have offered sooner.'

'Honestly, you don't need to ...'

'But I should ...'

My bag was so light that if I closed my eyes I'd have been hard-pushed to tell you which shoulder was carrying it. One T-shirt, one pair of socks, one pair of underpants, my darts, my toothbrush, some toothpaste, my phone and its charger. That's all it contained. I didn't exactly need a Sherpa to help me. But Steve wasn't taking no for an answer. He was taking my bag instead.

And I mean 'taking' in the most literal sense. He reached up and wrested it from my control and then slipped it on to his own shoulder saying, 'There, that's better ... it's only polite, isn't it?'

'Okay, then,' I said, happy to go along with it. 'That's very nice of you.'

But Steve had stopped walking. I didn't know why. I knew the bag couldn't have been weighing him down.

'Here we are,' he said, reaching his hands into his pockets. He pulled out a set of keys and unlocked the back door of a navy-blue transit van. After all his insisting he'd ended up carrying my nearly weightless bag less than six yards. 'I'll stick this in the back, shall I?'

I started to say that I could just as easily take it with me in the front but there was no point. The bag was in and the door was shut before I could even open my mouth.

'Hold on a minute,' said Steve, 'no central locking ...'

He climbed into the driving seat and I waited for a couple of moments while he leaned across and opened the passenger door from the inside. It was an old warhorse of a van. At some point in its life it had been in the building trade. The previous owner's name and number had been removed from the side of the van but their ghosts remained and they dated it just as surely as the rusty wheel arches: 'Tel: (01705) ...'

I knew that phone code and I knew it no longer existed. Before I had an agent I would spend countless hours each week calling various promoters looking for work. There was one promoter, Portsmouth Pat, whose phone number I could never forget on account of the fact it was just one digit different to my mum's. In Stafford, the STD code was (and still is) 01785. In Portsmouth it was 01705. The rest of their numbers were the same. And yes, I did once misdial. It's easily done when a telephone keypad has the eight directly above the zero. (Luckily it was a call that began with me calling my mum 'Pat', which is marginally better than one where I call Pat, 'Mum'.)

But this is all by the by. The point is that I knew Portsmouth's code had changed to 023 in the year 2000.[53]

---

53. 023 is a code shared by Portsmouth and Southampton. The two cities traditionally hate each other's guts and sharing an STD code doesn't appear to have given them any sense of unity. The Portsmouth code is often quoted as 02392 and the Southampton code as 02380. But that's a misunderstanding. The 92 and the 80 are, technically, a part of the local number. The code is just 023.

I heaved myself into the unfamiliarly lofty seat and pulled the door to. Steve turned the key, there was a belch of acrid exhaust fumes and we were on our way.

Steve's shaved head made it difficult to gauge his age. He could have been twenty-five or forty-five or anything in between. It's a look that can appear thuggish on some but not on top of Steve's rounded features. His puppyish, eager-to-please demeanour was anything but.

'So how do you know Lou, then?' I asked, as we made our way out of Portsmouth.

'Lou?'

'I think that was her name. Blonde girl. I met her in Lewes. She gave me your email address.'

'Lou? Lou? No ... not sure I know a Lou.'

'You said in one of your emails that she'd told you she passed on my address.'

'Did I?'

'Yes! Leather jacket? Lot of badges?'

'Hmmm.' He leaned forward, deep in thought, resting both forearms on the wheel. 'Nope. Can't place a Lou. I saw your thing on Twitter and emailed you about it ages ago.'

'Yeah ... I know. But then I emailed you because I met Lou and she ...'

'No. I emailed you and ...'

'No,' I scoffed. I knew I was right. 'I definitely ...'

'No,' snapped Steve. He sounded sharp all of a sudden and clearly didn't want to pursue the conversation any further. 'I don't know who this Lou is.'

Blimey. This was odd. Why would he pretend she didn't exist? Maybe she was his ex? Maybe it had ended badly? And recently.

'So, remind me,' said Steve, his voice now calm again. 'Did you say you were booking a hotel or did you want to stay at mine?'

'I've got a hotel,' I said, trying not to let any annoyance register in my voice. It was as if none of our emails had existed and every fact had to be re-established. Or, in the case of Lou, erased. 'All booked. They know I'm checking in late tonight. Will it definitely be okay to get a lift back into town later?'

'Sure. No problem. But you know you can stay over if you want.'

'Yeah, I know.' I smiled weakly. The offer of a place to stay was like the offer to carry my bag. He'd offered. And I'd declined. And he didn't seem to know how to stop offering. 'I ought to be on a train back tomorrow morning,' I added. 'It'll be easier if I'm waking up near the station.'

'I don't mind giving you a lift in the morning.'

'Well, it's booked now!'

'Fair enough.'

'Is it far, by the way?'

'A fair distance, yeah ...'

I hadn't really been paying attention to the journey. I guessed we were heading north. We had to be. We certainly weren't heading south. If we'd driven this far south we'd have gone through Portsmouth city centre and been in the sea by now. How far were we going to drive? All the way back to London?

As we left the urban sprawl behind, the sky darkened and the roads narrowed. The dim headlights of the van were probably exaggerating how narrow the lanes were becoming but the sound of the hedgerows brushing the sides of the van as we passed weren't. It was an eerie sound, amplified by the big empty van: an echo chamber on wheels.

'Hold on tight,' said Steve, spinning the wheel around. 'It gets a bit bumpy from here.'

Suddenly the track was more pothole than surface. The van bounced and rolled, each landing adding a vibrato stammer to our words.

'Th-th-th-this is wh-wh-why I d-d-d-drive an old-d-d-d thin-g-g-g lik-k-ke this,' s-s-said St-st-steve.

'The suspen-spen-spension m-m-must b-b-be kn-n-nack-k-kered.'

'Y-y-y-yeah.'

When the van finally came to a halt outside a small, white-walled cottage, it took a couple of seconds to get used to the idea that the ground wasn't shaking. Steve went ahead, opening the front door and switching on lights as he ushered me in.

'Come through, come through ... make yourself at home. Don't take your shoes off: I'm sure our floors are dirtier than your shoes! Ha ha. Tea? Coffee? Or I've wine if you'd like? Things are in a bit of a state ... we've been decorating ... I'm sure you won't mind. Did you say tea or coffee? Or wine? I don't mind. Don't drink myself but I don't mind. Would you like wine?'

'I'll just have a tea, ta. Could I just get my bag out of the van? Only it's got my phone in it and I'd like to ...'

'Oh, I doubt you'll have reception here,' said Steve. 'We never do. You can use the landline if you like?'

'Oh ... well, I'll leave it then.' I looked around the bare walls. 'Have you been here long?'

'A couple of years,' said Steve. 'I know ... it looks like we've just moved in, doesn't it? We're stripping everything back.'

'We?'

'The wife and I.'

'Is she around?'

'No. She's away at the minute. It's just us boys tonight. Milk and sugar?'

'Just milk. Thanks.'

'You said you're getting married soon?'

'Yep. Not long now,' I said. Steve handed me a mug – a big, satisfying-to-hold-mug – of good, strong tea. 'What about you? Been married long?'

'Seventeen years,' said Steve with justified pride. 'Now ... how hungry are you?' He was already fiddling with the oven. 'Shall we eat first?'

'Why not?'

'I feel like we ought to be painting these walls,' I said, one pizza later. 'It's the van, I think. Riding shotgun in a transit feels like the preamble to some work. Every time I've been in a transit it's been because I'm on my way to shift things, fix things or paint things.'

'Well, I won't stop you if you want to help out,' said Steve. 'Or we can play a game?'

'Hmm,' I pretended to be weighing up the options. 'Maybe we should just play a game.'

'Great!' Steve pushed his chair back from the kitchen table as he stood up. 'I'll go and get it. Why don't you make us another cuppa?'

I filled the kettle. I could hear Steve's footsteps making their way upstairs. I washed up our mugs. I could hear the creak of the floorboards overhead. I wondered what the game was going to be like. It could be anything. I had tried looking it up a few days before but IDVE wasn't a term Google seemed able to help me with. Like me, Google had first assumed it was a typo and that the word was meant to be DIVE. Then, when I insisted that I really was looking for IDVE, it had assumed I was missing the apostrophes in the contraction 'I'd've' (which looks so clumsy and wrong on the page but sounds so right when someone sings, 'If I knew you were comin' I'd've baked a cake.')

'Here we are,' said Steve coming back in and placing the box on the table. 'IDVE.'

I turned from the counter and passed Steve a mug of tea, taking in the game as I did so. My heart fell. I sighed a weary sigh. IDVE definitely wasn't 'I'd've' but if I'd've known in advance what it was, I'd've more than likely not boarded the train to Portsmouth that day.

IDVE stood for 'Intelligent Design versus Evolution'.

Oh, dear. I glanced at Steve, trying to see if he was smiling. Was he serious or having a laugh? Was his choice of game laced with irony or not? If it was, it was well hidden. But I didn't rule it out. Not yet. I mean: Intelligent Design versus Evolution? Really?

If you're unfamiliar with the phrase 'Intelligent Design', it is basically creationism by another name. As I understand it, the Intelligent Design movement exists to present creationism not as a religious doctrine but as a scientific theory. So, the creationist argument says: 'There's no way something as complex as the world we see around us could ever have happened by chance … it *must* have been made by God,' while Intelligent Design says: 'There's no way something as complex as the world we see around us could ever have happened by chance … it must have been made by, um, someone – not necessarily "God" y'know, just someone. Or something. Ahem. Sorry. Bit of a cough. By the way, while you're here, I've got some interesting books about the Bible, too …'

It's something like that. But look, I have no desire to lecture you on the subject. It won't achieve anything if I do. I'm pretty sure you already know where you stand on these things and I would have to possess extreme vanity if I thought adding my two penn'orth would contribute meaningfully to the debate. What's important, so far as this tale goes, is that you know what it is and what I think of it. Whether you agree with me is really neither here nor there.

I stared at the box. It was a very professional package. It wasn't something Steve had knocked up in his shed. I read the title again. This time aloud. 'Intelligent Design … Versus Evolution.'

'Yeah,' said Steve. He placed his mug on the kitchen table. His eyes narrowed. His nostrils flared. 'What do you think?'

'Honestly?'

'Of course.'

'Well ... *I* think evolution beats intelligent design ... but there's something about the box that tells me the game disagrees.' It wasn't actually a vague *something*. It was a very specific *something*. In the bottom left-hand corner of the box's lid was the following text: 'Educational, evangelistic and entertaining. You will uncover a wealth of powerful knowledge about the unscientific and unintelligent nature of the theory of evolution and the incredible fact of creation.'

That pretty much set its stall out. The title might suggest the two theories were going head to head, but everything else suggested the winner had already been decided.

Steve lifted the lid. It was a tight fit. As it came free, the box farted. We glanced at each other. We both giggled. It was a welcome break in the freshly minted tension. It was nice to re-establish some common ground. Even if it was just that we both found a fart noise childishly funny.

Steve unfolded the board. In the middle there was a picture of Darwin, alongside various images relating to evolutionary theory: a map of the Galapagos Islands, a skull and the classic 'ascent of Man' picture in which a modern man and various primate ancestors appear to be queuing for a bus. All of which was just dressing. It was a traditional roll-and-move game and the path our pieces would follow stretched around the board's perimeter. The last square was called 'The End Of Time' while the first was – with some wit, I thought – labelled 'In The Beginning'.

'I like that,' I said. 'Very good.'

'You see,' said Steve, the mood light again. 'This is going to be fun!'

He took out the playing pieces. Instead of traditional counters they were small rubber brains, each about the size of a walnut. (Or maybe they were just life-size model walnuts?) He placed two – one red, one green – on the first square. Then he dealt out two piles of cards.

'These' – he passed one of the piles to me – 'are your "brain" cards. You have ten to start with. The winner is the person who has the most brain cards when one of us gets to The End Of Time. Okay?'

'Okay.'

'You have to answer questions,' he continued, 'from this box here.' He placed a small rectangular box full of cards to one side and lifted the lid. It wasn't a tight fit. It didn't fart. 'If you get a question right, you roll a dice and move your brain … and then it depends where you land. The red squares are bad. The blue and the green squares are good. The yellow ones vary.'

'What about these squares?' I asked. 'The ones with pictures and photos.'

'They don't do anything.'

Oh.

'Right,' said Steve, rubbing his hands together, '… I'll let you go first.'

'Thanks.'

Steve definitely seemed to be taking the game seriously. Was he just putting on a poker face or was he for real?

He dipped into the box of questions and pulled out the first card.

'True or false?' he said. '"To illustrate Darwin's 'Natural selection', the *Encyclopaedia Britannica* used two photos, one showing a light-coloured moth and a dark-coloured moth against a dark background and the other showing them against a light background. This 'peppered moth' evidence of evolution was later proved to be fraudulent."'

'True,' I said without a pause. I'd got lost partway through the clumsily worded question but it didn't matter. It wasn't hard to work out what the answer was going to be given the game's rather obvious agenda. I had no idea if the peppered moth evidence had been proved to be fraudulent or not ... but seeing as this was an anti-evolutionary game, it was obvious that the answers were going to suit an anti-evolutionary argument.

'Correct!' It might have been the obvious answer but Steve seemed genuinely surprised that I'd got it right. He passed me the dice. 'Well done!'

'Thanks.'

I rolled. It was a four. I moved the red brain four spaces. It landed on a red square, which said the following:

DOUBT
'He that believes not God has
made Him a liar.'
Give Opposing Team 1 Brain.

'Ooh, unlucky!' Steve took one of my brain cards. 'My go. You ask me a question now.'

'Okay.' I pulled out a card. 'It's a multi-choice question. "How many ways are there to God? A) None? B) Many? Or C) One?"'

'One.'

'Correct.'

Steve rolled the dice. His green brain landed on a picture of Albert Einstein. He didn't have to give me any of his brain cards. But neither did he get to collect any.

'Is that your go over?' I asked.

'Yep.'

'Then bring on my question, please!'

'Okay,' said Steve, reading the card to himself first. 'You've got another true or false ... ready?'

'Absolutely.'

'Okay … "There is no scientific evidence for the existence of God. His existence cannot be proven; it's simply a matter of faith. True or false?"'

'True.'

'Incorrect.'

'What?'

'It's false.'

'What?'

'I'll read you what it says on the card,' said Steve. 'Here we go: "The word 'science' simply means 'knowledge'. Every person has the knowledge of God via the conscience and through creation. You cannot have a creation without having a creator. Creation is absolute scientific proof that there is a creator."' He held the card out for me to read it, too. 'You see. Oh … and unluckily it also says if you answered incorrectly, give the opposing team two brain cards.' He took two more of my brain cards. 'Right … my turn …'

And so it went on.

Certain types of questions were more popular than others. For example, there were plenty of Biblical quotes to identify. Another popular theme was which-of-these-three-people-you've-never-heard-of-came-out-with-the-following-state-ment-critical-of-evolution? And there were loads of peculiar riddles about how wonderful – and therefore how intelligently designed – the human body is, too.

There were 250 of these question cards, but oddly the game's creators hadn't managed to think of 250 separate questions to put on them. For example, these two came out of the box no more than fifteen minutes apart: 'What photo-processor has 130,000,000 light-sensitive rods and cones, which generate photochemical reactions that convert light into electrical impulses? A) The Panavision XPT Camera; B) The Kodak Super Cam; C) The human eye.' And then, 'What camera comes complete with automatic aiming, automatic focusing, automatic aperture control and automatic maintenance during the owner's sleep? A) Kodak's new HD video camera; B) Panasonic's award winning photo-processor; C) The human eye.'

I suppose *technically* that's two different questions … just not meaningfully so. Not that it really matters. You don't need to know anything to get the answer right, except perhaps the nature of the game you're playing.

'That's obviously a mistake,' said Steve after I'd read the second of the two aloud. 'They shouldn't have both those cards in.'

'Oh well – maybe the game isn't very intelligently designed,' said I.

It wasn't an especially vicious sideswipe at the game. It was just some poor wordplay, a weak joke that bubbled forth on some gag-reflex. It certainly wasn't an attempt to antagonise my host.

Unfortunately, it seemed to do just that.

'Just put the card back!' he snapped. 'Ask me another. Put it back and ask me another.'

'All right,' I said, trying to sound playful. 'Calm down! I'm only saying!'

'No! You're not just saying! You're enjoying the mistake!' He slammed his fist down on the table making an almighty bang. Then he repeated the action, adding an increasingly aggressive punchy punctuation to his words. 'Now!' *Bang.* 'Ask!' *Bang.* 'Me!' *Bang.* 'Another!' *Bang.* 'Question!'

Wow. Any suspicions I'd had that he was enjoying the game on some deadpan, ironic level disappeared rather suddenly. There was a silence. It was awfully tense.

I'd have welcomed a fart noise.

None came.

'Steve.' I spoke in a calm monotone. 'I've come to play a game. I came because you invited me. You knew what the game was about and I suspect you knew I wouldn't like it. I'm guessing that's why you didn't explain more about it in advance. I don't really know why you invited me. But I'm here. I've been honest. And I'm playing the game without complaint. I don't really know what else I'm supposed to do seeing as I've come this far.' I took a deep breath. 'Now ... if you're going to start punching the table then I'm not going to play.'

There was another long pause.

'Sorry.' The word was aimed at his shoes.

'I can't hear you,' I said. If I was going to be cast as 'Dad', I thought I might as well do it properly. 'Speak clearly.'

'Sorry.'

'That's better.'

How the hell had we found ourselves in this dynamic? What was going on? I was playing a creationist board game with an angry man! I was in his house! He was beating up his own kitchen table! And I was telling him off like he was my wayward ten year old!

I picked a fresh card out of the box. I don't know why. I guess I didn't know what else to do. I guess I was thinking it would probably be easier to just get to the end of the game.

'Right.' I looked down at the card. My life, this was getting more ridiculous by the minute. I tried not to let any sarcasm register in my voice. '"Why hasn't God punished evil? Is it: A) He doesn't care about justice; B) He doesn't see what's going on; C) If He had Judgement Day today every unsaved person would perish. He is patiently waiting for more to repent and trust the Saviour."'

That is a ridiculous question, isn't it? I mean, it's not a ridiculous question if you're a Christian. In fact it's a really interesting, perhaps fundamental, question for a Christian to ask themselves and to debate with others. But in *this* context, as a part of *this* game ... it's an utterly ridiculous question. In the same way that it would be ridiculous to have a board game called *Cats vs Dogs – Why cats are definitely better than dogs* and then load it with questions like, 'Who is definitely the best? A) Snoopy; B) Scooby Doo; C) Garfield.'

Steve wasn't answering.

'I'm going to have to hurry you,' I said, adopting the quiz-show host's argot in an attempt to jolly him up and along. (Why was *I* trying to keep *his* mood buoyant?) He still didn't answer. So I launched into my rendition of the *Countdown* clock music thinking that might work: '*Dah-ba-da-ba-dada, dah-ba-da-ba-dada, dah-ba-da-ba-dada, ba-dah, ba-dah, ba-da-da-da-bhoooooh!*'

'C,' said Steve, sulkily. 'If He had Judgement Day today, every unsaved person would perish.'

'Correct.'

'Including you,' he said. He was a grown man but he was speaking with the sullen tone of a difficult teen.

I wasn't upset at being damned to hell. But I *was* annoyed. I was annoyed because I'd travelled here ... for *this*! What was the point? What had he really hoped to achieve?

I stood up, crossed the kitchen and filled the kettle.

'Is it all right if I make myself another cuppa?' I asked tersely. There was no reply. 'Tell you what. You take your turn. Roll the dice. Move your brain. Do your thing. I'll make tea. Is that all right?' Pause. 'I'll take that as a yes.' Pause. 'Do you want one?'

Silence. It's strange how loud a teaspoon clinking on the side of a mug can sound when it's highlighting an awkward silence. I returned to the table.

'I didn't make you one,' I said. 'I *did* ask.' I looked down to see Steve's green brain had stayed where it was while I'd been mashing tea. 'You not rolled the dice then?' Silence. 'This isn't going very well, is it?' Silence. 'I don't suppose you fancy giving me a lift back into town then?'

Finally, he reacted. It wasn't necessarily the reaction I was hoping for, but after several minutes of stony silence at least it *was* a reaction.

Steve punched me in the face.

I think I preferred the silence.

I'm not a connoisseur but I don't think his technique was the best. It sort of started off as a dramatic punch but it was as if he tried to turn it into a slap at the last minute. It was the heel of his palm and his closed fingers that made contact with my face. He hit more cheek than bone. It hurt. But it was the wave of surprise that knocked me off my chair rather than the force of the contact.

'Ow.' I raised my hand to my face. My ear was ringing. Steve was standing with his backside pressed up against the oven door. He looked like he wanted to climb inside it. 'Or you could call me a cab if you'd rather …'

And then he ran. Into the hallway and up the stairs. I heard a door slam. And then silence.

Well, this was a bizarre one. I didn't know quite what to do. I looked at the stupid game. I didn't remember anything in the rules about throwing punches and running away, but I reckoned it probably constituted a forfeit. I gave myself the point.

I felt cool, calm and strangely unemotional. Nothing felt entirely real. It was as if I was seeing the world through a virtual reality headset. The colours seemed muted. The edges of the picture were not quite so distinct. I walked slowly and deliberately towards the front door. Was I in shock? I propped the front door open and walked out to the van. The doors were locked. I contemplated smashing a window and retrieving my bag that way. But what was the point? It wasn't going to make the evening better. Not as much as breaking a window would make it worse.

I wandered back inside. It was eerily calm. *I* was eerily calm. I climbed the stairs, one step at a time. I tiptoed the last few. My heartbeat quickened. This situation *was* real.

There was silence from behind Steve's bedroom door. As I approached, my anxiety grew. Should I knock? No. I turned left and drifted down the landing. Another door was open. The spare room. The same bare walls. A single bed. A neatly folded clean towel perched on the end of it. A bedside table. 'You can stay over,' he'd said. For some reason I was even less keen now. I used the bathroom. I twisted my head in the mirror trying to see if there was a bruise coming. If there was it was faint.

I sat on the stairs for a moment, unsure of what to do. I went back down and had a snoop around. Why did that make me feel guilty? There was no mail by the door. Damn. An address would have been helpful. I didn't know where I was. I didn't know the name of the nearest village. I didn't know how far the nearest neighbour was. There was nothing to physically restrain me and yet I *was* trapped. 'You can stay over,' he'd said. I might bloody well have to at this rate. Where was the phone? Not in the hallway. The kitchen? I hadn't seen it. This was ridiculous.

I stood at the foot of the stairs and called up. 'Steve?' Pause. 'Hello! Steve? I don't know where I am, Steve. My bag's in the van. I can't just leave, Steve. If you could just let me get my stuff and maybe call a cab …?'

There was nothing. What would I do if his wife came home? Did she know I was here? That's if he *had* a wife. What if he'd hurt himself? I had no idea what was true and what wasn't. Should I go and knock on his bedroom door? No. Not yet. Not just yet.

The game looked ridiculous sitting there on the kitchen table unplayed. I sat down and flicked through a few more questions.

> **BRAIN TEASER:**
>
> Which came first, the chicken or the egg?
>
> ANSWER: The chicken: 'And God said, Let the waters bring forth abundantly the moving creature that has life, and fowl that it may fly above the earth after its kind.'

That's *that* sorted then. A lot of people have been wondering.

> **BRAIN TEASER:**
>
> True or false? The Archbishop of Canterbury, Dr Rowan Williams (spiritual leader of the world's 77 million Anglicans), said that only evolution should be taught in science classes.
>
> ANSWER: True.

I put that one in my pocket. Naughty of me, I know, but it made me feel better. If Steve had an issue with my belief in evolution – and on balance, that seemed likely – then he didn't just have an issue with me but with mainstream Christianity.

Which reminds me. Some time ago, I told you about some pensioners in Cleveland, Ohio, walking out of a theatre because they didn't welcome my views on creationism. I said I'd tell you about another odd moment that occurred while touring that same show another time … and now seems as good a time as any. It's especially pertinent because it happened just up the road, in Portsmouth.

There was a vicar on the front row that night. It's hard to ignore a vicar on the front row. They stand out in a crowd.

When I got to the part of the story that involved me meeting the Senior Vice President of the Institute for Creation

Research I sensed some discomfort in the audience. My eyes darted to the vicar. He didn't seem troubled by it at all. But some of those sitting near him did. It was only a tiny part of the show – less than four minutes out of a ninety-minute story – so I contemplated just getting through that bit as quickly as I could. But I didn't. My instincts told me to do something else. I took a gamble.

I turned to the man in the dog collar and addressed him directly, saying, 'Excuse me, sir, but as a man of the cloth, you must have an opinion on this … would you mind telling me what you think about creationism?'

He stood up. He turned to face the audience. And in a loud, clear, pulpit-trained voice, he declared, 'Creationism … is bollocks!'

He received the biggest ovation of the night. (Which is a bit galling really. You put all that work into crafting a show, but the British public just loves a swearing vicar.)[54]

Still, it helped to settle the audience around him. Once they realised that being vaguely disparaging about creationism wasn't the same as being vaguely disparaging about faith, they stopped squirming on his behalf. Especially now that he was the star of the show.

I spoke to him afterwards. He was a real vicar. We've stayed in touch.

The floorboards creaked overhead. Steve was stirring. I heard his footsteps as he trudged downstairs. I heard the front door open. And then I heard his voice. 'Come on, then.'

---

54. It's not the *best* use of the word by a reverend. In 1977, a Nottingham record shop manager was tried for indecent advertising after a police officer saw his window display for the album *Never Mind The Bollocks, Here's The Sex Pistols*. The defence barrister was *Rumpole of the Bailey* author, John Mortimer QC. As an expert witness he called the Reverend James Kingsley – a professor of English studies at Nottingham University. He testified that the word was used in records dating from the year 1000, that it appeared in mediaeval Bibles, and that in the 1800s it had even been a colloquial term for a clergyman.

Was that it? Just 'Come on, then'?!

I walked through to the hall. He was already outside. I walked to the van where I was greeted by a splurt of exhaust fumes as he started the engine. I climbed into the cab and buckled up in silence. Off we went. Down the bumpy, pot-holed track. In silence.

I didn't have anything to say. Small talk seemed too small given the events of earlier. (And by 'events' I really mean 'event'. And by 'event' I really mean 'being hit in the face'.) But big talk seemed too big, too. Not in the confines of a transit van.

It wasn't until our surroundings had grown more urban – perhaps making us feel less trapped and alone – that one of us spoke.

'I'm sorry I hit you,' said Steve.

'I turned the other cheek.'

More silence.

'I saw you on stage once.'

'Most hecklers speak up on the night.'

'You were talking about creationism ...'

'Was it in Portsmouth? Were you there that night? The night with the vicar?'

'What? No.'

'Oh.'

'It was in Cheltenham.'

'Uh huh.'

'That bit upset me. I wanted to speak to you about it. That's why I invited you.'

'You've got a funny way of bringing it up.'

'I know. I'm sorry.'

He pulled up to the kerb and I let myself out.

I closed the hotel room door behind me and felt some of the tension fall away. It had been a very strange evening. One of the strangest. But it was over.

I started to run a bath. And then I called Beth.

'Hey … how was the game?'

'A bit weird.'

'How do you mean?'

'Um … well … it's nothing to worry about but … he, um … he was a bit angry and he … um … he hit me.'

'What?'

'He hit me.'

'But that's …' She sounded upset.

'I'm fine,' I said. 'I'm not hurt. I'm fine. There's nothing to worry about. I just wanted to let you know I'm okay. Because I am.'

'What do you mean he hit you? Are you sure you're okay?'

'I'm absolutely fine,' I said.

I told her the story. As best I could. Talking it through felt like a good exercise. I took control of the evening. I owned it. It didn't own me. I felt stronger. A bit less tense, at least.

And we talked about other things. And then we said goodnight. And then I had a bath. And then I went to bed. And then … I started sobbing. It came from nowhere and engulfed me. I didn't know why. I didn't feel upset or angry or scared.

I just felt like sobbing.

CHAPTER 27

The grey stone wall was cold to the touch. The heavy, royal-blue timber door looked stern and imposing. But then even the small, grey, plastic doorbell looked imposing that day.

My finger hovered. I rang the bell. There was a pause. And then the crackle of an electronically conveyed voice.

'Hello?'

'Hi. Is that Tommy?'

'Aye.'

'It's Dave. I'm here to play–'

Bzzzzz.

'Come on in. We're on the third floor.'

I put my shoulder to the door and it swung open. I stepped inside. It swung back to with a bang. I started to climb the stone steps, each one worn down to a shallow bowl-shape by a hundred years of footfalls.

My holiday-in-instalments was nearly over. My two-days-a-week working life was the exception not the rule. It existed in the vacuum created when my planned pre-wedding holiday had instead become a traditional post-wedding honeymoon. I wasn't going to have this kind of free time again for a while.

I could tell you what game I was going to play that day … but I think that would be to miss the point. I'd turned up. That was the point.

It doesn't matter what the game was. And it doesn't matter whether I won or lost. It doesn't matter how many games we played that day and it doesn't matter how I was doing against the Rest of the World. What matters is that I rang the doorbell. What matters is that I climbed those stairs.

I didn't lose the mind game. I didn't lose my mind. I didn't lose my *me*.

My experience with Steve had affected me. I'd run through the events of that night many times since. I'd thought about Steve a lot. In truth I still do.

Of course, I can only guess at what was in his mind. I certainly don't think it panned out the way he wanted. Then again, I'm not sure I know exactly what he wanted. I'm not sure he did, either. That doesn't really matter now.

Maybe I should have been sarcastic about his choice of game. Maybe I should have rolled my eyes and told him it was nonsense. Maybe then he'd have had his day. Maybe then he could have reeled off a few, *Well-actually*s and a couple of *I-think-you'll-find*s and he would have felt a whole lot better? Maybe what annoyed him most was my failure to take the bait?

If only I'd known it was bait.

'You don't have to go, y'know. They'll understand if you want to cancel. Anyone would be shaken up by something like that.'

Beth's words. She was right. And I had cancelled a couple of games already. But it was time to make a stand. It was time to board a train.

We'd be married soon and, of course, I was thinking about that, too. About all that it meant. It meant everything.

As the train rattled north I thought about sitting in the dark in an attic in Splott. And about standing naked, statue-still, privates cupped, in a Windsor shower. I recalled a Scouse cabbie's advice – 'Just be careful, eh, mate? Whatever it is you're up to … be careful' – and the small bout of doorstep paranoia it had induced. Ridiculous little moments, all. And I thought about Steve punching me in the face. And I thought about Steve punching me in the face. And I thought about Steve punching me in the face. Not so ridiculous.

None of these thoughts left me that day. They swirled through Edinburgh's brisk September air as I strode down Leith Walk. Towards the docks. Towards Tommy's flat. Towards my next game.

It would have been easy to retreat: 'Sorry, I can't come … the wedding's getting close and there's still a lot to do.' That's all it would have taken. As excuses go, it's watertight. I might even have been able to convince myself that it was true. And in two or three weeks it would be irrelevant, anyway. The games I'd planned were nearly over. A new life – married life – would soon be starting.

It was tempting. It was very, very tempting.

But it would have been a lie. It would have been an excuse for closing myself off from the world and trusting it a little less.

It was tempting. It was very, very tempting,

But I didn't want to be that man. I didn't want Beth to marry *that* man. I wanted Beth to marry *me*. I wanted Beth to marry the man I've always tried to be. A man who trusts others. A man who can be trusted.

Why should I let my worldview be shaped by Steve? Why not let it be shaped by others? Weren't most people nice? I thought about Rhys and Rob. About Andy, Clive, Elliott and Caroline. I loved Victor and Joyce. And Martin and Rich. And so many more.

There were lots of them. And there was just one Steve.

The truth was that I didn't trust the world as much as I once had. But I wanted to. I didn't want to stop being curious about the world. I didn't want to stop playing in the world. I didn't want to stop playing with the world.

That's why I made myself board the train that day. That's why I rang that doorbell. That's why I climbed those stairs. Because that's how I proved to myself that I was still me.

*

And it's why this story doesn't have an ending: because I haven't stopped playing games. I've continued. When I have the time. When I can. When it looks like fun.

The offer's still there. Do you play any games? Real life, not computer games. Would you like a game?

If you'd like to play a game I'll see you over at
www.davegorman.com/game.html

APPENDIX: TEXAS HOLD'EM

In Texas Hold'em everyone is dealt two cards face down. These are your 'hole cards'. Only you see them.

The dealer changes with each hand, moving clockwise around the table.

Two players – the two sitting to the left of the dealer – are 'forced' to bet: if there were no chips to win there'd be no point in anyone betting. These are 'the blinds'. The player to the left of the dealer is 'the small blind'; the player to their left is 'the big blind'.

At the start of a game these blind bets are, typically, very small. In a game where everyone starts off with 1,500 in chips, you might set the small blind at 10 and the big blind at 20. They're there to ensure that *something* happens every hand.

As the game goes on, at pre-arranged intervals – say, every hour, or maybe every twelve hands – the blinds increase. This means if you don't win a few hands – or if you choose to do nothing – your stack of chips will eventually just disappear, getting eaten up by the blinds.

When everyone's hole cards have been dealt, there's the first round of betting. You're betting on potential here. You don't have a complete hand. But clearly a pair of aces is much stronger than a 2 and a 7 of different suits, for example.

The person sitting to the left of the big blind gets to act first. They have three options. They can a) fold their hand, b) call – that is, equal the bet made so far (at this stage, the big blind), or c) raise.

The betting continues round the table with everyone having the same option. Fold, call or raise. This includes the two blinds. If they fold, they lose their chips.

If anyone raises, the betting simply continues going round. It doesn't matter how much you've bet so far, if someone bets more than you, you need to match them before anything else happens.

If one player bets enough to persuade the others to fold he takes all the chips committed so far, and it's time to shuffle up and deal another hand.

But if two or more players are still in the hand, then it's time for 'the flop'. The flop consists of three cards dealt face up in the middle of the table. These are community cards. Your hand will be the best five-card hand you can make combining the two cards unique to you *and* the community cards.

Another round of betting follows the same pattern. This time, the first person to act is whoever is sitting nearest the dealer's left.

If, when this round of betting concludes, two or more players are still in the hand, the dealer turns over another community card, known as 'the turn'.

There's then another round of betting.

Another, final, community card follows – 'the river' – and then another, final, round of betting.

If everyone but you folds, you take the pot. You don't have to show them what your two cards were. They haven't paid for that privilege – you've successfully bet them out of the pot.

HAND ORDER

Royal Flush: 10♦ J♦ Q♦ K♦ A♦

Straight Flush: 4♣ 5♣ 6♣ 7♣ 8♣

4 of a Kind: J♥ 6♥ 6♦ 6♣ 6♠

Full House: 5♣ 5♥ 9♥ 9♠ 9♦

Flush: 2♦ 5♦ 7♦ 9♦ Q♦

Straight: 7♣ 8♦ 9♥ 10♣ J♠

3 of a Kind: 3♠ 8♣ 8♥ 8♦ K♠

Two Pair: 7♦ 7♣ J♥ J♣ 2♠

One Pair: 4♠ 4♣ 6♦ 10♣ J♦

High Card: 2♣ 7♦ 8♥ Q♠ A♥

TOURNAMENT POKER

The most common form of Hold'em on TV – and the only type I really play – is tournament poker.

In tournament poker, you can't think, 'Wow, I'm 2,000 up, I think I'll leave now, cash these in and get the night bus home.'

You all commit the same amount of money at the start. You all get the same amount of chips in return. You all play until you're out. Or until you've won all the chips.

There is pre-agreed prize money for first place, second place and as many other places as you see fit. It depends on how many players you start with.

GLOSSARY

Blind: A mandatory bet posted before the cards are dealt

Board: The five community cards can be referred to as 'the board'

Button: Whoever is dealing a given hand is 'on the button'

Connectors: Any two consecutive cards, e.g. 2 and 3. 7 and 8, etc.

Flop: The first three community cards. These are dealt simultaneously

Fourth Street: The fourth community card

Hole cards: The two cards dealt to each player

Kicker: A hole card that isn't used to make your hand but could break a tie. If you have A,K and your opponent A,Q then you have the better kicker

Nuts: The best possible hand given what's on the board is 'the nuts'

Pocket pair: When your hole cards are paired

River: The fifth and final community card

Set: Three of a kind

Suited: Two hole cards of the same suit. So 2♠ 3♠ would be suited connectors

Trips: Three of a kind